ACTING GREEK TRAGEDY

"In this book I shall be giving an account of an approach I have been using in the studio over a number of years, and which I have developed through a longer period studying the theatricality of ancient Greek tragedy . . . The approach I have found to be best is one that draws on an essentially dramaturgical analysis in the actor, and which then applies that understanding in and through performance. So a more accurate title for the book might actually be 'preparing to act Greek tragedy', since it concentrates on methods of preparation for a testing realization in a workshop performance in the studio."

from the author's Preface

Graham Ley is Professor Emeritus of Drama
at the University of Exeter

ACTING GREEK TRAGEDY

Graham Ley

UNIVERSITY
of
EXETER
PRESS

First published in 2014 by
University of Exeter Press
Reed Hall, Streatham Drive
Exeter EX4 4QR
UK
www.exeterpress.co.uk

British Library Cataloguing in Publication Data
A catalogue record for this book is available
from the British Library.

Paperback ISBN 978 0 85989 893 5
Hardback ISBN 978 0 85989 892 8

Cover design by Holly Rose and Stephanie Sarlos

Typeset in Sabon by
Kestrel Data, Exeter

Printed in Great Britain by
Short Run Press Ltd, Exeter

Contents

PREFACE

WELCOME

In this book I shall be giving an account of an approach I have been using in the studio over a number of years, and which I have developed through a longer period studying the theatricality of ancient Greek tragedy. I would not in the first instance call it a form of actor-training, since it is not primarily concerned with a regime to develop voice and movement skills, nor does it have a hard focus on inhabiting character. The approach I have found to be best is one that draws on an essentially dramaturgical analysis in the actor, and which then applies that understanding in and through performance. So a more accurate title for the book might actually be 'preparing to act Greek tragedy', since it concentrates on methods of preparation for a testing realization in a workshop performance in the studio.

There are sound reasons for this, which go beyond the obvious need to prepare well before you enact. These are that modern productions of ancient Greek tragedy must and do show a bewildering variety of different forms, according to the inclinations and inspirations of the practitioners who are taking the initiative to put them on. It is necessary for actors to be open-minded and flexible in their attitude to productions, and to the direction and mise-en-scène that will animate the performances;

but it is unreasonable and unwise to expect actors to go into a production process unprepared.

Actors need to be able to develop confidence in their ability to handle any material, and Greek tragedy is a potentially daunting prospect. I would suggest that trust in a director to supply all is inappropriate, since the performance of Greek tragedy may be just as much an unknown to directors as to actors. There is nothing wrong with a path of discovery; but discovery with trained actors is a far more dynamic process than wandering around totally in the dark, searching for the beginning of that path.

So why would thoughtful actors (or directors) be unprepared for Greek tragedy, especially if they have already been through a sound course of training? The answer to that is that ancient Greek tragedy is at risk, despite its distinct appeal over the centuries, of being culturally locked in. This is as true of the beliefs that activate its characters as it is of the form in which it operates, which is unlike anything that we find in theatre today. This combination means that it is not truly accessible to the kind of training in interpretative acting that may prove highly effective with later European drama. Clearly such training will give an actor a fair start, but it is not sufficiently specific to go beyond a certain point, and any performance will contain far too many leaps of faith for comfort.

Some may ask at this point why a contemporary actor would want to bother with Greek tragedy at all, let alone take on the questionable burden of a specific approach to acting it. The answer to that is that it supplies some of the best available classic roles for women as well as outstanding roles for men. The fact that those roles were not originally written for performance by women is not an obstacle: the female characters are no less seriously conceived than the male, and they represent women at all ages of life. It is a remarkable resource, waiting to be exploited and opened out to audiences.

While I would hope that you might work happily as an actor from this book without already knowing much in advance about Greek tragedy or the ancient theatre, I would recommend that you do take a good look at the broader picture. I am going to assume that you will find out elsewhere about the three tragic playwrights, Aeschylus, Sophocles and Euripides, and the relationship between performers and audience expressed in the ancient playing-space, amongst other important information. There are many ways of doing that, but you can find informative guidance in my own *A Short Introduction to the Ancient Greek Theater* (second edition) which is published by the University of Chicago Press, and is readily available.

I shall not delay the Introduction any further. What I shall be doing there is to outline a concept that will be central to my approach, and illustrate it before adopting and deploying it throughout the rest of the book. That concept is not itself culturally specific, but it serves as a means to unlock the beliefs and the forms of expression used in dramatic texts such as those from antiquity. Once the idea of it is grasped, it can be applied consistently across all four Workshops that form the main substance of this book.

So these opening words serve as a welcome and an invitation to work that—if it is undertaken with commitment and given sufficient time—will undoubtedly change your ability to perform Greek tragic scripts.

INTRODUCTION

Food for Thought
and First Steps

The key to performing Greek tragedy well is to understand the action. I do not by this mean the plot, taken in the large sense, or indeed the incidents that make up the plot, although they bring us closer to the kinds of action I mean. The plot and the myth very often exercise a strong fascination on us, which is a crucial excitement. But a fascination with myth may lead to a fixation on heroic or mystical qualities in the material, which can result in a particular style of presentation. Such styles may be either imaginatively or badly judged, but they will not in themselves secure firm ground for an actor's performance, and can often prejudice it, providing at best a kind of tight-rope walk without a net. No performer likes to be exposed, and productions of Greek tragedy can be very exposing and hazardous.

The term I would like to introduce as food for thought is that of 'transaction', which is familiar to us from a business context, and may also be familiar from a social or linguistic context as well. The business context reveals very little about the word or the idea it contains, since we think of our most common transactions as cash withdrawals from an ATM, which for most of us prove to be all too frequent an experience for our financial wellbeing. A transaction involves at least two parties, and is in some senses a 'bit of business' conducted between them. In this case, I suppose that the use of our card and PIN in an agreed setting (the ATM till, or 'hole in the wall') authorizes our bank to release money to us directly: there are two parties involved, ourselves and the bank we have chosen for our deposits.

In the case of the purchase of an item, the release occurs by means of a slightly different machine to another party, the seller, who then becomes a third party in the transaction. In more traditional terms, we might simply hand over cash for an item to the seller, or in still more traditional terms hand over another item in exchange, in what is called barter. Our purchase may be of an item or of a service, which is interesting because it may well entail further transactions in order to be accomplished. So if we book a holiday with a travel agent, our payment is one transaction. But the agent may then conduct a series of transactions with other agencies (the flight or ferry company, the hotel) to implement the first transaction successfully and faithfully for us.

We might think of these relatively familiar and everyday transactions as lacking emotional texture, of being 'business' in the sense that we sometimes use the word. While this may be true to some considerable extent, we have only to think of occasions when things go wrong to realize how much hangs on such transactions. If the ATM fails to deliver, it is often only a minor frustration. But if the holiday booking has been made wrongly, then all hell may break loose, with screaming kids, irate partners and rooms that are not available. A very great deal hangs on transactions, and we can see that most clearly when we consider them in the social context.

The simplest examples of social transactions may well be everyday, and not apparently charged with feeling or consequence. Such are our greetings, which in the best if not the normal form do require or expect an acknowledgement. I am sure a human behaviourist would insist that for human society a great deal hangs on greetings, and an anthropologist would insist that it always has done. If we say 'How are you?' we do expect or hope to hear 'Good!' or 'Not bad', according to our culture, while in many cultures greeting remains far more formal and brings with it a similarly formal expectation for the reply or acknowledgement. If the greeting fails, we may feel snubbed, whether at the breakfast table or with the CEO, and I shall return to that emotional sense of failure later, since with others it is an important aspect of transactions which applies in drama.

Of course, we also 'do business' with each other in countless ways and all the time, and it is fair to say that human life could not take place as it does without transactions. We can see that easily in the family debate about which film to see on the day out, or in partners considering in a long process which singles or couples they wish to ask to an evening meal, and which they think will fit together. At the graver end of the spectrum, the formalities of wedding or of civil partnership are public transactions that advertise the results of previous, private transactions. On reflection, such transactions may appear to us now, under the influence of anthropology, to be rituals, as are those connected with death and burial. Yet burial is all too plainly a transaction between the living as well as between the living and the dead, and we can find that in the emotive cliché that such events are comforting because they bring about a 'closure'.

Indeed, it may be helpful to some performers to speak of transactions in the same breath as rituals, and to regard our everyday behaviour as carrying rituals within it. If we look back in our cultural history, this approach may seem to bear more weight; but I would maintain that ritual behaviour has features which it is not helpful to expect of all transactions. An argument between two people may have few ritual features if any, and it may be that there are few ritual components in the culture available to the participants. That would be the case with most 'modern' arguments. Yet arguments similar to these still play a crucial role in the evolution of the plot in older dramatic texts. There they will sit alongside more explicitly formal disputes, which may have ritual components in them, such as oaths or curses taken and sworn.

Older, pre-modern dramatic texts do contain many highly formal transactions, where acts of persuasion or dispute or commitment between two or more people are accompanied by forms of public or religious validation. Authority or status may have much to do with this. An autocratic ruler may be expected to have the right of condemning individuals, commonly expressed in drama through identifying supposed traitors and dealing out banishment or death. But status does not necessarily mean power of the kind we think we can recognize across cultures. In Greek tragedy, a messenger may be required or charged to deliver a report, and the delivery of that account to specific individuals to whom it is relevant is a transaction. In fact, any report that is required of an individual is likely to be a transaction, and I shall explore that further in the first chapter.

Many of these more formal transactions connect closely with what the linguistic philosopher J.L. Austin identified as 'performatives', **words** (usually verbs or verbal phrases) that contained or implied decisive **actions**. While Austin picked on the words of the marriage ceremony as his example, we might well consider banishment or condemnation to exile as the kind of authoritative pronouncement that is, in Austin's terms, a performative (J.L. Austin, *How to Do Things with Words*. Oxford: Clarendon Press, 1962). These pronouncements sometimes fall under the broader term 'utterances' used in linguistics or discourse analysis. But although that may be worth noting, 'utterance' is not an idea that is likely to bring scripts to life in our minds or in the studio. 'Performatives' has a little more appeal, and while Austin was very much concerned to hunt out verbs that were 'performative' in his sense, my approach is far more interested in identifying transactions, which may or may not contain specific, performative verbs.

By fixing on the correlation between words and actions, and specifically by identifying those words or forms of words that were decisive, Austin incidentally offered an immense insight into the functioning of dramatic texts. While we should certainly not expect to find 'performatives' keying-in subsequent actions in plays, in a kind of linguistic demonstration piece, the idea of 'performatives' alerts us to the intimate and intricate connection between words and actions. In many pre-modern societies, words are decisive and thoroughly consequential, and the pronouncement of them is taken very seriously indeed. To put that another way, words play a very large part in pre-modern societies, and pre-modern plays dramatize the impact of the spoken word.

It is my intention to indicate the significance of transactions in the course of the analysis of scripts undertaken in the chapters that follow. I would rather do that than go into a great deal more explanation right here, in advance, in theory and in the abstract. But it may be helpful just to turn away from Greek tragedy for a moment, and indeed to turn away from tragedy of any period, to see a transaction in process and to cement an early impression of how pervasive transactions are in dramatic texts, and in the evolution of action. The example I have chosen is from a comedy, Shakespeare's *As You Like It*, and is taken from relatively early on in the play (Act II, sc.3). The reason I like it is that it is relatively obscure, perhaps the slightest of the scenes that occur in the first part of the play, and one that it is easy to ignore, even to forget. It is a two-hander, between the attractive but down-on-his-luck Orlando and an old retainer of the family, who is loyal to the memory of Orlando's father and to Orlando himself. Here it is.

Enter Orlando and Adam from opposite sides

ORLANDO: Who's there?
ADAM: What, my young master? O my gentle master,
O my sweet master, O you memory
Of old Sir Rowland, why, what make you here?
Why are you virtuous? Why do people love you?   5
And wherefore are you gentle, strong, and valiant?
Why would you be so fond to overcome
The bonny prizer of the humorous Duke?
Your praise is come too swiftly home before you.
Know you not, master, to some kind of men   10
Their graces serve them but as enemies?
No more do yours; your virtues, gentle master,
Are sanctified and holy traitors to you.
O, what a world is this, when what is comely
Envenoms him that bears it!   15
ORLANDO: Why, what's the matter?

ADAM: O unhappy youth,
Come not within these doors; within this roof
The enemy of all your graces lives.
Your brother—no, no brother—yet the son—
Yet not the son, I will not call him son   20
Of him I was about to call his father—
Hath heard your praises, and this night he means
To burn the lodging where you use to lie,
And you within it. If he fail of that,
He will have other means to cut you off.   25
I overheard him, and his practices.
This is no place, this house is but a butchery;
Abhor it, fear it, do not enter it.
ORLANDO: Why, whither, Adam, wouldst thou have me go?
ADAM: No matter whither, so you come not here.   30
ORLANDO: What, wouldst thou have me go and beg my food,
Or with a base and boisterous sword enforce
A thievish living on the common road?
This must I do, or know not what to do:
Yet this I will not do, do how I can.   35
I rather will subject me to the malice
Of a diverted blood and bloody brother.
ADAM: But do not so. I have five hundred crowns,
The thrifty hire I saved under your father,
Which I did store to be my foster-nurse   40
When service should in my old limbs lie lame
And unregarded age in corners thrown.
Take that, and he that doth the ravens feed,
Yea, providently caters for the sparrow,
Be comfort to my old age. Here is the gold;   45
All this I give you. Let me be your servant.
Though I look old, yet I am strong and lusty,
For in my youth I never did apply
Hot and rebellious liquors in my blood,
Nor did not with unbashful forehead woo   50
The means of weakness and debility;
Therefore my age is as a lusty winter,
Frosty, but kindly. Let me go with you,

6

I'll do the service of a younger man
In all your business and necessities.   55
ORLANDO: O good old man, how well in thee appears
The constant service of the antique world,
When service sweat for duty, not for meed!
Thou art not for the fashion of these times,
Where none will sweat but for promotion,   60
And having that do choke their service up
Even with the having; it is not so with thee.
But, poor old man, thou prunest a rotten tree
That cannot so much as a blossom yield
In lieu of all thy pains and husbandry.   65
But come thy ways, we'll go along together,
And ere we have thy youthful wages spent
We'll light upon some settled low content.
ADAM: Master, go on, and I will follow thee
To the last gasp with truth and loyalty.   70
From seventeen years till now almost fourscore
Here lived I, but now live here no more.
At seventeen years many their fortunes seek,
But at fourscore it is too late a week.
Yet fortune cannot recompense me better   75
Than to die well, and not my master's debtor.

When you look at any passage from a play with transactions in mind, then many come crowding in for attention. So it may be as well to think of a core transaction for the scene, one that sums up what we can call the function of the scene in moving the play forwards. In this case, the core transaction is the desire and attempt of the old servant Adam to prevent his young master from entering the house, and correspondingly to send him away, for his own safety. This core transaction passes between two people, and we can see from the nature of the dialogue in the first part of the scene that Adam has the initiative: he is stepping forward to do the warning, and to make the prevention. In order to do this effectively, he has to use persuasion—waving red flags or shouting 'danger' to a brave young man like Orlando will not have the right effect. So the transaction, as we might expect from a verbal form like Renaissance drama, is achieved through words and quite complex argument; Adam uses persuasion.

We might then immediately note one further, conspicuous transaction that is closely related to the core transaction, which is that Adam offers money to support his young master, and in addition offers his own support and companionship. We might take it that these are aimed at consolidating the persuasion, and so bringing about the desired effect. In fact, this subsidiary transaction in the second half of the scene is balanced by another subsidiary transaction in the first, one that is equally necessary and equally related to persuasion. Adam opens the dialogue and keeps speaking in order to shock Orlando, because his aim is to get Orlando to do something counter-intuitive, which is to realize that his home is no home, and his brother no brother. He tries to make Orlando see the paradoxical truth that in some circumstances his apparent virtues will act against him, almost treacherously (lines 2–15). As we can see, this is too much for Orlando to take on (16), but the seed of doubt is sown, and Adam continues (16–37) with assertive evidence to back up his insistent instruction.

So by line 29 the first part of the core transaction is achieved, in that Orlando is at least persuaded of the dangers of entering the house. In that respect, we may say that the first subsidiary transaction has been successful, has achieved a result. But there is now an intermediate transaction (29–36), a kind of bridge that has to be crossed before anything further can happen. There is a necessary debate about where to go and how to survive without the maintenance the house can provide, meagre though that may be, as the audience has seen in the opening scenes of the play. This short section results in a temporary failure for Adam in the core transaction, since Orlando cannot see the way forward; but it prompts the second subsidiary transaction (38–55), in which Adam decides to commit his life-savings and his person in order to persuade Orlando and secure success.

We might call the final section (56–76) a coda, if we like musical terminology, or just note that it is a conclusion. But it does also contain a transaction, which is hidden amongst other things. Orlando actually issues a warning to Adam that he is and probably will always be unable to pay him back the money he is offering, and that in order to find a living of some sort they will probably have to accept a far lower status in life. For Adam, the situation and the prospects are indeed serious, and he does admit to disappointment. But this further transaction between them is successful, because Adam notes that loyalty matters most to him, this being loyalty as much to his now-dead master as to Orlando, since the meaning of 'master's' in line 76 is ambiguous.

I hope this analysis is reasonably clear. There are two points that I would now like to make about it. The first is that transactional analysis is inherently dynamic: transactions move things forward, they represent the script in motion as a set of actions which make a play. In that sense, a good transactional analysis should always be convincingly organic. It should be drawn directly from the script, and closely represent what the script actually 'is'. What I have called the core transaction of a scene should be formulated in such a way that it explains what that scene does to move the play forwards. In this case, Orlando is sent out into the wilds, so to speak, which is actually the end of the beginning, since all the sympathetic 'players' are now in or heading for the forest.

The second point is that in talking about transactions I have had to use the term 'success' and 'successful', with the related ideas of aim, purpose, or effect. These characteristics of transactions are organic to them, and the simplest formula is to note that any transaction will either be a failure, a success, or inconclusive. Had Adam not thought of offering his life-savings and his personal support, then Orlando's sense of personal dignity might have meant that the core transaction of the scene, initiated by Adam, would have been a failure: Orlando would not have left the house and the city. But although success is important in this case, the failure of a core transaction can at times move the action of a play forwards just as effectively as a success. Unless we are dealing with a very incompetent playwright, then an inconclusive transaction will also be placed in a script for a sound dramatic purpose.

If we listen carefully, transactions will also tell us about the beliefs of the audience, or at least what the playwright felt assured were the prevailing beliefs. Beliefs are closely associated with sentiment, and in this case we can still sense the sentimental quality of the scene. We are invited to feel sorry for the young man, and to feel a kind of pride for the old servant. We can be almost certain that the ideological charge in the scene is the buzz that is given by the thought of a loyal, faithful and self-sacrificing servant. This presumably must appeal (perhaps admittedly in different ways) not just to those who retain servants, but to those who may identify with them. This buzz is attached to the time-honoured cliché about how 'things ain't what they used to be' (56–62), which draws its conviction from the evident certainty that the relations between servant and master nowadays are very cynical.

In fact, for this nexus of sentiment to have its full effect, another minor transaction has to take place, which might be called an internal transaction, since it is achieved by one character on himself. While Orlando's father was alive, Adam was loyal and faithful to him, but on his death Adam by rights should be loyal and faithful to the new master of the household, Orlando's mean and cruel brother. Again by rights, Orlando is not really Adam's 'young master', and he has to justify to himself what amounts to a very drastic transfer of loyalty from the older brother to the disfranchised, younger son of old Sir Rowland.

So in the first part of the scene, apart from attempting to persuade Orlando by the means we have discussed, Adam is also achieving the persuasion of himself, or perhaps the moral justification of what will prove to be the transfer of his worldly wealth and his body: he is treating himself like a chattel, in fact, a piece of property that Orlando will now inherit. He does this subtly, despite the rhetorical character of the language, by insisting that Orlando is the 'memory of old Sir Rowland' (lines 3–4), which suggests that he is the true imprint of his father, which is confirmed by his virtue and its knightly qualities (5–6); and in his second speech by the corresponding assertion that Orlando's brother is in truth no brother, nor can he be called the son of his father: Orlando alone is due that distinction. So the evidence that Adam adduces of Orlando's brother's evil nature not only persuades Orlando, but is also successful in internally persuading Adam himself that his true loyalty should and must lie with the true son of his former master.

While we correctly think of the scene as containing a transaction that matters most to the action of the play in so far as it affects Orlando, it is fair to say that it paints an emotive picture of a massive transformation in the life of a far more humble man. This is a scene that matters greatly to both, and the moment is difficult for both. If we seize on the sentimental qualities of it without any sense of affliction, then we have purchased it too cheaply. Although it may be very helpful when building a performance of a pre-modern play to have research and information about the society of the day in hand, one should not neglect the evidence about beliefs and values that the script brings forward to us, notably in the course of the achievement of the transactions. The playwright will invite us through the structure of the scene, and the substance of the specific transactions, to notice and perhaps subscribe to certain beliefs, and to be swayed by feelings that relate to them.

There is no need to guess at these in the process of preparation, and subsequently in performance to slap an emotional layer on top of an unconvincing stabbing at sense. Whether we approve of them or not, these past feelings and beliefs will be to a large extent comprehensible, once they are carefully located, despite our understandable prejudices about the antiquity of the pre-modern and our own unassailable modernity. It is worth remembering that modern society has just as many servants as Renaissance England, and some of them are less well-paid than Adam. What is required is a reliable means to unlock those beliefs, and I have found the approach offered by the idea of transactions does just that.

In the following Workshops I shall be applying this idea to Greek tragedy, and shall at the same time be considering aspects of dramatic form and presentation used by tragedy. I am going to give these four Workshops successively a focus on monologue, dialogue, three-actor scenes, and scenes with properties. These structural characteristics are discernible components of script-composition in tragedy, and they require specific attention from a modern actor, since they work in certain ways that can be identified. I aim to provide sufficient illustrations to give a firm sense of the approach I am recommending; there is always a case for more examples, but I think that a number of different angles may be as good as a multitude. I have discussed between four to six scenes in each of the Workshops, which gives a good basis for intense work from a group of moderate size, who can divide the scenes between them.

The translations that I am using are by friends and colleagues, in the case of Aeschylus and Sophocles for the most part, or are my own: details of those I have used are given at the back of the book, in 'Thanks'. I have made new translations of all the passages taken from tragedies by Euripides specifically for these Workshops. We all have worked to the same principles, which are that our translations should be put through a workshop by actors in a studio, if not a full performance, and tested in that way. The rhythm that we use varies between four and six stresses in the blank-verse line, to give us the necessary flexibility in rendering the original, ancient Greek in translation. The English language naturally works by stressing certain syllables, and an alternating rhythm of stressed and unstressed syllables can at times emerge as a natural pattern in everyday speech. The Greek verse line for the spoken roles of actors, which are what this book considers, is called the iambic trimeter, which means that in its normative form it conjoins three sets of four syllables of alternating sound, short and long. It was a kind of verse that was easily memorized and spoken, but it was written in an elevated language, with the strength of ordinary speech enhanced by a poetic vocabulary, and turns of phrase that were not colloquial. In those respects, it was not that dissimilar to the blank-verse line used by Shakespeare and his contemporaries.

The nature of the language and the verse line is a useful indicator for the question of style in contemporary reproduction. Style is something at which most sophisticated theatre-people grimace when it is mentioned, although all of them ineluctably participate in creating one of their own when they perform. The way in which the spoken parts of Greek tragedy are written should tell us that driving exclusively towards the colloquial in a contemporary performance will be working against the grain, while creating an elaborate formality will be imposing a stilted quality which the original avoids. Greek tragedy did not sound everyday in its own day, but neither did its characters sound like stuffed shirts or symbolic values. It was written for an audience who wanted to understand what characters said, did and felt, but who were willing to be taken out of the realm of average experience, and the language caters for both of those requirements. That to my mind poses a good theatrical challenge, one that is susceptible of countless, different contemporary interpretations.

While I am concentrating in this book on the building-blocks for any modern reproduction, which must be the extensive spoken parts for actors, I have included some comments on the involvement of the chorus in spoken scenes. For the workshop performances envisaged here, I am happy for the actors to treat the other workshop members either as audience or as chorus, or as a combination of both. While this approach ensures the maximum engagement of all in a workshop conducted in a studio, it may not always transpose easily and readily to a full production. Nonetheless, it is my belief that abolishing any notion of a fundamental gap between performers and audience, and between audience and chorus at some times, is the best way to ensure the vitality of Greek tragedy in contemporary performance.

In this connection, it is as well to note my view that individual actors playing characters performed in the open playing-space of the *orchestra* (which means a dancing-place) in the ancient theatre, and indeed played to the chorus in that space almost the whole time. So there is a close relation between all the performers in the original playing-space, and I have found that this translates readily to the studio. What we cannot replicate there is the vastness of the auditorium, or what might be considered the original 'blocking' of the scenes, in front of a constructed scene-building (the Greek word is *skene*) and with actors interacting in a broad space with a full chorus. But if an audience is present in the studio, then the address of the individual actors to them alongside a representative group for a chorus is fully effective.

Similarly, we may suppose that the delivery of tragic actors in ancient Greece relied on specific skills and capacities directed outwards and upwards towards that vastness of the auditorium. But no contemporary performance needs to feel inadequate simply because it is not imitating them. Nor should a performance in modern, usually interior conditions feel obliged to use masks, which originally enveloped the whole head, not just covered the face or part of it. These were designed for that vast, outdoor space as part of a distinctive, probably unique form of expression, and one major aspect of their function was to allow male actors to play women characters. Specific exploration of their value is fascinating, and I have been involved with it often, but it will not form part of the basic approach set out in this book.

I do not intend to go into great detail here about all the possible attributes of a workshop, since these will in any case differ according to taste, culture and circumstances, and that is fine, so long as the participants are relaxed and happy. In general terms, there is always a place for such staples as warm-up of body and voice, concentration exercises, collective or individual loosening, and group trust or confidence exercises. But I do have some specific ways of working which I would recommend. I ask performers to read the whole tragedy, at least twice, before the first practical session, and always to walk through the particular piece at a very early stage, simply to hear it while in movement. The sooner that movement is involved the better, because it will prove vital to cast aside any notion that Greek tragedy is best performed by actors creating a set of barely moving, classical statues, intoning their lines and looking half-asleep or bored off-cue. Movement was implicit in scripts composed for a large, open space, and it will be translated into similarly fluid work in the studio.

I also recommend gaps between studio sessions, because individuals and pairs need to discuss and work together to make progress. It is no good compressing the process, or believing that nothing can happen unless all are together in one place undergoing one experience, preferably intensively. Intensity very often reinforces existing assumptions and practices, since it comes through to the nervous system as pressure for results, the obligation to 'present to peers' or 'perform and survive'. What is needed is an atmosphere in which learning is possible, releasing and unmaking some mental and embodied practices, and working through failure or uncertainty into a changed approach that is capable of being realized in performance.

The guidance that I offer in live workshops is substantially represented in the narrative discussions of the scenes that follow in these four Workshops, although in live sessions it occurs in dialogue and response. No performer or set of performers will ever work on more than one scene at once in a live workshop, and that principle *must* be carried across to reading from this book: do not attempt to take on board at once everything that is contained about all the scenes in any one Workshop in the book. It will prove to be overwhelming and counterproductive: confine yourself in the first instance to the discussion in the book of the scene on which you are working. You cannot draw any real value from thoughts on a scene which you have not encountered. Once you have worked on a scene or scenes, and perhaps seen workshop presentations of others, you may well be able to draw down value from further discussions in the book by reading the relevant scene in advance, and posing questions to yourself about how you would work with it.

In live workshops, I expect performers to work through their speeches, scenes or sequences in detail, after establishing for themselves what they feel about the larger context, which is the play as a whole, and what leads up to their scene. You may find it helpful to mark-up your copy to indicate the different phases of the speech or scene as these are explored in my discussions. Extended work with each other by participants on the analysis is followed by extended work on the realization in space, with critical input from me as the workshop leader, or from another outside eye. Decisions can be made in that second phase about where the other participants in the workshop will be placed, and how they will be involved, in the presentation.

I shall be making further comments about the use of space as the sequence of Workshops unfolds. But as a preliminary caution, it is fair to say that what may seem satisfactory at an early stage will seem quite obviously wrong later. That is precisely what should happen: rather than being given a rubric for performance at the beginning, performers must acquire a sense of the right choices as their understanding progresses. This has to be an organic process; it cannot be a set of instructions given at the outset, because it is a matter of judgment rather than of rules.

This dynamic use of space is not one that can be reproduced in the recordings—available on the dedicated website www.actinggreektragedy.com—which directly accompany this book, and which serve principally as illustrations of the discussions of a number of the speeches or scenes in the four Workshops. They are performed well, but they are recorded end-on and uniformly, in a studio space that is bare of other participants, apart from the occasional, indicative chorus member. So they can only be glimpses of how a kind of presentation can be artificially extracted from the holistic qualities of a workshop to show to others. It is extremely helpful to see how other people 'do it', and frustrating if you are deprived of that opportunity. But do not forget the purpose for which they were made, and the strict conditions in which they were recorded.

Lastly, what do I mean by a 'studio'? I have worked in large and small studios, and it is just possible that one could work on some aspects of Greek tragedy in a cupboard. But I would recommend having six by five metres/yards, or five metres/yards square as a minimum, with a larger space definitely to be preferred, and do not be afraid to people your space from the centre outwards. There is, as we shall see, very often a central focus of some kind in the scenes. Although the engagement of a chorus and an audience with the action may call to mind the concentric qualities of the Greek theatre, no one should aim to reproduce its component features solely as an attempt to create the stamp of authenticity for their work. In our preparation we may well need to know how scenes were conceived for specific performance conditions in order to understand them well. But it is the organic relationship of elements that matters now and today, not the superficial reproduction of the whole as we believe it to have been. If we manage to recreate the vitality of Greek tragedy, then we have recreated Greek theatre.

FIRST WORKSHOP

Monologues

I always start the full sequence of Workshops with what can be called for convenience 'monologue', although there is more to that term, which I shall soon explain. The fact is that monologues are familiar technical territory to many actors, and it is possible for workshop participants to work in pairs on the same piece, which I think is constructive at an opening stage. We then also get a taste of a good range of Greek material, seen through the experience of individual dramatic characters. All this makes the work accessible and relatively easily assimilated in the first steps, since there is a great deal to take on board. Just about everything to do with acting Greek tragedy requires an adjustment to assumptions or set practices, and there is little point in making an assault out of the process of learning.

The second, convenient quality of working from monologues is that it is possible to introduce a large number of the important considerations attached to the idea of transactions without heading straight into the core of the idea itself. It is not so much that the core idea is difficult to grasp; but when you are adjusting in almost every way as a performer, integrating and implementing what can seem initially like a central concept can be daunting and counterproductive. The temptation will then be to go for the concept at all costs, when in fact the supposed concept is a formulation of what should take place through analysis and realization.

Another advantage of starting with monologue is that although each piece should be studied in its context within a scene, and in the larger movement of the play, it can be played almost anywhere and anyhow. This is really quite important when a great deal is being taken on board. I have known actors who are listening and thinking and learning from the word go, but who will cover their early learning by playing an old game, pitching a few casual tricks into a tentative presentation of what they see in the script at present. This is fine in the first instance, and almost always dissolves by the time of the second Workshop. In particular, I invite participants to locate the monologue anywhere in the studio they choose, avoiding attempts to reproduce a picture of the conditions of the ancient Greek theatre in miniature.

In fact, almost any assumption about conventions of space is initially preferable to that attempt to show us Greek theatre and how it was played. Some monologues feel best as if played indoors, and seating is also fine if anyone feels inclined that way. But there should be no pressure about space and its definition at this point. It is something that builds very well over the full extent of the Workshops, and rushing at it is unnecessary. That is not to say that I will not gradually make suggestions about how the workshop participants may be used as a chorus and as an audience. But I expect those suggestions not to register very strongly at this stage, or—if they do—not to register effectively in space. The monologue gives a performer the chance of the comfort zone of the self, the actor as unit in a supportive environment, and that is just fine to get people over the threshold.

Monologue is a word that is Greek in formation, with *monos* meaning 'alone' or 'by oneself' and *logos* meaning (in this instance) 'the spoken word'. Monologue means the same as soliloquy, which is derived from Latin, in the corresponding two parts of meaning. There is no philosophical difference between them, although at times critical thinking is inclined to use soliloquy for a reflexive, internal monologue. Now in Greek tragedy it is very rare indeed for any character to be completely alone with the audience, since the chorus is constantly present once it has first appeared, which is early in the play. There are only one or two exceptions to that in the surviving plays, when a chorus is removed for a short period, and I shall mention one of these in a moment. Before the chorus appears, characters may be alone for at least a while in those introductory sections which are conventionally if rather misleadingly known as prologues, since they are not necessarily separated from the rest of the play. But the explanatory prologue by the character of a god, which is rather remote from the human characters in the dramatic action, is indeed a feature of some of the tragedies of Euripides.

So in these prologues, and on those few occasions when the chorus is temporarily absent during the course of a play we may get characters 'speaking alone'. In such circumstances, their isolation may be a significant factor. When Ajax commits suicide in Sophocles' *Ajax*, the chorus has left the playing-space in one of those rare instances I mentioned, and he is resolutely on his own as he speaks for the last time. When the Watchman introduces us to the scene and setting of *Agamemnon*, the first play of the tragic trilogy *Oresteia* by Aeschylus, he is conscious of letting us into a secret which he can speak aloud only by virtue of his lonely job, stuck up on the roof of the palace at night. When gods tell us what they think, feel or intend to do at the beginning of a play, as an audience we sense that this is something that we are privileged to hear, and gods are autocrats in will and intention. Just listen to Dionysus at the beginning of Euripides' *Bacchae* or Aphrodite at the beginning of his *Hippolytus* and, as the catchphrase has it, be very afraid.

One might then say that these are true monologues, but Greek tragedy is full of speeches of considerable length, and it is this characteristic that merits specific attention. If we turn to the other end of the spectrum, many speeches are counterpoised to a speech by an opposing character in the same scene, in an overtly formal structure that may even constrain the speeches to a similar length. Other speeches are delivered to a community represented by a chorus, still others to characters waiting apprehensively for news. Characters may also be addressed by a god, to be told how pitifully they have erred and what they must subsequently do. Many speeches fall into one of two categories: they participate in an almost legal atmosphere of trial, often in accusation and defence, or they act as reports given to the chorus or to characters, not always but often by slaves, soldiers or working people who might be classified as 'messengers'.

Clytemnestra telling it how it is (not), from Aeschylus' *Agamemnon*

Let's now take some text, and handle it with a relatively light touch. This is Clytemnestra in *Agamemnon* by Aeschylus, the first play of the *Oresteia* trilogy, on the occasion of the return home to the city of Argos of her husband Agamemnon, successful in the war against Troy:

CLYTEMNESTRA: Men of the city, Elders of Argos, I   855
am not ashamed to speak of how I love
my husband. Time erodes
all reticence. I have not learned from others—
I shall tell you of my wretched life
for all the time this man was camped before the walls of Troy.   860
First, for a woman to remain at home
alone, without a man—that is unbearable:
she has to hear so many fresh and wounding rumours—
one herald comes, and then another brings a tale of woe
worse than the last, crying sorrow for the house;   865
indeed, if this man here had suffered from
as many wounds as rumours said
which reached us, he'd have more holes in him than a net.
And if he'd died as many deaths as stories claimed
he'd be a second Geryon with three bodies   870
and he could boast that he had got a triple cloak   872
of earth, a death for each of his three shapes.
Because of all these stories that came back,
they often had to hold me forcibly   875
and free my neck from nooses I had strung from up above.
That's why your son's not standing here
as he should be, the guardian of the pledges made

by me and you, Orestes; do not be amazed;
our faithful ally's looking after him,   880
Strophios the Phokian. He alerted me
to dangers on two sides: first, your peril in the war
at Troy, and then the chance that popular
revolt might overthrow the Council,
since men often give a further kick when one is down.   885
So this excuse of mine bears no deceit.
But as for me, the gushing fountains of my tears
have now run dry, and not one drop is left.
With waiting late at night my eyes are sore
as I cried bitterly because the beacons for your victory   890
always refused to light; and in my dreams
I was awakened by the gentle rushing of a gnat
buzzing aloud, since I saw you suffering more
than could have happened in the time sleep shared with me.
Now I've endured all that, with joyful heart   895
I would proclaim this man the watchdog of a farm,
the saving forestay of a ship, a high-roofed house's
solid pillar, or a father's only son,
to thirsty travellers a flowing spring,
and land for sailors suddenly in sight beyond   900
their hopes, a fair day dawning after storm.
These are the words in which I think it right to honour him:
may Jealousy stand far away; we have endured so much
before. And now, my dear beloved, step   905
out of this chariot—but don't permit your foot
to touch the ground, my king, the foot that conquered Troy.
Women, why do you wait? I have instructed you
to clothe the area with fabrics where he has to walk.
Create at once a crimson path, where Justice may   910
lead him into a house he never thought to see.
All else a mind not overcome by sleep
will justly make, with gods' help, reach the fated end.

This is not a particularly long speech by the standards of Greek
tragedy, nor by the standards of Clytemnestra in this play, who
delivers speeches throughout the action, deferring only in the end

21

to her lover Aegisthus. It is a delightful piece, and perhaps some of the exaggeration communicates itself without much sense of context: the gnat buzzing is a wonderful moment, and the set of comparisons between lines 895 and 901 lays it on very thick. The character is seen to be enjoying herself as a public speaker, something a woman is not meant to be in ancient Greek culture, proving her rhetorical skills. This display is not lost on her husband, who in the rejoinder that follows drily compares her speech to his absence, in that both were very long.

It is also an immensely deceitful speech, since it conceals the fact that Clytemnestra detests her husband Agamemnon, and in his absence has taken his cousin Aegisthus as her lover. This has been hinted to us as an audience, if we did not already know the myth, and so we hear the account of her painful waiting with great irony. She may have been strung out, but if so it would be in hoping to hear of his death, and strung up she would not have been. Nor was she on her own at night. But this is the saga of the faithful wife, and it conceals very violent thoughts about triple deaths, and a net like that in which she will eventually trap her husband. Later in the play Clytemnestra will be seen standing over the dead bodies of Agamemnon and his lover Cassandra in such a net, and she will then inform the chorus and the audience with relish that she has spoken a great deal in deceit until this moment that all is accomplished.

But what in particular I would like you to notice is that Clytemnestra addresses her speech to the Elders of Argos, who are the chorus, and not to her husband. She does later address Agamemnon directly during the speech, in the passage on their son Orestes, who is notable by his absence, and subsequently in her picture of nocturnal misery and grief. But she then returns to addressing Agamemnon in the third person, as 'this man' (896) and 'him' (902), before swinging into 'my dear beloved' at 904. This speech is indeed a speech, and not part of a conversation: one can imagine Agamemnon standing in his war-chariot or carriage, and being the 'subject of discussion' until he is told to move. This is a monologue that is a long way from private thought, although its public aspect conceals very private thoughts.

It is also a speech that balances another, the opening speech made by Agamemnon on his arrival home from war as a victorious general and as monarch of Argos. Neither 'he' nor we as the audience may be expecting a balancing speech from Clytemnestra to follow; but on the other hand, what we as an audience have heard from her up until this point might suggest that it could. Once it does, and once the sense of balancing visions from two contrasting characters appears, we may begin to detect another important aspect of the scene, namely that these two characters are bidding for command and control.

Until this point in the play, which is many years after Agamemnon's departure for Troy, Clytemnestra has been in charge at Argos, and she has spoken authoritatively to the chorus of Elders. They welcome Agamemnon, and with his speech he starts to reassert his authority. Clytemnestra's speech counterbalances that bid on his behalf, and assertively continues her insistence on commanding the attention of the chorus, and writing the story on her own terms. As so often, Greek tragedy is strongly shaped by the relationship between one leading character and the chorus, and Agamemnon despite his status and his victory is unable to displace Clytemnestra in her control of the playing-space. He is the leader that the Elders want, but he is not the one they actually have.

We might readily discuss this scene in terms of transactions. The explicit transaction of the scene, as it opens, is the return of Agamemnon to Argos: his greeting to the gods of his land and thanks to the gods for victory, and his transformation from a military into a civil leader, which he anticipates in his speech. His return has previously been announced by a Herald, who has also announced the victory to the chorus, so this is potentially a climactic transaction since it would entail the displacement of the interim authority of his wife. He wishes to complete his transformation by making an offering to the gods of his house (this is the palace, elsewhere called the halls).

The transaction that Clytemnestra has in mind pays no attention to any of this at all. As she hints darkly here (lines 910–13), and reveals clearly later after the act, she has planned for a long time to murder Agamemnon in revenge for the sacrifice of their daughter, Iphigenia, at the time that the fleet sailed to Troy. She plans to get Agamemnon (and indeed Cassandra) into the house where she will immediately carry out her revenge. So she flatters him, sells him a story about her grief and fidelity, and hopes with her elaborate deceit to persuade him to enter his house in an arrogant way, treading over tapestries that are fit only for gods. Ultimately she succeeds, he gives in to her, and walks in to his death. Her transaction is successful, his is a lamentable failure, and both transactions are suspended against a backcloth of the governance and welfare of Argos, and ultimately of the nature of justice in Greece, which the trilogy takes as its major and concluding subject.

As you can see from this example, what a workshop must do is to address the context of the monologues. That means looking at the scene in which they are cast, and looking out to the play as a whole. It may be that proves a great deal to take in; but it is an exercise that is operative even in the first stages, and will have effects. I would advise performers in this instance to look at the speeches that Clytemnestra makes before and after this scene, to see how the character uses speech to exercise control, and how that control works in response to different stimuli in the tense continuity of events that the play represents. Time presses on characters in Greek tragedy, even if there has been a long run-in to this point: Clytemnestra may have had a long time to plan, but she is responding in the moment, with complete consciousness. Her articulate self-confidence grates on male senses of 'a woman's place', and she relishes that in everything that she says.

All Greek plays start with a situation that is at least tense, and which is tipped into almost frantic action soon after they open. The cliché that Greek tragedy is static is laughable, almost as ridiculous as the belief that it is classically serene and composed: it is frantic, urgent and explosive. Each scene adds further urgency to the evolution of the action, and characters struggle to keep pace with events. Hardly a character is allowed to occupy stable ground, and winning or retaining the conviction and support of the chorus is a challenge for almost any leading tragic character. Authority is assertive, fragile and flawed, and that is how tragedy declares to us its democratic origins, which are suspicious of any individual authority.

One further point emerges from this first view of a monologue and through it of a scene. What we call 'Greek' tragedy was an Athenian creation, and the city of Athens at this time was an innovative democracy, as I have just mentioned. What that meant fundamentally was that political decisions were made in a public assembly by voting citizens, as opposed to by aristocrats in a restricted council of their members, and that the legal system was trial by a large jury of fellow citizens, as opposed to judgment by an aristocrat. These were the two major components of the democracy, and both depended on public speaking and on the capacity to listen to arguments with excitement. The democratic habits of Athens account for the delight in extended speeches in Greek tragedy, and for the high expectations of them.

That sense of delight in speaking is also carried through to description and narration. In a society and culture with no smart form of distance-communication (Clytemnestra's beacon-chain in *Agamemnon* is a form of 'telegraph' which actually remained in place in Europe until the nineteenth century), news was dependent on the fastest form of movement, which could well be a runner in mountainous terrain such as Greece (and so we now, for example, have 'the Marathon' race). The impression of what had happened depended on spoken report: one might draw a picture in the dust, but the remarkable flexibility of language was far more capable and reliable. No doubt a dull report of an exciting and successful battle would be tolerated, but the desire would always be for a description that matched the achievement. So we have monologues that are vivid descriptions. These often have a tremendous impact on the play and certainly on characters. But they also serve to enhance tragedy for the audience as an experience, to bring the outside world of the play to life at a crucial and pitiful moment.

The Herald telling it how it was, from Aeschylus' *Agamemnon*

While these reports may be made by an incidental character, they may at times be delivered by a specialist, someone whose role in life was to convey official messages or reports formally. These figures are usually called heralds in English translation. Earlier in *Agamemnon* news of the capture of Troy, originally conveyed by Clytemnestra's beacon-chain, is confirmed by the arrival of just such a Herald, who delivers a report in three parts. In his first speech he greets the land of Argos and the gods on his homecoming, praying for their good will and welcome, and also greets the palace and the gods associated with it. There is then an exchange with the chorus, in which the chorus admits to grieving for the absence of the army, and living in fear of someone. The Herald then offers his second part.

HERALD: Yes. The outcome has been good. Over a span of time
you'd say some things have fallen well—
and others badly. Who except the gods
lives through his lifetime free of pain?
Suppose I told you of our sufferings—bad quarters,   555
narrow gangways, lousy bedding—what did we not
complain about? Each day brought every form of misery.
Then when we landed things were even worse:
we had to sleep close under hostile walls;
and from the heavens and the meadowland   560
dew drizzled down on us, a constant plague
making our woollen garments verminous.
And then the winter, death to all bird life,
intolerable cold brought by the snows of Ida—
or scorching heat, when the sea fell into sleep,   565
a noon siesta without wind or wave.
What reason to lament all that? The pain has gone!
It's gone for us, and for the dead
there is no fear they'll ever have to rise again,
while for what's left of all the Argive troops   570
the gains are won, and not outweighed by sufferings.

26

Why should we count the number of the dead like votes,
why should the living grieve that Fortune wounded them?
Myself, I want to bid a fond farewell to misery,
since we can rightly boast here, in the sun's bright gleam,   575
words that will soar on wings above both land and sea:
'We are the Argive force that once took Troy;
these are the spoils we nailed, throughout the length of Greece,
upon their temple walls as everlasting glory for the gods.'
When men hear that, their duty is to honour both   580
this city and its generals; so will we pay our debt to Zeus,
whose favour gave this prize to us. That's all I have to say.

There is much in this speech that is immediately inviting to
actors, because it is so evocative. Its movement is, however,
subtle and repays some care and attention. What the Herald is
apparently doing is to steer away from misery and fear towards
relief and celebration, but as he does so he passes through much
misery that sticks, and touches on the terrible cost of warfare
and victory. His narrative concludes in direct speech (lines 577–
79), issuing a claim on behalf of the conquering force which
requires others to honour the victors: the claim indicates that the
conquerors have paid their tithe of spoils to the gods, their 'debt
to Zeus' and other gods.

But the central dilemma is that of death. It is clear that suffering is capped by death, that many have indeed been lost, and he
is going to be vague about those numbers. As a herald, he might
well be expected to know the count of the dead and be able to
report it, and also to be able to report the names of the dead. The
most telling phrase is the reference to votes (572), because the
sense that comes forward here is that if these men had been able
to vote on it, they would have chosen to live, perhaps not to go to
war, perhaps to condemn those who led them to death. The hint
is that voting might be an obstruction to militarism, although
sadly that was as uncommon in ancient Athens as it proves to be
today.

It is only the living who may be said to have gained, since all
they experienced was a suffering that proved to be temporary,
lasting through many summers and winters admittedly, but

finally coming to an end. Yet these are the pictures that we remember and that strike through to us as an audience, vividly, as they must be meant to. First there is the cramped voyage on board the warships, then the constant sleeping in the open, exposed to the elements, the extremes of cold and heat, the vermin in the unchanged garments. All these are factors known well to an audience of active Athenian sailors and soldiers, who regularly conducted campaigns. But they are an unusual counterpoint to glory in the mouth of an official spokesman, and they are followed by the blunt lack of compensation to the dead, who need not 'fear . . . to rise again' (569).

So while this speech aims to accomplish a successful movement from fear and misery to success and acclaimed glory, justified to the gods by due offerings, it does not achieve that transaction without the shadow of another, which threatens to convince us of unrequited suffering and disenfranchisement of death. Just before this scene the chorus has sung of how 'the gods un-failingly mark out/those who've killed many' (lines 461–62 in the same translation), and how the ashes of loved ones killed at Troy provoke angry murmurs against 'the leaders of this cause' (451). There is an ominous counterbalance to the idea of success and celebration, and in the third part of his account (636–80) the Herald is pressed by the chorus to tell of Agamemnon's brother Menelaus. This is difficult for him, for it entails revealing 'the storm of anger from the gods against the Greeks' (649), which has wrecked so much of the returning fleet, with unknown dead, and the fate of Menelaus uncertain.

Have a look at how one young actor took on this central speech, and saw it though its movements while keeping that dual sense of transactions in mind (**Recording 1**). The use of space is no more than a sketch, with a sense of chorus conveyed by a marker, and the audience presumed to be behind the cameras. The actor must respond to the chorus but also extend beyond them to the audience, whose experience has to be conjured up in sympathetic imagination, although for many audiences this hard touch of the war zone is alien. What is clear is that Aeschylus achieves effects in a compressed manner; this is concise, strong, dense but finely tuned. It must be traced and followed through, not slammed out like a slab of rhetorical emotion or assertion.

There is something else of the greatest importance that needs to come out from this speech and the discussion of *Agamemnon* in general, which concerns the relationship of actors and the chorus. The Herald expects to address the chorus when he arrives in the playing-space/at his home city of Argos, and he does. Even when Clytemnestra speaks, which she does just after the chorus of Elders has responded to this speech, the Herald does not speak to her, although she charges him with a message to her husband. In the plays of Aeschylus it is apparent that the expectation is that characters will address the chorus rather than each other, and although there are only two actors required for the early surviving plays (*Persians, Seven against Thebes, Suppliants*), the action does not move forwards by exchanges such as conversation or dialogue between characters. This remains largely true even in the *Oresteia*, for which three actors are required.

I shall look into this further in the second Workshop. But for the time being it is worth registering this basic fact, and as a consequence how important the chorus is to any conception of acting Greek tragedy. It is not a matter, as might be expected, of mostly paying attention to interaction between characters and building the actor–audience relationship. In many circumstances, the core relationship is with the chorus, notably in the case of a leading character but not only then, as we have seen with the Herald. Despite its intensity of revelation and emotion, Greek tragedy is a public form, and much passes through the chorus on its way to the audience.

The central relationship between a leading character and the chorus is cemented by the identity of the chorus. In *Agamemnon*, the chorus of male Elders is almost inherently bound to be opposed to the rule of a woman, so there is an acidic mix of opposition, suspicion, distrust and hostility in the fascinating set of exchanges right through the length of the play. Clytemnestra challenges the chorus and taunts them, displacing the person whom they see as their rightful leader. Other relationships between a chorus and a prominent character can be apparently supportive, although support is also fragile in the evolution of tragic action, which divides leading figures from their community very readily. Leading figures can ask too much of the chorus, or lead it to places that are repulsive to its feelings of piety, alienate its sympathy, or pull the wool over its eyes.

The world according to Hippolytus, from Euripides' *Hippolytus*

In *Hippolytus*, Euripides allows Phaedra a sympathetic chorus. Towards the beginning of the tragedy, this is not difficult to do. Phaedra is a sick woman, wife of the absent Theseus, king of Athens, and she needs support from the women of Troizen, a dependent city where she is at present living. Euripides uses the device of bringing a chorus into the playing space out of curiosity and concern for a leading character, and their concern coincides with Phaedra's appearance from the palace, helped out by the Nurse. Despite the desperate revelation about the source of her sickness, extorted from her after an emotional siege by the Nurse, the chorus remains sympathetic if rather horrified at the thought of a forbidden passion for her stepson, Hippolytus.

By contrast, Hippolytus himself is denied the continuing support of a chorus, only allowed a quick song of camaraderie towards the opening of the play from a subsidiary group of huntsmen who never appear again. He is the object of Aphrodite's animosity, since he refuses to pay her homage, and indeed finds the erotic repellent. Instead, he is biased to a dangerous degree in favour of Artemis, goddess of the wild, and in favour of his own extreme idea that chastity is equivalent to piety. He is a man in isolation from most people other than dependants, or so we sense him to be, and it is a drastic mistake on the part of the Nurse to try to tempt him to take advantage of his stepmother's infatuation. She means well, this interfering and intriguing figure, but she has misjudged all the leading players about as much as one might.

We pick up the scene after Hippolytus has charged out of the palace in a rage, followed by the Nurse. He rushes into the open air, calling on Mother Earth and the Sun, and after fending off the Nurse bursts into the following diatribe.

Hippolytus—lines 616–68

HIPPOLYTUS: Zeus, why on earth did you pass off this fake coin on us,
colonizing the light of day with debased women?
After all, if you'd wished to propagate the human race,
we didn't need to have women to provide for ourselves!
We humans could have come to your temples   620
to trade either gold or iron or heavy bronze
and purchase child-seed, each man getting
what the value of his property determined; we could then
live like free men in our homes, without any trace of women.   624
I'll give you plain evidence of what a monstrous evil women are: 627
the father, who spawned and bred her, throws in a dowry
when he pitches her out of doors, just to be rid of bad rubbish.
Then the man who takes this pestilential creature into his house 630
is overjoyed to load his pernicious idol with the finest
gear, putting the finishing touches to her wardrobe and his own
distress, taking everything that he adds from his family wealth. 633
Look, it's easiest if she is a nothing, a woman who just   638
sits there uselessly around the house, innocent in her stupidity.
It's the clever ones I hate. God forbid I should ever   640
have a woman in my house who's smarter than a woman should
    be.
You know why? Because Aphrodite breeds sexual misdemeanour
far more readily in the clever ones. The witless woman doesn't
have enough initiative for debauchery; she's spared by her lack
    of brains.
I say that you should not let a servant near a woman.   645
Better to make them settle down with animals that
bite but are dumb. That way they'll have no one to talk to,
and there's no chance of them hearing any reply.
But as it stands, the enemy within dreams up schemes
of depravity, and their servants spread them abroad.   650
Just like you came to me, you embodiment of evil, to involve me
in your illicit dealings with my father's inviolate marriage.
Something that I shall expurgate with fresh, flowing water,
sluicing out my ears. How do you think I could be so debauched,

31

when hearing it suggested is enough to make me feel impure?   655
Just get this straight, woman; it's my piety that saves you.
If I had not been caught off-guard in my oath to the gods
I could not have prevented myself from declaring it all to my father.
As it is, so long as Theseus is out of the country
I shall stay away from the palace; I shall say nothing.   660
But I shall return as soon as he sets foot here, and watch
to see how you and your mistress will look him in the face.
I hope you die, all of you. I shall never have enough of hating
women; I don't care if people say I'm always talking about it.
Women are always bad, in one way or another; so there you
   are.   665
Either find someone who can teach them how to control
   themselves,
or leave me alone to trample, and keep trampling on them.

Let's take a look at how this speech works in sections or phases.
The opening appeal to Zeus leads directly into Hippolytus'
obsession with worship and the transactions that constitute
religious life. The standard Greek practice of dedication made in
the sanctuary of a god, to back up a prayer and win the support
of the god, is turned by Hippolytus into a cash-mart for fertilized
human seed. This mart will be for free men, and is based on
class categories, much as the tax system at Athens was assessed
on wealth (lines 616–24). This appeal is likely to be delivered
up to the heavens, since that is how Greeks prayed, with arms
raised, although this is an appeal rather than a prayer. As far
as Hippolytus is concerned, a free man should live in a house
of his own, and a crucial part of that freedom is freedom from
women (624).

This idea of women as a blight in the house of a free man
with wealth is developed in the following phase (625–33),
where the general tone is that of evidence offered in support of
condemnation, as if in a court. This evidence is based on the
dowry system, which Hippolytus adduces to prove that a father
has to bribe a husband to take his daughter away (628–29).
But he then adds the further evidence that a woman is a kind
of infatuation, alluding here to the tradition that springs from

the myth of Pandora. Not content with the dowry, the husband allows the woman to eat away at his own inherited family wealth by spending on luxurious clothes.

In this phase, Hippolytus seems to be transferring his address from Zeus and the heavens towards the human audience, and it must be the audience because he has no relationship with the chorus, who are women, and whom he completely ignores. There are men in the audience, and the full effect of this speech must be that Hippolytus assumes that many agree with him, while those who may doubt his wisdom or his sanity will feel caught awkwardly by sympathy for a woman, Phaedra, whose conduct is hardly acceptable in their eyes.

The next phase (638–44) has a far more conspiratorial tone to it, a 'come here and let me tell you how it is' quality. The tone is indeed frightening, with prejudice against clever women compounded by the taunt that cleverness leads to debauchery, with a corresponding insult for stupid women, who only abstain because they have not got the wit to err. The bile rises still further in a suggestion (645–48) that women should be 'stalled' like animals, and deprived of that standard appurtenance of the free Greek, a slave or servant. It is clear that what Hippolytus hates above all is the fact of women talking, which plainly is a vital part of his definition of the clever woman.

Hippolytus now prepares to shift his address back to the Nurse, who is a living illustration of the kind of depravity which he has generalized. With a brief transition (649–50) to that effect, he turns on her to condemn her and to assert his own purity and piety, promising himself a ritual act of purgation (653–54), and insisting that if his ears need purifying after merely listening to a proposal for debauchery, the rest of him would always be unassailable, the act itself unthinkable for him (654–55). He is bound to keep silent by his own oath, which the Nurse extracted from him inside the house before she made her declaration to him (656–58). But he commits himself to a cleansing absence from contact with her and Phaedra until the return of Theseus, the king and his father, restores male authority and allows him to exercise the only action his oath permits him, which is silent enjoyment of their hypocrisy (569–62).

Curiously, in the final and climactic phase of his tirade he does briefly address women in general (663), but only as part of a climactic self-justification. He claims for himself the right to abuse women unless they reform themselves, and absolutely rejects their right to existence, in a revisiting of the idea with which he opened his speech. He also swings out and away from the playing space when he has finished speaking, in accordance with the commitment to absence that he has made.

Part of the problem of acting Greek tragedy is dealing with sense, working out how to break down long speeches into sense-blocks, or phases as I have called them, and trying to avoid sliding over shifts of emphasis and idea indiscriminately. The whole of a monologue is made up of its parts, and it is likely to be an argument or a presentation. It works forwards insistently, but is neither vague nor merely bombastic, and it should not be dominated by one emotion, something that quite often proves a temptation even to serious actors. In this instance, it might well be constructive to play around with identifying the different emotions which are ruling Hippolytus—contempt, anger, pride, loathing, disgust, bigotry and prejudice, aggression and fear at least spring to mind. He is arrogant, he is also fastidious to an extreme degree, and we might try to attach all kinds of familiar psychological terms to him.

All of this pre-med will be highly valuable if it loosens the temptation to slap down one strong emotional colour throughout the speech; but this kind of subsidiary work should not become a substitute for the close interpretation of the sense-blocks. Why is that? It is because the speech activates itself through sense-blocks, not through inarticulate emotions: the chosen emotions should feed into the sense. Whatever we think of Hippolytus, he presents an argument, taken through as he chooses on what we would call a twisted logic. He is a speaker with public-speaking skills, as we would expect of an aristocrat and member of a ruling family, and he is enjoying himself in venting his indignation and self-righteousness. He is not out of control; sadly, this particular event has done no more than confirm his prejudice against women in the house. He is probably, granted his predisposition, more satisfied by it than truly surprised.

Take a look now at the two recorded versions of this speech (**Recording 2** and **3**), and see if you think that the actors have found the direction of the whole, and built it from differentiated phases in the speech as outlined above. Have they lost the plot through selecting and then being taken over by a dominant emotion? Do we detect an emotional rhythm modulating through the different sense-blocks? Is Hippolytus' misogyny adequately expressed? Do we feel addressed as an audience, and to an extent put on the spot as the speech seems designed to do?

In its explicit and shameless misogyny, this speech is compelling almost without a further context, and actors can work on it effectively so long as they know the prompt to it, in Phaedra's affliction and the Nurse's declaration of it. Yet although the chorus is ignored, the chorus is present, and more to the point so is Phaedra. There is nothing to suggest that Hippolytus suspects that she is present; but clearly this is a case when a speech has the most profound impact on a listener. The transaction here is an elaborate and appalling rejection, and the humiliation that is an immediate consequence leads to tragic results, with Phaedra driven to suicide and also to revenge, falsely accusing Hippolytus of rape in a suicide note, and so ensuring his death. The Nurse believes that all is not lost, but with the presence of the chorus as a witness to her shame and her sense of honour, Phaedra refuses to meet Theseus face to face and dishonour herself, him, and her sons.

There are, in addition, considerable implications for a full realization in space, with Phaedra initially listening by the door as the Nurse makes the proposal to Hippolytus, and then probably shielded by the chorus as Hippolytus bursts out of the door of the palace. As an audience, we will register that tension, and implant our feelings of horror on to the chorus and the woman they are concealing or sheltering. The Nurse is the one visible object of Hippolytus' venom and abuse, and he directs the rest of his speech up to the heavens or away to the men in the audience.

The outside, public space of the ancient Greek theatre, with its connections to other outside spaces dedicated to the political and religious life of the community, seems to our preconceptions a strange environment for some of the actions of tragedy. At such times, it is as if characters are forced out into the open air by the conditions of performance, and it is easy for us now to imagine them and their actions taking place indoors. It is certainly true that the script is always very well adapted to a sense of exposure and the public, but some of the transactions or dilemmas strike us as being inherently private.

Medea in reflective mode, from Euripides' *Medea*

This tension is true for Medea who has been deserted by Jason in Euripides' tragedy in favour of a marriage to the King of Corinth's daughter. Medea's grief and trauma are first experienced by the audience as cries emerging from the house, on which a commentary is made by a Nurse. But she does prove capable of encountering a public, in front of her house, in the form of a chorus of women. Although her suffering can be presented readily enough for sympathy in that setting, her plans for revenge are more naturally secret, since they are violent and indeed dangerous. Even more private would seem to be the hesitation and uncertainty which surrounds planning of that kind. Yet it also proceeds at least in the presence of a chorus, whose members at one stage later in the play object strongly to Medea's resolve to kill her own children.

Medea is given a series of monologues by Euripides, who is clearly fascinated by her pathology, and allows the turn of events to accentuate and torture her intentions not to be humiliated. The series is introduced by a great public speech to the women of Corinth who form the chorus, and who have come to the house out of concern and curiosity. Medea makes a case for women in a man's world in this first speech, stirring up sympathetic feeling for herself, and ultimately inducing the members of the chorus to commit themselves to silence, should she find a way of taking revenge on her husband Jason. In some senses, that opening monologue is almost an inversion of the monologue of Hipploytus that we have just explored. It is not just a matter of the argument and its content. While Hippolytus in his bigotry pointedly ignores the dramatic chorus of women in order to address the leading male god and the men in the audience, Medea in her first speech addresses herself directly to the chorus of women, since she is unlikely to find sympathy in the masculine prejudices of the audience.

But the second major monologue from Medea is drafted in a very different way from that opening speech, and poses some very interesting problems. What is apparent is that Euripides has pitched this particular monologue somewhere apparently between the chorus and the audience, but with the unusual effect that it is not really directly addressed to either constituency.

Medea—lines 364–409

MEDEA: Things are really very bad, all round. Who would
   disagree?
But this isn't how it's going to end, don't think it is.   365
These newly-weds still have a struggle in front of them,
with pain on the grand scale for those who made the marriage.
Do you imagine I would ever have crawled to this man
if I did not have something to gain, and some scheme in mind?
No, I would not have spoken to him, or let my hands touch him. 370
But he has come to such a pitch of stupidity that he has
allowed me to stay here all today, when he could have
thrown me out of his country and shackled all my plans.
Well, in that one day I shall make corpses out of
three of my enemies, the father, the daughter, and my husband. 375
There are many roads to death that I can choose for them,
and I'm not sure which I might try first, my friends.
Perhaps I'll set their house on fire, a bridal torching.
Or maybe I'll stick a sharp sword into their guts,
creeping into their house soundlessly, right into their bedroom. 380
But there's one thing against me there: if I am caught
darkening the doors of the house with some scheme in mind
I shall be put to death, and my enemies will laugh at me.
There's a straight road I can follow, and it's the best. I'll
take them out with poison; I'm clever most of all with poison.   385
Well then.

Let's say they're dead. Which city will take me in?
Who will act as my friend, offer me sanctuary on his land,
provide me with a safe house and secure my person?
There isn't anyone. So let me wait a little while yet,
and see if some tower of strength and safety appears.   390
In that case, I shall do this murder silently and secretly.
But if there's nothing for it except the disaster of exile,
I shall take a sword in my hand, even risking death,
and kill them. I'll see it to the end, come what may.
For by my mistress Hecate, whom I revere most   395
of all the gods and choose to be my accomplice,
who lives in the recesses of my hearth-place,
none of them will escape to cause me grief.
No, I shall make their marriage bitter, a grim reality,
with a bitter price for my exile for the father of the bride. 400
Come on then; don't hold back on anything you know,
Medea; let that knowledge shape your plans and schemes.
You face a test of your courage: walk forward to terror.
You can see what's being done to you. You can't afford
to let Jason's Sisyphean marriage make a mockery of you,   405
you, whose father is of blue blood, himself a child of the Sun!
You have the knowledge. And after all, we are
women, completely hopeless at great achievements but
clever as can be at constructing all kinds of evil.

In the first phase of the monologue (lines 364–67), Medea appears to be responding to the chorus, who have just cried out to her, wondering where she can find refuge and support. She has, at her own request, been given one day of reprieve from banishment by Creon, the king of Corinth, but the chorus cannot see where she can go. Her acknowledgement of the gravity of her situation is initially an answer to their concern (line 364). But she changes the sense of a turnaround (365) to refer ominously to her ability to inflict suffering on the pair of Jason and the king's daughter and, in a more veiled expression, on those who helped make the marriage contract.

Explicitly, there can be no doubt that Medea keeps referring what she says to the chorus in the first part of the monologue:

once again she says 'you' (at 368, following on 365), and later she addresses the women of the chorus as 'dear friends' (377). Yet this second phase of the speech (368–75) leads her climactically to an open statement about her intention to kill not just her husband Jason, whom the chorus regards as deserving punishment, but also the king and his daughter (375). It is as if the chorus is put into suspension by the playwright at the same time as he has his leading character rely on them, since it is hard to see that a threat of this kind to their royal family would be of no consequence to them. Later in the play they do respond forcefully to the threat to kill the children that is also expressed in a monologue.

There is only one solution in performance, which is to add a third point of address to those of the chorus and the audience, and that is the self of the character. This speech is to an extent, and despite some appearances, an internal monologue, a form to which the term soliloquy is often applied. The challenge for the actor is to reconcile that idea with the open, public delivery associated with address across to the chorus and out to the audience. Medea at moments happily refers to the chorus, but where another character might alternatively or alternately rely on the audience, Medea substitutes for that an open address that takes in both chorus and audience, but addresses neither directly.

So this second phase must be understood as having Medea track from address to the chorus, in a kind of rhetorical question (368–69), through gloating at Creon's simplicity and her own subtlety (370–74), to the unacceptable announcement of her intention to murder (374–75). At this point she places herself beyond the kind of address that might expect a response, and she confirms this distance with the final reference to them ('dear friends', 377) in the monologue. This almost demands to be seen as a patronizing but dismissive gesture which accompanies her accelerating detachment, taking an internal train of spoken thought through openly in a public space.

The third phase of the monologue (376–85) is characterized by the displacement of this final external reference to the chorus by a series of questions about methods of murder, which Medea puts to and answers herself. The short series of possibilities seems to be characterized by a shift from the attractions of a hands-on involvement at the scene of the crime, after a virtual break-in, to the advantages of distance-killing. At the centre of this shift lies what seems to be relish at the impulse of thrusting a sharp dagger right through a liver (379), contact-killing in the bedroom, something that would bring the greatest satisfaction. Self-preservation catches her in the act and withdraws her from the imagined scene, placing her back where she is, and deploying her art as a skilled woman, which for Euripides in this play is as a potion-woman and poisoner (385). Medea must not fail, and must not be laughed at by her enemies for failure (383): this is a consistent motive for Medea for the most extreme actions, one that is ironically and commonly elsewhere both male and Greek.

The principle of self-preservation characterizes the fourth phase of the monologue (386–94), which actually looks forward to the later appearance of Aegeus, king of Athens, who will provide Medea with sanctuary in a trade-off for fertility drugs. Running through this play is a deep concern about belonging or not, about the rights that a full citizen has and the insecurity of the outsider. For the chorus, a concern for refuge occupied their brief intervention to which Medea responded at the opening of this monologue, and they return to that worry in the second half of the choral song that follows it. What Medea calculates is that if she can find somewhere secure to go, then she can murder by stealth, so ensuring her own safety, which would be preferable (390–91). But the problem is that it is hard to see how any foreign friend would feel able to provide a refuge for a person tainted by murder (386–88). She is operating in very tight time, but she is willing to wait and see if something turns up. If she has nowhere to go, then she might as well slip in with a sharp sword, deliver the blow herself, and expect to die (392–94).

Both the third phase of her reflections and the fourth have led to the same firm conclusion, that she is determined to punish and deliver pain to her enemies. In the fifth phase (395–400), she confirms this by an invocation to an ominous goddess, Hecate, who is associated with the moon, the night, curses and magic. As a sorceress, Medea sees Hecate as a patron deity who provides strength to her practice, and by invoking her Medea is effectively cursing the bride and groom, relying on Hecate to make it certain that Medea's enemies will not escape vengeance. Yet although we might call this an invocation, it still stands as part of the mode of reflection rather than as an outright prayer, since Medea insists that the shrine to Hecate is indoors, by the hearth, conventionally the location for a far more benign, family goddess, Hestia (397).

The invocation has provided her with strength and divine backing, even though at present her plans are still open in relation to method. No one harms Medea and remains happy (398), and in the final phase she summons up all her skill for the challenge that lies ahead (401–403), and recalls again her refusal to be laughed at by her enemies (404–405). She regards her genealogy as far more impressive than that of the union of Jason and Creon's family, whom she despises as descended from the trickster, Sisyphus, the legendary founder of the city of Corinth (404–406). Right at the end of the monologue she adds a final twist. It is not just that she has the knowledge to achieve her ends; she is also a woman, and that makes her practically useless at doing good, but a most clever architect of evil (407–409).

With this comment, Medea sardonically turns Creon's condemnation of her as clever in the preceding scene into a threat and a taunt. We can confidently see Creon's condemnation as a social prejudice of the time, since Hippolytus shares the same masculine apprehensions, adding detestation and hatred to fear of clever women. As a dramatist, Euripides can create in Medea and Phaedra characters who turn these apprehensions into reality when placed under intense, traumatic pressure. His perception is that women who sense their own dignity will turn on those who harm them when they are insulted gravely, and he is offering these insights to his audience. Whether such women are Greek and honourable, as Phaedra is portrayed, or non-Greek and volatile as Medea is shown to be, it is the abuse of them by men which activates their intelligence to a vindictive and profoundly destructive purpose.

This final comment also acts as a gesture of inclusion to the chorus as women themselves, although it is hardly one to which they would rush to subscribe. Their emphasis, in the danced song that immediately follows the monologue, is firstly on the abuse and slander of women by men, and then on their continuing concern about a place of refuge for Medea. It is as if they have not heard what she has just been saying, but are exercised in a continuity of preoccupation with the general situation laid out to them in Medea's first public speech, which was addressed openly and directly to them. This broad preoccupation is actually maintained in a second danced song after the scene with Jason that follows. They only break out of their own world of consciousness when Medea finally declares that she will murder her children, an announcement which shocks them into a dialogue of protest with her.

If everything points to this speech being an open form of address that contains an internal monologue, one which has no distinct effect on the chorus or another character, then we should also expect the transactions to be internal in this case. So they are conducted in the internal debate about the methods of murder and their consequences for Medea the perpetrator, with poison preferred; and the related debate about places of refuge, which qualifies the doubts over methods, since direct action will be preferred if no place of refuge emerges. Once these debates have been taken through their phases, then support from Hecate is brought in to confirm the principle of revenge taken on an enemy. The final transaction is Medea's assertion that she has a more impressive genealogy than that of her enemies, and impressive qualifications for her task. The overall transaction of the monologue is that of achieving the resolution to take revenge on those who have hurt and insulted her, a revenge which will satisfy, and will either result in personal security or a bloody and violent gesture.

A new ruler and his public: Creon and the chorus, from Sophocles' *Antigone*

Both Euripides' Creon and Aeschylus' Agamemnon are characters who might expect to have the security of a sound relationship with the chorus in their home cities, but who are decisively marginalized by women who are able to maintain their purpose in the insistent beat of tragic time. What is apparent from all three tragedies that we have visited to date is that the house or palace contains a great deal, and is often a source of horror for the males of tragedy, whose patriarchy is subject to subversion, and whose lives may be terminated or wrecked. So alongside the playing-space there is the looming presence of the scene-building, into which characters enter and from which they may appear. The role of the scene-building in each play should be carefully considered, as it often provides a reference point for the construction of a scene, or has implications for the evolution of the action. It is the interior space of Greek tragedy, which is hidden from us but which often impinges on the consciousness of the characters. It may be a palace, a more humble house, a temple, a military tent, or even a cave.

In Sophocles' *Antigone*, another Creon summons elders of the city of Thebes to join him in front of the palace, which has become his on the death of the two sons of Oedipus in battle on the day before. The city is to an extent celebrating its relief from a siege, but it is also oppressed by the turbulence of dynastic struggle in the family of Oedipus, a struggle that has only now apparently ended. Creon inherits authority from his sister Jocasta, married to Oedipus, and despite his name he has no connection to the Creon of Corinth in Euripides' *Medea*: the name 'Creon' in Greek simply means 'ruler'. In *Antigone*, Creon is the new ruler in town, and in front of what is now 'his' palace he holds forth in the playing space, to a chorus that owes deference to his authority. Here is his first public speech in power to his council of Elders:

Antigone—lines 162–210

CREON: Well, men, the gods have shaken up our city with gigantic waves
but now they've set it safely straight on course again.
I chose to send my messengers for you, selected from
all of our people, first because I know how constantly   165
you gave respect to Laius' power when he was king,
and then, when Oedipus was ruler of this city,

[my sister's husband, you were loyal too.]
After he died, you stayed true to their sons.
Now they have also perished, falling on one day   170
by a twin fate—they hit out, they were struck,
and were polluted by the stain of kindred murder.
I hold all power and the throne,
because I was the next of kin to those who've died.
It is not possible to know a man's whole character,   175
his mind and judgement, till he has
been tested in administration and in framing laws.
Now I believe that if the man who guides the city
as a whole does not cling firmly to the best advice,
but keeps his tongue locked tight because of fear,   180
that shows he is and always has been worthless.
If a man regards his friends or relatives
as more important than his native land, him I count as nothing.
May Zeus, who sees everything, know this:
I would not stand in silence if I saw destruction looming up   185
for people of this city in place of security; nor would
I ever make a man who was this country's enemy
my friend. I know our country is our saviour;
if she stays upright, and holds a steady course,
then we can make true friends.   190
These are the principles by which I'll make this city great.
And now I have proclaimed an edict, close related to them,
to our citizens about the sons of Oedipus;
Eteocles died fighting for this city, and
achieved surpassing merit in close combat; so   195
we will entomb him, and pay all the sacred offerings
which go below to the most excellent among the dead.
As for his kinsman—I mean Polynices,
who was exiled and came back intending
to burn down from the citadel his fathers' city   200
and its native gods, taste kindred blood
and sell the rest of us as slaves:
it is proclaimed to Thebes that no one can
give him the grace of burial or sing laments for him;
his body must be left unburied, food for birds   205

and dogs to eat—mutilated in the sight of all.
That's what I want; people who harm us will
not ever get more honour from me than the just.
If anyone is well disposed towards this city,
I will honour him in death and life.   210

With a speech of this kind, the tragic character addresses the
chorus and through them the citizenry of Thebes, while the
tragic actor expands this dramatic role to speak and perform to
the chorus, but above and beyond them to the audience. Tragedy
here reproduces the political form of speaking that was so
familiar to the Athenians, seating the audience as if they were in
their own political assembly. The most significant difference is
not so much in the language and topic, but in the fact that Creon
is an autocrat and dynast. While this is unexceptional in tragedy,
it would be anathema in the politics of democratic Athens, and
such tragic characters are inherently tainted with a tone and
expectations that jar on popular feeling.

Nonetheless, Sophocles gives Creon some good, stirring
lines, which start in the first phase of the speech to flatter the
attendant chorus of Elders, whose constancy and loyalty have
been outstanding over three generations of the dynasty (lines
164–69). What he also indicates, by the opening gambit and his
telling summary of how the sons of Oedipus slaughtered each
other, is that his succession is not just an event. With this last,
dreadful and dual killing the gods have not only shaken the
city (162) but have also categorically brought the dynasty of
Laius and Oedipus to an end. The pollution of this most recent
kindred murder (170–73) is and must be the last of a tainted
family. Although Creon is kin, he is not of the blood line. So he
is implicitly claiming a dual authority, that of being next of kin
but also that of not being of the same tainted blood that the gods
must abhor. It is a very strong pitch to make, and it is elaborated
and pressed home with care.

Creon is determined to be a thoroughly public man, whose
natural home is in public space, and whose natural form of
speech is open speech, addressed to the chorus, the audience,
and to any character who happens also to be found in the public

playing-space. In the second phase of this speech, he sets out his stall, a political and personal manifesto that contains issues that could well have been advanced in the political assembly at Athens by a speaker. What runs through this creed is that intertwining of the personal and public life which can be associated with those from powerful families who enter politics, and the need to guard against it. This was still as true of democratic Athens as it is of many apparent democracies and other regimes now, and the suspicions of favouritism for family members would be live in the audience.

Curiously, Creon opens this set of considerations with a platitude that would seem not to apply to him, namely the need for a man to be tested in the mechanics of power before people can pass judgment on his worth and ability (lines 175–77). It may be that this is a gambit aimed at buying him tolerance for the moment, but he quickly follows it with some strong political signals (178–81). In ancient Greece, to speak of 'the best' and 'the worst' people (here translated as 'worthless', 181) carried political connotations of class, the 'best' indicating the wealthy aristocracy and the 'worst' either the poor or those who had no inherited wealth. So Creon is here implicitly asserting the value of the advice of the chorus of Elders, and how he as an aristocrat himself will naturally tend to follow it. But buried in that comforting and flattering idea is an insistence on the need to speak out and to be decisive after taking the best advice (180), something that Creon sees as applying to himself in the current situation.

That current situation then presses forwards in the next step of the argument (182–83), with Creon asserting that the fatherland (here translated as 'native land', 182) must matter more to a political leader than those close to him, friends or relatives. As I have stated, those in power were always suspected of favouritism, and Creon has every reason to wish to make an unequivocal declaration about it. As he has shown in the opening of the speech, he is acutely aware that he has come to power in the aftermath of the threat and destruction caused by the obstinacy and dynastic arrogance of the sons of Oedipus, his nephews (and at the same time great-nephews, if you wish to press the point!). The city, while relieved, is wounded by that struggle, and he must set out a clear distance from them, while retaining his title to power through his relation to them. It is a delicate balance.

The final part of this phase of the speech brings all-seeing Zeus in as a witness (184), and reiterates the theme of speaking out. Creon is preparing the ground for what he has determined to do, which is to show that he can distinguish without sentiment between those who defend the city and those who are a threat to it. That is the hint that lies in the commitment never to let his country's enemy be his friend (186–88). In place of the aristocratic and dynastic code, which sees the national interest as an extension of private interest, Creon advances the principle that the security of his country is the soundest basis for a man in forming friendships (187–91).

All this looks like solid backup for what Creon is about to do, but Sophocles likes to hang his leading tragic figures out to dry, pre-soaked in irony. The righteous assertion about the duty of speaking out when you see 'destruction looming' (185–86) is something that Creon will himself ignore, when he is confronted later in the play by the priest and soothsayer Tiresias and his own son Haemon. Both of them see 'destruction looming' in the dire effects of Creon's decisions, but they are both dismissed on different specious grounds by Creon himself, who forgets his own principle of the duty of speaking out.

The opening and the second, middle phase of the speech have led up to its climactic third phase (192–210), in which Creon passes from the general principle to the specific instance. Significantly, he calls these political principles of operation 'laws' (191), which is precisely the term Antigone later uses for the principles governing her own conduct, what she calls the 'unwritten laws'. As Creon says in the translation, his new decree is 'closely related' to the principles he has stated (192); the Greek text actually uses the word 'brother', which in the circumstances is almost an unwitting pun on Creon's part. The distinction between the brothers, the sons of Oedipus, is absolute. Eteocles fought with 'surpassing merit' in close combat and for his city, a combination that leads to the highest acclaim, and brings

47

him both burial and the full dignity of 'all the sacred offerings' (194–97). Both 'surpassing merit' and 'excellent among the dead' use the aristocratic value term of 'the best'.

What follows is indeed a climax to the whole speech, and for all its apparent emotion is actually a formal proclamation and decree of ritual exclusion from burial. It is rather similar to a decree of exile, and indeed it connects with that status for Polynices, who was previously exiled in Creon's thinking. In fact, he was due to take on power in an arrangement made with his brother, who then refused to resign and effectively declared Polynices a traitor. This Polynices certainly became, when he brought an army to besiege and attack his native land and city. So this is a transaction that comes at the end of a disastrous series of transactions, involving not just the dynasty but the city and the land and its people. Creon is also overriding the reciprocal responsibility of the brothers not only for the conflict but also for the polluting 'stain of kindred murder', as he himself has expressed it. They are, in truth, both horrendously guilty, and it is only a reliance on his guiding principles that allows Creon to distinguish between them. The whole of the speech, in its intricate pursuit of argument, is essential to get to this point.

It is bound to be the case that Polynices will be given a dreadful portrayal, in contrast to the short and sweet account of the aristocratic virtues of his brother. Polynices was an exile who returned, which is in itself a crime, but in his case returned to attack his own city and its shrines, intending to 'taste kindred blood' and sell his fellow-citizens into slavery on their defeat (199–202). Accordingly, his body is denied burial, and he may not even be lamented (203–204), lament being a ritual procedure normally carried out and certainly led by relatives. Here we see the full force of all the general principles so carefully enumerated by Creon earlier, since he is condemning a dead relative of his own and ordering other living relatives in the family of Oedipus to abstain from burial rites. What will happen to Polynices is mutilation and so humiliation: he will be eaten by birds and dogs in place of the protection of his body by burial (205–206). This is an ultimate dishonour, and for

Creon it is the counterpart to honouring those who are 'well disposed' to the city (207–10). Creon is a leader who will enact his stated principles, and not compromise them through family or personal interest.

If the decree is a transaction achieved by the proclamation of it in this public speech, then the speech to the Elders of the chorus is a parallel transaction aiming to bring them round to supporting both the decree and their new ruler, Creon. Greek tragedy dramatizes the insecurities of power with great acumen, and it achieves this often through modulations in the relationship between the chorus and a leading figure. This is true of Creon and the Elders in *Antigone*, and those who work on this tragedy should note that Creon is the figure who is exposed throughout the full length of the play, and wrecked at the end. At this moment, in the short exchange that follows the speech (211–22), the chorus make a commitment not to take sides with anyone who disobeys. They will find this increasingly difficult.

Feedback and rounding off

In this first Workshop, actors should aim to establish a good working practice, which is supportive and alert in its feedback. Although groups may decide to range over a broad set of criteria in feedback on the final presentations, I would myself suggest that it would be wise to stick principally to two: the extent to which the progress of argument through phases is made apparent, and the degree to which a sense of transaction(s) is communicated. These will focus the minds of all participants on the task in hand, and concentrate on the essentials.

The second of these criteria (on transactions) may not, as I indicated at the beginning, have been an explicit objective of the work at this initial stage, but it is a quality of the script that may start to emerge from the work, and it may add a compelling note. In making their final presentations, performers should also provide a contextual introduction for the monologue, leading the rest of the workshop participants up to the moment of the spoken action. This should be concise, and should attempt to represent the action of the play as it tips forward to this point, not the encyclopedia entry on the myth. It is an art of summary, and should reveal the awareness of the performer of precisely how and when the monologue steps into the play.

While the analysis and the interpretation of the script has been the substance of my outline here, it is also obvious that the relationship of characters with the chorus is a vital ingredient of understanding, as it is of the structure of tragic experience excruciatingly explored in the plays. This groundwork is very important, since it is radically different from any assumptions a modern actor is likely to have acquired. A full tragic character is to some extent inconceivable without a chorus, as he or she would be if considered without reference to the public and open aspect of ancient Greek performance. Modern productions may attempt to translate the tragic mode into an interior action; but they will be on stronger ground if they have first acknowledged and worked on the public and exterior quality of the script. In this first Workshop, it may have been helpful to feed in another participant as an indicative chorus and a reference point. But even if that is not done, the learning should take place, and the monologue must allow for the chorus to be addressed quite as much as the audience.

While the contemporary audience is always in front of us, it should also be apparent that a sense of the ancient audience must emerge from working on tragic scripts. Although some extrinsic information is always going to help, much of what is needed can be drawn by the actor from the script itself, which after all was precisely drafted to work on the feelings, beliefs and perceptions of its original Athenian audience. But it should be no surprise if these are at times, or even fundamentally, contradictory in their nature.

To take one prominent instance, Athens was both assertively democratic in its institutions and attitudes and also still actually led within those structures by those from wealthy and upper-class families. Tragedy exists within this paradox of feeling, which is suspicious of all aristocratic tendencies, but also still inclined to admire aristocratic qualities, and use language that reflects them. The audience might admire such characteristics in the dynastic, mythological figures brought to ruin in front of it, but also sense relief and justice in the destruction of their arrogance and obstinacy. It is not as difficult to understand this as we might care to pretend: all we have to do is look around us at our own societies, and perhaps even at ourselves as contradictory beings.

SECOND WORKSHOP

Dialogues

While some may think of the lone performer in space as the essence of theatre, others would contend that dramatic theatre only really takes place when there is the capacity for dialogue. Greek tragedy offers both of these elements, but also subjects both of them to the presence of a chorus, who as we have seen in the First Workshop may have the script almost entirely directed to them.

There is something elemental about Greek tragedy in its basic resources, and there are limits to the extent to which these elements are exploited. So we may learn that a general rule seems to have fixed the number of individual actors in tragedy at three, with some possible exceptions. Yet only rarely do we find three characters speaking together in a scene, and some of those interesting moments will form the theme of the Third Workshop. Similarly, the total number of characters in a Greek tragedy is never very large, with one leading actor taking a main role, often throughout the play. The other actors then share the remaining roles in what often seems to be a pragmatic arrangement, allowing time for the change of mask and costume for a new character.

There are many thoughts that might spring from core

observations such as these. Some of them may not prove to be very relevant to the modern theatre. We do not, for example, actually need to worry long over the intriguing question of the skills required in switches between male and female characters, since we have actors of both genders, something which the ancient Athenians denied themselves. But we may need to adjust sharply to some of the implications of one seemingly less fascinating feature, which is that tragedy increased the number of its performers over time, from one to three.

Most of the surviving Greek tragedies do in fact come from the period in which three actors were available, and they were certainly available at the time of the production of the *Oresteia* by Aeschylus, in 458 BC. Yet just a few years earlier it seems that two actors were the norm, since they were for his three other surviving tragedies (*Suppliants*—463 BC, *Seven against Thebes*—468 BC, and *Persians*—472 BC, to put these in reverse chronological order), and probably for most of his life as a playwright. How far back we would have to look for just one actor is impossible to judge, since this phenomenon is unfortunately hidden from sight by the absence of anything other than fragments of other early plays.

Now there is no inherent reason why the number of actors should worry us at all in practical terms. But we should be attentive to assumptions that may arise about the history of the increase from one actor to two, if not from two to three, for the simple reason that it is almost irresistible to see this initial increase as an evolution, a natural search for the possibility of dialogue.

Despite its compelling attractions, this theory is totally mistaken. In the two-actor tragedies of Aeschylus there is virtually no dialogue between characters, and there is very little even in the (three-actor) *Oresteia*. This is because characters usually talk, or address themselves if we put that more formally, to the chorus. The principle is that the collective character played by the chorus is moved by individual characters appearing in succession to it: if you doubt me, try reading or even leafing through *Persians*, *Seven against Thebes*, or *Suppliants* with that principle in mind, or even *Agamemnon*, the first play of the *Oresteia*. The chorus in these plays is virtually the centre of gravity, the defining element in our awareness of location and situation, and a register of the developing or accelerating trauma that forms the tragic action.

So it follows that the second actor could not have been introduced for the purpose of discovering dialogue, but in order instead to make the duplication or addition of roles possible, to broaden the scope of dramatic embodiment in tragic performance. Nonetheless, dialogue does emerge as a consequence of this increase, or perhaps more accurately of the increase to three actors, when it may have become more obvious that two might be held in an exchange, with a third ready to come forward to change or vary that picture.

What this means is that the scripts of Greek tragedy may indeed offer up dialogue to us on occasions in what we would regard from our standpoint as a simple and interpersonal form. But the dialogic exchanges of tragedy may also form part of a pattern of address to the chorus, which may incorporate speeches or monologues, as we have already seen contextually in the First Workshop. These may be delivered as relatively free-standing components, or in a balanced form with the feel almost of a trial, or at least the representation of two contrasting points of view. For the most part, we should not expect tragic dialogue to be conversation, and this is partly because it is carried on in public.

As we have seen in relation to monologue, the presence of the chorus places the transactions of Greek tragedy in a public setting, something which is also inherently a part of the implications of performance in the open air, in an open space in front of a building of some kind. The scene-building as a construction is present at the back of the performance space from at least the time of the *Oresteia*, and according to its definition within the play it impinges on our sense of the action and often on the consciousness of the characters. But the chorus is a living presence, and its involvement in exchanges between characters and scenes of dialogue may reflect its close relationship with one leading character, or divided loyalties between the two characters.

So we shall find that the chorus is regularly used as a sounding board in arguments or contending cases submitted by characters not so much to each other as to public opinion, which will be partly represented by the chorus. In these Workshops the role of the chorus remains crucial, but it is not the role that is so often considered by directors and critics. They are concerned with its substantial contribution through song and dance, at performative moments that in a modern context may be seen to punctuate the action. What matters to us in all these Workshops—on monologue, dialogue, three-actor scenes, and properties—is the role of the chorus as an almost hidden 'mass' that, when taken into account, can explain the movement of other bodies. With some few exceptions, the scripts are nearly always best understood by allowing for the presence of the chorus, and for a default assumption by dramatic characters of the potential significance of that presence.

Throughout the tragic exchanges and dialogues featured in this Second Workshop we shall find the constant thread of transactions. These are never more apparent than in the business conducted by two people directly with each other, but in tragedy they are often subject to the variations introduced by competing purposes. So it may be that one character will appear to be leading the opening transaction in the space, but it may also prove to be the case that the second character introduces a contrasting transactional purpose to the occasion in response to that first impetus. Transactions may register themselves as leading or secondary, and tracing their interlaced pattern of purpose will be a crucial part of the approach of this Workshop.

Contrasting authorities: Oedipus and Tiresias, from Sophocles' *Oedipus the King*

Let's now look at a script-sequence that illustrates these two important aspects well, the presence of the chorus and a powerful transaction, in this case one that is absolutely central to the play. The sequence between Oedipus and the blind prophet Tiresias comes from relatively early in Sophocles' *Oedipus the King*, for which in some ways a more telling title might be 'Oedipus in Power', and the sequence is embedded in a larger scene. That is helpful to us, because it prompts the observation that the context must always be drawn in by participants, even to detailed and localized work on the text.

I encourage actors to provide an introductory summary to their presentation, to bring the other Workshop members up to the point at which the chosen section of script begins. What this means is that they must explain what I call the opening situation of the play, and then track the action through to the relevant point. This might seem simple, but it is actually as demanding as any form of understanding can be. What I mean by the 'opening situation' bypasses what I call the encyclopedia-entry on the myth. Instead, I draw attention to the fact that tragedies have, at the start, a kind of unstable stability that is tipped into full instability by the first action of the play, and the tragedy then moves forward with urgency at an alarming and precipitous rate.

So let me explain these terms of reference in relation to *Oedipus the King*. I would not want to hear about the Sphinx and the long saga of Oedipus' family and personal history, because the first arrives as a reference point in the script itself, and the second is brought out in the substance of the action. What I want to hear is that the city of Thebes is suffering from a plague, and its king Oedipus is found at the start of the play standing at the centre of suppliants who are asking for his help. Some action must be taken, and that he has already done, sending to Delphi for divine advice from the oracle of Apollo. As the opening scene of supplication progresses, his brother-in-law Creon arrives from Delphi with the response of the oracle: the killer of the previous king of Thebes must be found and expelled, for he is a source of pollution.

Greek tragedies are set in motion by actions, which in keeping with the Athenian temperament are often motivated by decisions and reasoning; as an audience, we are free to see how flawed that reasoning may prove to be. The relative stability at the opening of a tragedy may have lasted a long time—it is about ten years since the fleet left for Troy at the opening of Aeschylus' *Agamemnon*—or it may be calm after the storm, as it is in the opening of Sophocles' *Antigone*, on the dawn of the day after a threatening siege has been repulsed. Yet it is unstable because tragedy chooses the moment when things will change drastically. That is unstable stability, and the tipping point comes with an action: the return of Agamemnon from Troy, the decisions of the new ruler in *Antigone.*

In *Oedipus the King* the tipping-point is the arrival of the advice from the oracle, but it would not work without the determination and commitment of Oedipus as the figure in power to use his authority to search for, identify, and banish the murderer of the previous king. All in Thebes are now certain about the root-cause of the plague that is devastating their city and its fertility, and the tragic action has its driving purpose, represented in the will and authority of its current ruler. What the chorus does as it arrives in the public space in front of the royal palace is to dance and sing invocations to many Olympian gods in succession, calling on them to come to the aid of the city in this crisis, but also at this moment of potential resolution.

It is only with the arrival of the chorus that Oedipus the king has a body that is representative of the political citizenry of Thebes, of the responsibilities of the free adult population. He can now indicate to the gods and to the citizenry the seriousness of his commitment to civic purity by issuing an oath declared to the chorus, following his promise of impunity for anyone denouncing the guilty man with a decree of ritual exclusion from the land of Thebes for the man himself. This pronouncement to the chorus, and by extension to all in Thebes, forms the first part of the larger scene in which our dialogue occurs, which is the subsequent exchange between Oedipus and Tiresias.

How vital the presence of the chorus is to this exchange should be apparent from the invocations made to the gods by the chorus on behalf of the city and from this pronouncement by Oedipus. The bridge to the arrival of Tiresias in the space is constructed by a short dialogue between Elders of the chorus and Oedipus. Here they not only declare their own innocence in relation to the murder of Laius, but strongly recommend summoning Tiresias to take advantage of his advice in complement to that of Apollo. So if the opening situation provides the larger context, the presence of the Elders and the respect shown to them by Oedipus as solemn representatives of the city provide the immediate context into which Tiresias slowly steps to take up his position.

What this means is that some of the participants in the workshop should be involved as chorus members in the exchange between Oedipus and Tiresias, and both performers should be profoundly aware of their presence in the space. I shall not attempt to indicate here what kind of disposition in the space might be adopted in any particular workshop, since this will depend on how the work is developed organically on the occasion. But it is always useful to consider whether all workshop participants should form a chorus, or if a distinction can be usefully made between a chorus and the rest of the participants as an audience. To take one example that should now be familiar, in the monologue from Euripides' *Hippolytus* discussed in the First Workshop some participants might well take the part of the female chorus, while others form the male audience whom Hippolytus addresses. These groups, no matter how they may be organized in themselves, would need to be widely separated in the space to help the performer build his performance—in his address to those separate groups, and to the Nurse as an individual character—strongly and clearly.

In this sequence from *Oedipus the King*, participants might all be involved as a chorus. But it should never be assumed that placing a chorus in a huddle (still less in a 'formation') will somehow release the true 'Greekness' of a scene or a section of text. The chorus is there to be addressed by the characters, who will also 'perform' their projected purpose to it: for example, a denunciation gains its validation from the impression it makes on the chorus and/or on the audience, not as an insult thrown in the teeth of another character. To put that in metaphorical terms, a chorus needs to 'ring' the space; that is, its presence needs to be felt throughout the space, not just in one tidy corner of it. If a group of performers representing a chorus is compressed, their collective voice and character are considerably constrained, potentially 'caged'. The chorus outlasts potentially any character; it cannot restrict them much in their actions, but if we think in terms of modern politicians (characters) and their acute sensitivity to public opinion (chorus) we shall not be far wrong.

As a character, Oedipus is almost the embodiment of a meticulous obligation to the welfare of the city on the part of a political authority. It is not just that he is a man who is sensitive to public opinion, although that is abundantly true, but that his pride rests in being dutiful and successful in preserving the city-state. His relationship with the Elders is solid, founded on their respect for his achievements and good judgment in the past. He is, at this stage of the play, supremely confident that he will guide the search through to its conclusion, and that includes not being misled.

In fact, he could hardly be more securely placed, with a trusting chorus around him, and with what he sees as a mandate to seek out the killer who is polluting the land. Here is the script.

Oedipus the King—lines 300–462

OEDIPUS: Tiresias, you know all kinds of things,	300
what's learnable, unnameable, earth-bound or divine.	
And though you cannot see, you clearly know	
how sick the city is. We find in you	
alone, my lord, a leader and a saviour.	
The god, Apollo—in case you haven't heard—	305
sent back this answer to our embassy;	
release from our affliction would come only	
if we discovered Laius' killers, and	
killed them or sent them out from Thebes in exile.	
Therefore do not begrudge us auguries from birds	310
or any other of your ways of prophecy.	
Protect yourself and Thebes, protect me, and	
protect us from infection from this corpse.	
We are in your hands. The best thing you can do	
is use what you have got, what you can do, to help.	315
TIRESIAS: Oh. How awful to be wise and yet	
not profit from that wisdom. And how well	
I knew that, but suppressed it. For I should not have come.	
OEDIPUS: What's this? You were not eager to come here?	

TIRESIAS: Send me home. You bear your burden, I'll   320
bear mine. It's easier, believe me now.
OEDIPUS: Holding back auspicious words is neither fair
nor friendly to the town which nurtures you.
TIRESIAS: I see that in your case your statement's not
appropriate. And I won't make this same mistake   325
OEDIPUS: If you know, before the gods, don't turn
away—we're on our knees, all suppliants.
TIRESIAS: You all don't understand. I won't disclose
my anguish so as not to expose yours.
OEDIPUS: What are you saying? You know but will not speak?   330
Have you considered this betrays us and ruins Thebes?
TIRESIAS: I'll not distress you or myself. Why question
to no purpose? You'll not learn anything from me.
OEDIPUS: Won't you—you utter coward—ever speak?
I mean you'd drive a rock to fury, really.   335
Must you be adamant, leave things so unresolved?
TIRESIAS: You blame my temperament but you don't know
your own which lives with you. Still you find fault with me.
OEDIPUS: Who could hear what you have said—insulting
words to Thebes—and not become angry?   340
TIRESIAS: I cover up with silence . . . it will still come.
OEDIPUS: If it will come, then mustn't you tell me?
TIRESIAS: I'll speak no further. There it is. And you
can rage as fiercely as you wish.
OEDIPUS: Oh yes, I will. I'll leave out nothing—I'm   345
so angry—that I know. It seems to me
that you helped cultivate the crime—you did it,
but not with your hands. If you could see,
I'd claim the crime was yours and yours alone.
TIRESIAS: Is that so? Then I tell you; abide   350
by the decree you have announced, and from
this day, don't speak to these here or to me,
for you are this land's ungodly pollution.
OEDIPUS: How can you come out with this so shamelessly?
What grounds do you think will give you leave?   355
TIRESIAS: I have my leave. The truth's the strength I cherish.
OEDIPUS: Who's taught you this? It's not come from your craft.

TIRESIAS: You did. You urged me speak against my will.
OEDIPUS: Speak what? Well, speak again so I learn better.
TIRESIAS: Don't you know already? Or do you test me?   360
OEDIPUS: Not so as to say it's known. Tell me again.
TIRESIAS: I say that Laius' murderer whom you seek is you.
OEDIPUS: You'll regret that you've repeated this disgrace.
TIRESIAS: Should I say more to make you angrier still?
OEDIPUS: Whatever you like. Your words will not affect me.   365
TIRESIAS: I say you're unaware that your love for
your partner is shameful; you don't see your misery.
OEDIPUS: Do you think you can keep saying this and not regret it?
TIRESIAS: Yes, if there is any strength in truth.
OEDIPUS: There is, but not in you. You have no strength   370
for you are blind in ear and mind and eye.
TIRESIAS: You poor man, you cast in my face insults
which everybody will soon cast in yours.
OEDIPUS: You're nursed in never-ending night. You can't
disable me or anyone who sees the light.   375
TIRESIAS: It's not your fate to fall by me.
It's fitting that Apollo cares to make it happen.
OEDIPUS: Creon! Has this idea come from him?
TIRESIAS: Your misery's not from Creon—it's from yourself.
OEDIPUS: Oh wealth and power and cleverness   380
beyond all cleverness, an emulated life,
how much envy is secured by you,
if on account of this pre-eminence, which Thebes
thrust, though unasked, into my hands, a gift,
if for this the loyal Creon, my friend of old,   385
in secret conned me, wanted me thrown out,
concocted schemes with this here king-maker,
this crafty fakir who has eyes for profit
only, but in practising his craft is blind.
For, tell me, where are you a true seer?   390
How come when the bitch-sphinx sang her song
you uttered nothing to release these people?
For sure, the riddle was not for the first
man there to explain; prophetic power was needed.
You did not emerge with any knowledge   395

61

from some god or from the birds. No, I came,
knowing nothing, Oedipus, and stopped her,
with intelligence, not with bird-lore.
Me, whom you're trying to throw out, with thoughts
of standing close beside the throne of Creon.   400
You will be sorry, sure, and he who's framed
the murderer's exile. If you didn't look
so old, you'd know through pain how rash you are.
CHORUS: My view is that the words of this man and
yours, Oedipus, compare—uttered in anger.   405
We don't need this; we need to look to how
we best discharge the god's oracular word.
TIRESIAS: Authority is yours, but we are equal
in my right to answer and I claim it.
I'm not your servant; I'm the prophet-god, Apollo's.   410
Nor do I subscribe to Creon's patronage.
I tell you, since you've taunted me with blindness,
you have sight but cannot see your misery,
not where you dwell, not with whom you live.
Do you know your parents? You don't even know   415
you're an affront to family in and on the earth.
The stroke of curses from your mother and father
will one day drive you out of Thebes in terror.
Now you see all right, but then darkness.
What harbour will there be for your howls then?   420
What part of Cithaeron will not resound
when you understand that marriage, and the house,
no haven, you sailed into, on your 'lucky' voyage?
You've no idea of the scale of other ills
which will make you level with your children.   425
So throw your mud at Creon and at what
my mouth has uttered. There is none alive
who will be rooted out so foully as you.
OEDIPUS: Should I put up with hearing this from him?
No, be damned! Now, at once! Go back.   430
Go on, get away! Leave my house!
TIRESIAS: I'd not have come if you had not called me.
OEDIPUS: I didn't know you'd say such stupid things,

or there's no way I would have brought you to my home.
TIRESIAS: I am precisely, from your point of view,   435
stupid, but from your parents', your begetters', smart.
OEDIPUS: Who are they? Wait. Who then did beget me?
TIRESIAS: This day begets your birth and your destruction.
OEDIPUS: You talk in riddles, entirely in the dark.
TIRESIAS: If so, aren't you the best to interpret them?   440
OEDIPUS: You now throw in my face what makes me great.
TIRESIAS: And this same lucky chance has brought you down.
OEDIPUS: Well, if this city's saved, then I don't care.
TIRESIAS: It's time to go. Here, boy, take me.
OEDIPUS: Yes, take him. For here, you're in the way,   445
a pain; once gone, you won't distress me more.
TIRESIAS: I'll say what I came to say, then go.
I don't fear your face. You can't destroy me.
I tell you this; this man you have been looking
for, among your threats and your decrees   450
about Laius's murder, he is here,
a resident stranger it seems, but soon
to be revealed as native Theban, a circumstance
without delight. For blind—though now he sees—
and poor—though now he's rich—he'll use a stick   455
to guide his steps into another land.
He'll be revealed a brother and a father
to his children in his house, husband
and son to her who gave him birth; wife-sharer
and the killer of his father. Go   460
inside, and work it out. And if you find me wrong,
say that I know nothing of prophecy.

Oedipus greets Tiresias (300–15) as someone whom he can expect to help him in his search for the murderer, as someone whom he has summoned to him, and as someone whom he may have to encourage to speak out and act on behalf of the city. In this respect, the transaction is palpable: Tiresias is charged with a responsibility by the king to use his arts (reading the flights of birds, or other ritual means, 310–11) to contribute to the search. The implication of the transaction as it is set out by Oedipus is that Tiresias might not have offered anything had he not been sent for and specifically asked. The transaction looks like an invitation and a request. But just as Oedipus had previously shown some suspicious impatience at the need to send two messengers in succession to Tiresias (287–89), the invitation barely conceals a command.

To take on its full form the transaction requires an appropriate response, and so it is significant that at the very first that response is stalled by reluctance. Undoubtedly, Oedipus has been greeting and instructing Tiresias (300–15) as he makes his slow and blind progress into the performance space, guided by someone who is later identified as a boy (444). By coming up to Oedipus in the space, Tiresias registers his willingness to be obedient to political authority; but what he now finds impossible to do is to speak, to provide the response that Oedipus has demanded.

In Athenian drama, Tiresias is seen as a prophet or seer with civic responsibilities; that is, he is tied to Thebes and its inhabitants, and has his seat of augury there. He acknowledges allegiance to Apollo, but there is not a sense that he is a cultic priest of Apollo, serving in his dedicated temple. In that respect, he may be unlike the priest of Zeus who leads the suppliants at the start of the play. Even if this tie of loyalty to Thebes allows the transaction initiated by Oedipus to exercise its hold on Tiresias and bring him in, his natural space of operation is larger than the locality. As a seer, he is like Apollo, as the chorus says (284–86), and his comprehension looks upwards and outwards in order to see what is the case, the truth (287–89). Apollo sees everything because he is identified with the light of the sun that permeates everywhere. Apart from insight that may be gained from Apollo, whom he regards as his patron, Tiresias relies on birds, which fly high and wide, potentially overseeing what we as humans do. His physical blindness detaches him from the exercise of mundane authority, but he has vision that exceeds the limitations of this space and this time.

So what we have in this scene is a contrast of authority that is rooted in a sense of space. For Oedipus, Thebes is a place that he rules, with all the people in its boundaries, amongst whom is Tiresias. For his part, Tiresias recognizes that political authority, and acknowledges his own civic responsibility. But the space of his own authority is far wider, certainly not confined to the kind of power that rests confidently in the here and now. For the chorus, who have the deepest respect for both men, there is a conflict between two kinds of authority, and that is now realized in two different interpretations of where and who we are when standing on any ground. To put that evocatively, for Oedipus the performance space has walls around it, while for Tiresias the roof is lifted off.

It is helpful to see scenes in phases, much as I have advised looking at monologues or speeches in phases. Once Tiresias has fully arrived he speaks, and the first phase of the dialogue (316–53) extends itself as a continuing attempt to make Tiresias declare what he knows, which Oedipus believes will help to preserve the city. Oedipus is shocked by the prophet's refusal to speak, and he moves from flattering Tiresias in his opening greeting—'We find in you/ alone, my lord, a leader and a saviour' (303–304)—to insulting him as both a condemnation and a provocation: 'Won't you—you utter coward—ever speak?' (334). Here the Greek word for 'lord' (*anax*) from the opening speech is one that would as readily apply to a supreme king, and is the standard term applied to Agamemnon as leader of the Greek army in Homer's epic *Iliad*. At the other end of the spectrum, the word for 'coward' (*kakos*) in the subsequent insult does mean that, but also indicates an absolute lack of class status or moral stature.

In this opening phase, we seem to see Tiresias moving into the performance space and coming to rest, uncertain whether to go or to stay. We also seem to see an elaborate gesture from both the chorus and Oedipus himself—'don't turn/ away, we're on our knees, all suppliants' (326–27). The language here is quite vivid and explicit (the translation might ideally include 'on our knees *to you*'), and we should recall that the play opened with an elaborate scene of supplication of Oedipus himself by the priest of Zeus and others. So there is no reason to regard this as a purely metaphorical expression, and it may be that this posture was adopted towards the end of Oedipus' welcome speech. If so, then Oedipus will rise from it as he gets angry and presumably before or by his insult. But the sense is that Tiresias is still for the time being at the centre of some kind of arc or circle of appeal, even if the chorus too is loosened from a clearly defined position by the intensity of the argument.

This phase moves forward by exchanges of two lines each, in a pattern that picks up intensity as Oedipus breaks out of respect into an insult that takes up three lines (334–36); is briefly resumed as Tiresias keeps his cool, but then given a quick charge of pace with a one-line exchange (341–42); and which breaks open into a more expansive climax with the reciprocal accusations made by the two men. It is important to see here (345–49) that Oedipus understands Tiresias' reluctance and refusal to speak even under extreme pressure as explicable by only one thing, namely that Tiresias was himself involved in the murder. For his part, Tiresias concludes that he now has no choice but to point the finger back at Oedipus, if only to defend himself. It is hard not to see this moment as indeed one of literal finger-pointing, as the two furious men face each other in what had been intended to be a ring of respect.

While the argument provoked by Tiresias' refusal to declare what he knows has been almost a surprise to both men, and caught them off-guard, there is now an opportunity for Oedipus at least to exploit his listening public in a manner that will satisfy him. We should note that the transaction which had been carefully prepared, with an orchestrated reception in the space and a flattering welcoming speech, has become a complete fiasco as far as Oedipus is concerned. In the subsequent phases of the dialogue, after the accusation made by Tiresias (350–53) that Oedipus is the proper object of his own curse and decree of banishment, Oedipus is convinced that he is dealing with a kind of despicable conspiratorial defamation, and sets out to make that plain to the chorus.

The irony in the line-by-line exchange that follows is, according to Tiresias, that Oedipus ought not to be speaking either to the chorus or to him. But the exchange speeds forward relentlessly, on the technique of picking up on words or ideas voiced in the previous line and throwing them back at the speaker. Insistent on the idea of defamation, Oedipus presses Tiresias to 'say that again' (359) and repeat the condemnation he has made, and this phase of the dialogue concludes with insults from Oedipus on the blindness of Tiresias (370–77). Oedipus aims to establish how dismissive he is of Tiresias' and his supposed knowledge, and Tiresias fends him off with a reference to the power of Apollo (376–77). Yet the true climax of this phase is a logical conclusion to Oedipus' insistence on the idea of defamation, as Oedipus suddenly brings Creon into the picture as a conspirator, the man behind the accusation that is supposedly being 'staged' by Tiresias.

In constructing this picture of a conspiracy to remove him from power, Oedipus returns to the self-belief and confidence in his own abilities which had been his hallmark as a ruler. His monologue (380–403) is expansive in feel, played to the chorus and the audience for approval and conviction, and as an expansive speech it may well be supported by movement. It is played in two phases, the first (380–89) appealing to a kind of common wisdom about the nature of envy, and the sense that all those in power have of the possibility of betrayal. What emerges from Oedipus' extravagant estimation of his own 'cleverness', and his insulting ridicule of the blindness of Tiresias for anything except money, is that he understands Tiresias' hostility to stem from a kind of professional jealousy.

This idea is part of the contempt expressed in the second phase of the monologue (390–400). Tiresias failed to come forward with a solution to the riddle of the sphinx, and Oedipus believes that he is now keen to remove Oedipus to have his authority restored, to end up through the conspiracy 'standing close beside the throne of Creon'. Tiresias is doubly condemned: he has no real powers of insight, so his accusation against Oedipus is fraudulent, but that accusation also reveals that he is a conspirator, aiming to complete the job that he and Creon started when they murdered the previous king. This is the view that Oedipus makes completely explicit when he later confronts Creon himself with it (532–42). Disappointed in the transaction with which he had opened the scene, Oedipus now constructs another transaction, an accusation which seals him off from any guilt or danger.

Yet both the chorus and then Tiresias refuse to let Oedipus

conduct this transaction to his satisfaction. The chorus insists that what Oedipus wishes to see as a convincing condemnation of the prophet is no more than the expression of anger (404–407). Tiresias counters by insisting that although Oedipus may have political authority, that does not give his voice the right to pass judgment without defence or contradiction (408–409). Tiresias' reliance on the god Apollo as his patron is firm, since he regards himself as protected by religious authority rather than subject to dependence on Oedipus or Creon (410–11). He is, effectively, asserting that he is untouchable, and he then goes on to unnerve Oedipus by needling him on his ignorance of his origins, and suggesting a curse on him to come from within his own family (415–25). This represents an abrupt and disturbing change from the previous charge that Tiresias made, which was directly connected with the curse on the murderer of the previous king. It allows Tiresias in turn to taunt Oedipus with blindness, and the ensuing dialogue shows that Oedipus is now highly agitated, his second transactional bid temporarily in ruins.

His first reaction is to order Tiresias to leave (429–31), no doubt turning away himself. But as Tiresias starts to go, Oedipus is provoked into treating Tiresias as the authoritative prophet he has claimed that he is not: 'Wait. Who then did beget me?' (437). Tiresias enjoys now taunting Oedipus with his ability as a riddle-solver, and it is clear that his anger has made him more buoyant. Although he does decide to go (444), he delays his departure to add more fuel to the fire, to say finally what he originally came to say, since he has now conquered his own fear (447–48). Yet he casts his revelation in the form of an enigma, a riddle that is built out of apparent paradox: a stranger who is a Theban, a man who sees who will be blind, who is rich but who will be poor, who is both a brother and a father to his children, a husband and a son to his mother (449–60). As the scene ends, Tiresias seizes the initiative and recasts the transaction as a riddle to be solved by Oedipus, in this explosive conflict of powers and status between the two men.

Sisters alone in private and public space: Antigone and Ismene, from Sophocles' *Antigone*

Conflict may also occur where the overall sense is one of power-lessness, and it may be helpful at this point to bring into view a very famous scene, the opening of Sophocles *Antigone*.

Antigone—lines 1–99

ANTIGONE: Sister! My dearest, closest sister Ismene,
is there a single suffering from Oedipus which Zeus
does not inflict upon us two who still survive?
There is no suffering, disaster,
shame or deprivation, which I have   5
not seen in your misfortunes and in mine.
What is this edict which they say
the general has recently imposed on all the citizens?
Do you know? Have you heard? Or is it hidden from you that
our dear ones will soon suffer at the hands of enemies?   10
ISMENE: To me, Antigone, no word about those dear to us
has come, pleasant or painful, since we two
lost our two brothers on one day,
when they struck each other down.
And since the Argive army vanished   15
earlier this night, I do not know whether my life
is now more fortunate, or I have suffered more.
ANTIGONE: I knew it! And I brought you out,
beyond the courtyard door, so you might hear alone.
ISMENE: What is it? Clearly some dark news is troubling you.   20
ANTIGONE: Has Creon not decided that of our two brothers one
deserves the honour of a grave, and one does not?
They say he's buried Eteocles beneath the earth,
according to our laws and customs; he'll receive
full privileges down below among the dead,   25
while as for Polynices, who died wretchedly, he has
apparently proclaimed to the townspeople that
no one may bury his body or cry laments for him;

he must be left unwept, unburied, a sweet treasure-trove
for birds who spot him to enjoy as food.   30
That's what they say the good Creon has now
proclaimed for you and me—yes, I mean me—and he
is coming here to make his proclamation clear
to all who do not know it. He means business;
anyone who does these things will be sentenced, and   35
the people of the city will stone them to death.
That's what you're up against; you will soon show
if you are true-born, or disgrace your noble family.
ISMENE: My sister, this is terrible; but if it's true, what help could I
give weaving or unweaving such a tangled skein?   40
ANTIGONE: Work with me, help me now.
ISMENE: What must I dare to do? What do you mean?
ANTIGONE: Help my hands lift the corpse for burial.
ISMENE: You're going to bury him, although the city is forbidden
    to?
ANTIGONE: Yes. He is my brother—yours as well, although   45
you may not wish it; I will not be caught betraying him.
ISMENE: How are you so determined, when Creon's opposed?
ANTIGONE: He has no right to keep me from my own.
ISMENE: No! Think, sister, how the father of us two
died hated and despised, when his own search   50
revealed his ghastly past, and he struck out
both eyes with his own hand; then his mother—
twice his, because she was his wife as well—
destroyed her life by strangling in a woven noose.
Third, our two wretched brothers on one day   55
fought hand to hand and killed each other,
bringing down upon themselves a common fate.
Now we two girls are left alone—so think
how terribly we'll perish, if we go against the law,
defy our rulers' votes and powers.   60
Consider this: we were born female,
so we can't fight men—and we are ruled
by people stronger than ourselves; we'll have
to bear in silence this command and others even worse.
So I will beg all those below the earth   65

to pardon me, since I am now compelled,
and will obey those in authority. There is no sense
in going further than we can.
ANTIGONE: I would not ask you; later, if you change your mind,
I would not welcome any help from you.   70
Be what you want to be, but I
will bury him. When I do that, death will be beautiful.
Dear to him, I will lie beside a dear one; I will be
a pure and holy criminal, for I must please
the dead below far longer than the people here.   75
I will lie there for ever; you, if you behave like this,
pay no respect to values which the gods revere.
ISMENE: That is not true—but I don't have
the strength to go against the other citizens.
ANTIGONE: That's your excuse; I'm leaving now,   80
to make a tomb for my own dearest brother.
ISMENE: You'll suffer for it; I am terrified.
ANTIGONE: Do not feel fear for me; just sort out your own life.
ISMENE: At least tell no one else what you
are doing. Keep it secret; so will I.   85
ANTIGONE: No, shout it out aloud! You will be even more my
    enemy
if you stay silent, and do not tell everyone.
ISMENE: Your heart is very warm for such chill deeds.
ANTIGONE: I know I'm pleasing those I am most bound to please.
ISMENE: If you can do it; your desire's impossible.   90
ANTIGONE: I'll do all that I can; then I will stop.
ISMENE: We should not even start to strive for what we cannot do.
ANTIGONE: If that's your attitude, I'll hate you, and
you'll rightly lie beneath the hatred of the dead.
Let me, and my own 'foolishness',   95
suffer this dreadful fate: I will not suffer anything
so much as if I do not die with true nobility.
ISMENE: Go, if you must. Know this, that you
are mad, but truly dear to all that love you.

This is an excellent sequence for use in the dialogue Workshop in
many ways, and one of these is that it offers the relatively unusual

challenge of the absence of the involvement of the chorus, who first arrive in the space after the scene has ended. The space itself is interestingly defined, because the script itself contains very little that to our eyes immediately does define it. But these are two young, unmarried women who are outside their home, which is the royal palace (18–19), and they have come outside to be at least private, and beyond that conspiratorial. Women seen outside, and so potentially in public, strike a jarring note in the consciousness of Greek tragedy and its audience, and their behaviour supposedly must be circumspect. Powerful women, in charge of households or perhaps charged with regal authority, such as Clytemnestra, are allowed a limited licence; but unmarried girls or young women can easily be criticized or constrained. So there is a nervous edge to the sight of these two young women, and a feeling must develop that for some reason the scene-building behind them contains a potential threat instead of security.

The second aspect of definition of the space derives partly from an awareness of time: not just that an edict has been imposed 'recently' (7–8), but that as far as Ismene is concerned it is still night (16). So this is early dawn at best, and not just any dawn, since this is the dawning of the day after a siege was lifted and an opposing army has vanished (15), leaving the two brothers of these sisters dead. The first reference is to 'the general' who has imposed the edict 'on all the citizens' (7–8), which in the Greek is the 'city in its full assembly', and this suggests that the announcement was made while the people were still standing to arms during the night, or in the earliest dawn. The general proves to be the new ruler, Creon, who first appears in the play in the scene that begins with the monologue discussed in the First Workshop.

So this is a space full of private and public tension, one that offers little security to these young women, and which has until recently been fraught with danger, or at least ringed by that immense threat. We might say that this definition, which emerges quite swiftly in the first twenty lines of the script, here takes the place of any definition that can be offered by the chorus. These are young women alone, and for my part I prefer to see Antigone alone in the space to start with, since her agitation can be registered strongly like that, and the script does indeed start with intense and laboured agitation. She can welcome Ismene from the scene-building and bring her away from it, granted her motives and intentions (18–19); and while Ismene plainly does not share her nervous energy there must be some intimacy between them, whether physical contact or close proximity.

Antigone is excited by her sister's lack of awareness of the most recent developments ('I knew it!', 18), and as she overwhelms her sister with the precise details of what Creon has announced (21–36) she builds to her transactional purpose, introducing it indirectly at first (37–38). There is a curious irony in the fact that Creon's edict has separated the fate of the brothers, since it will also separate the sisters; but initially Antigone claims to expect that Ismene will show dynastic solidarity. Antigone's proposition is introduced to her sister precisely, as an initiative from Antigone and an action in which Antigone takes the lead (41–48). This is a clear transaction by now, one in which Antigone is inviting Ismene to join her in a ritual act of family duty, fulfilling the functions normally carried out by female relatives for the dead.

Yet the invitation fails, and a gap opens up between the two sisters which will never be restored. Ismene lays out a path of logic (49–68): the sisters have been deprived of male support, in the self-mutilation of their father Oedipus following the suicide of their mother Jocasta, and the mutually-inflicted deaths of their brothers only the day before. They have no advocates, no protectors under law, and as women they are incapable of contending with men by themselves. So it is that Ismene not only contradicts and frustrates Antigone's attempted transaction, but also counters it with her own. She intends now to stop her by inviting Antigone to recognize her own weakness, and to avoid intractable dangers. To do this, she has to ask and expect to gain pardon from 'those below the earth' (65–66) for her justifiable inaction and obedience to political authority.

There is now an unbridgeable distance between the two young women. While Ismene may be able to appeal to the prejudices of the audience in making her argument and plea, Antigone seals herself up in the isolation of conviction (69–77). Antigone does

73

not believe that there is anyone present who shares her values, and her vision is of an inevitable and justified death, reuniting her with her brother, after conducting a sacred ritual act which is a crime to some human eyes. She refuses to allow Ismene to join her should she change her mind (69–70). In the final dialogue, Sophocles mixes two-line and single-line exchanges, and while Antigone is making to leave, by one of the side-passages out of the performance space, Ismene is still actively trying to dent her sister's resolve, or protect her.

She asks Antigone to keep her plans silent, and is scorned (84–87). She hints that the task is impossible to carry out (90), and seems to gain a concession from Antigone: 'I'll do all that I can; then I will stop.' (91). But as Ismene attempts to build on that, by suggesting—in her rationalizing way—that it is better not to start something that you have no power to finish (92), she prompts her sister into a final, vehement denunciation of her and her impious reasoning (93–94). It would be our conventional phrase to say that these lines are 'spat at her', and it is hard to see this moment any other way. But Antigone achieves her underlying purpose in some final tranquillity, because she wraps herself as she leaves in the comforting and satisfying conclusion that her act will allow her 'to die with true nobility' (97).

Although it by no means fails to acknowledge the harsh realities of power or the ruthless effectiveness of *realpolitik*, tragedy is happy to allow apparent powerlessness to carry through its purposes. The subversion of power is one of tragedy's most consistent enactments, and performers should beware of assuming that anyone is particularly strong or particularly secure in an artform that trades in instability. Of course, tragedy also deals in loneliness on the massive scale, as we have just seen, and there are few means that can establish this more effectively than dialogue.

Putting pressure on an autocrat: Medea and Creon, from Euripides' *Medea*

Apart from the opening scene, in which two actors in the performance space are joined by the voice of a third from the scene-building, Euripides' tragedy *Medea* is unusual—in a period when three actors were available—for working dramaturgically by a succession of scenes for two actors. The earliest of these comes after Medea has emerged from the scene-building to address a sympathetic chorus of women of the city of Corinth, setting out her own suffering in the context of the lives of women subject, as wives, to men. The father of her children, Jason, has left her to marry the daughter of the king of Corinth, (that other different) Creon, and she has been distraught at this outcome. At the end of a brilliantly emotive and persuasive monologue, Medea asks for and gains a pledge of silence from the chorus should she work out a plan of revenge on her husband. In the opening scene, before she comes outside, we have heard a rumour that Creon intends to banish Medea and her children, and this proves to be the catalyst to action.

Medea is surrounded in the playing-space by the chorus, who are as close to her at this moment as a chorus might be, sharing her feelings and agreeing to abide by her will. She is in front of her house, which we understand to be a household capable of supporting a female and a male slave; but this is a dysfunctional household, and a house that provides her with no security. For Creon, who comes on from a side-passage into the playing-space that leads to and from the city and from his own palace, Medea's hold on space is tenuous: he knows that he has authority over this area and all that surrounds it. He is also about to detach Medea from that space outside her house, and from the house itself, since he intends to banish her. What transpires is a battle to secure the space, and use of the house, for a short time, a contradiction to his automatic authority which will surprise him. Granted the nature of his mission, it would be strange if he did not come attended by men, slaves or free, to whom he refers at one point.

Medea—lines 271–356

CREON: You there, Medea, scowling and raging against your
    husband—
I've proclaimed that you must leave this land
and go into exile. Take your children with you

and make haste about it. I am here to execute
this order, and I shall not go back to the palace   275
before I have thrown you beyond my country's borders.
MEDEA: Ah! This is the end. I'm lost, completely ruined.
You see, my enemies have fully unfurled their sails,
and there is no easy landing to give disaster the slip.
But even as a victim I shall still ask a question: 280
why are you sending me out of your country, Creon?
CREON: I shan't cloak the truth in words: I fear that you
will cause some irremediable harm to my daughter.
There are many bits of evidence contributing to this.
You're a clever woman; the wide knowledge you have is evil.   285
You're wounded by the loss of your husband from your bed.
And I gather from the reports that are brought to me
that you're threatening to do something to the bride and groom
and to me. So I'm taking preventative action before it's too late.
It's better for me to earn your hatred now, woman,   290
than to be indulgent and be bitterly sorry for it later.
MEDEA: Oh!
This isn't the first time, Creon, it's happened many
times that rumour has done me immense damage.
It's essential that any man of good sense should never
overeducate his children and make them too clever.   295
Apart from the charge of idleness they also experience
resentment and hostility from their fellow-citizens.
With stupid people, a man who introduces clever new ideas
will get a name for uselessness, not for being clever.
As for those with a reputation for knowing a thing or two,   300
once the city rates you higher, you'll find you'll offend them.
I am a clever woman, and for that reason I share
in what happens to men like that. Some people hate me,   303
some find me uphill work. Yet I'm really not too clever.   305
But you fear me. Frightened you'll suffer something dreadful?
You don't need to be afraid of me, Creon. I'm not
in a position commit a crime against men in power.
And after all, what harm have you done to me? You've given
away your daughter as your heart has prompted. It's my
    husband   310

76

that I hate. In my view, you did what you did thoughtfully.
As things stand, I don't resent your affairs prospering.
Go for the marriage; I hope it's successful. But let me live
in this country. Even if there has been an injustice,
I'll keep quiet about it. Victory goes to those who are stronger.   315
CREON: What you say sounds submissive. But I dread to think
what kind of evil plan may be forming inside your head.
I'll tell you why I trust you less than before:
a woman with a quick temper, just the same as a man,
is easier to guard against than the clever, silent type.   320
Get out right away, and don't waste your breath.
My mind's made up. You're my enemy, and for that reason
I'm not letting you find a way to stay here with us.
MEDEA: No, by your knees, which I grasp, your newly-wedded
   daughter.
CREON: You are wasting words. You could never persuade me. 325
MEDEA: I'm begging you; won't you show respect? You can't
   expel me?
CREON: Yes I will. You're not as dear to me as my own family.
MEDEA: Oh my own country, how keenly I remember you now.
CREON: Yes, apart from my own children, mine is closest to my
   heart.
MEDEA: Ah, what a calamity love is to us all!   330
CREON: In my view, that would depend on luck and
   circumstances.
MEDEA: Zeus, make sure you see who is responsible for these
   crimes!
CREON: Don't be ridiculous. Get out, and relieve me of a problem!
MEDEA: Relieve you of a problem? I have enough of my own.
CREON: We're getting to the point where my men will use force
   on you.   335
MEDEA: No, no, don't do that, I'm still begging, Creon.
CREON: Am I to understand you still insist on being annoying,
   woman?
MEDEA: I'll go, I'll leave, exile. That's not what I'm begging for.
CREON: So what do you want to force from me? Why won't you
   leave?
MEDEA: Let me stay here for today, just for one day more,   340

to get sorted out in my mind where I can find a place
for me and my children to start a life in exile, since
their father hasn't taken any care to provide for his children.
Have pity on them. You have children yourself, you
are a father. I'm sure you must feel kindly towards them.   345
I'm not thinking of myself, you see, in this exile,
but the idea of what may happen to them is distressing me.
CREON: I don't have the right temperament to be a ruler.
   Not at all.
I have ruined far too many things by being considerate.
And even now although I can see I'm making a mistake,   350
woman, I'll grant your request. But you mark my words:
if the divine light of the sun on the day following this
sees you and your children inside this country's borders
you will die. This proclamation is one of absolute certainty.
As it is, if you have to stay, then stay for one day.   355
You can't, on that basis, carry out the kind of outrage I fear.

We know that Creon is conscious of his authority, and he comes
ready to conduct the transaction in person, and to wait to see
it successfully completed (271–76) with Medea's immediate
removal. Although he undoubtedly has the power, this abrupt
announcement must strike the ears of the chorus very hard
so soon after the complicity of Medea's speech, since the only
accusations he brings against her are that she looks hostile and
is angry with her husband (271–72). In fact, he may be directing
his command right at her, but he must be aware of the presence
of the chorus and of who they are. He is in public whatever he
may have envisaged, and it is already a little awkward, although
he is likely to override that.

   For Medea, Creon's ruthless order is an almost perfect embodiment of the male prejudice that she has been conjuring up. She
can revert to emotion, prompted not only by her own feelings
of abandonment and desperation, but also by the opportunity
to display her hopelessness and innocence to the chorus. It is the
latter context rather than the former that provokes her question,
and makes it predictable: 'Despite my dreadful suffering, I shall
ask this question nonetheless:/ what reason do you have, Creon,

for sending me away?' (280–81). It is easy to imagine Medea here close to the chorus, speaking to Creon from their shelter, or certainly playing to them, with Creon at a distance, which he would himself prefer.

Creon is now put on the hot spot: he must have a reason, and it must be one that is acceptable to this public. It would be safe to assume that any representative group in a Greek city would allow news to diffuse, even if its members belonged to a ruling elite like Sophocles' imagined elders in *Antigone* or *Oedipus the King*, who might see it as part of their responsibility to disseminate governing intentions as much as to advise those who govern. As the tone of his short speech (282–91) indicates, Creon is talking as much about Medea as he is speaking to her, and he leads with his suitably emotive reason, that he fears that she may harm his daughter (283). Although he condemns her as a clever woman, he defines that as having an ability to do a great deal of mischief (285), and he claims to have been given reports that she has been making threats against the bride and groom, and against himself (287–89). So his justification is that he is acting to protect himself and his family—a pre-emptive strike, so to speak; were he to soften, presumably at her distress, he might well regret it later.

Creon has had to adjust his purpose. The transaction he had in mind was to execute an eviction immediately; he now has to settle for arguing the case, and listening to an opposing case, which may seem persuasive to those who are hearing it. Like Creon, Medea knows she has to appear to be reasonable, not just to have an outside chance of persuading him, but to work on Creon through the opinion of the chorus. So she goes for self-pity, with a vague appeal to the sad case of people reckoned to be cleverer than average, who suffer prejudice for doing—as she implies— nothing very much at all (292–305). So we are supposedly meant to assume that she too poses no threat, since after all she is by no means 'too clever' (305).

While this rather specious argument may be directed disingenuously to the chorus as much as to Creon, she must turn to face him to bring home her point in the second phase of this impromptu personal statement: he need not fear her, since she is not the type to do harm to men who are kings (307–308). After all, why should she anyway? He has done nothing to her; it is her husband whom she hates. She flatters Creon's judgment in making the marriage, has no grudge against him, and hopes the wedding goes well (309–13). Her attention flits around him, with undoubtedly pacifying tones, aiming to confuse his judgment, and to lead him to let her stay (313–14). How can the weaker harm the stronger? She will suffer in silence (314–15).

Medea is now releasing her own transactional purpose, gradually taking the initiative away from Creon, who has remained static while she is mobile. It may take him a moment to shake off the spell, and he perhaps has to move away to do it, before turning back to be even more resolute. He spurns her approach, and sends her back to the women, because he fears the pretence of a softer, long-suffering Medea (316–20). Her bid is about to be quelled, and he will carry through his initial purpose into action: she must go, right away (321–23).

The dialogue then tumbles into a line-by-line exchange, whose urgency and discomfort comes from the fact that Medea has dived to the ground to grasp Creon's knees in an act of supplication, at or just before 324. This is probably the worst that Creon could fear in public, since it is an act which demands at least some respect and possibly clemency. It also places Medea overtly in the protection of a god, Zeus, whom Medea invokes as part of her physical siege of the Corinthian king's will (332). Once again, the appeal is as much for the chorus as it is to Creon, and the pressure does not seem to be telling. She is clutching at straws, and he is about to call on his men to remove her forcibly (335), when she hits on a stratagem. She offers the compromise: she will go into exile, but as a suppliant she is seeking something else (338). In his relief at the first part of this, Creon just wants to be released from her grasp, her grip on his hand (339), and he fails fatally to see what is coming.

Medea has used supplication to gain what she wanted, which is mounting pressure for what appears to be a minor concession to be made. It is extremely difficult for Creon to deny it to a suppliant, since he has apparently gained what he wanted, which is her exile from Corinth. Presumably she cannot let go of him, or his hand, until he has agreed to the day's respite (340) that she humbly requests, in order to make arrangements for the care of her children in the absence of provision from their father (340–47). After all, Creon is a father himself, as he has repeatedly emphasized (344–45).

There is nothing that Creon can do in the circumstances. To refuse would be tyrannical, as he says, although this almost seems to suggest, in his terms, that he is unsuited to be a king, since he often shows too much respect for others (348–49). He has to give in to the suppliant, and be seen to give in, even if he knows he is making a mistake. He can only reconcile himself to it by seeing it as a postponement of his purpose, since she has to be gone by tomorrow (351–54); but in fact he is acceding to Medea's growing purpose, which is ruthless revenge. She releases him, perhaps when she first senses that he must and is going to agree (348), and once he has spoken he takes his leave.

The effects of the public presence of the chorus are subtle and varied, reflecting allegiance to the characters in front of them and the situation in which those characters are placed at a given time. The chorus may not be able to see the outcome, but it is generally aware of the evolution of the action, a sensitivity that is mediated through its danced songs. In the tragedies of Aeschylus, this activity is the central dynamic of the drama, an articulate and evocative energy that the characters direct, attempt to restrain, or provoke. In the tragedies of Sophocles and Euripides their evocative power extends and amplifies our awareness of the resonance of the evolving drama, and also allows the chorus to move forward in their consciousness of the action. The chorus may give out a moderating voice, but it is able to do so precisely because it is listening and 'following' the evolving argument. With song and dance such a predominant feature of the tragic performance, it is perhaps inevitable that the chorus will appear to be still when the characters are fully engaged in transaction and interaction, as is the case in dialogue. But it is not the stillness of inertia and disengagement.

Public exposure: Clytemnestra and Electra, from Sophocles' *Electra*

Our next text carries some of those subtle variations in the effect of the presence of the chorus on the dialogue. It is the embittered exchange between Clytemnestra and Electra from Sophocles *Electra*.

Sophocles *Electra*—lines 516–659

CLYTEMNESTRA: So! You have escaped, you're roving round
   outside again.
Aegisthus is not here—and he has always kept you from
disgracing your own family, a woman out of doors.
Right now he is away, and you don't care at all
about how I feel; you have told so many people   520
that I'm arrogant, I have no right to rule,
and I do violence to you and yours.
That is not true! I speak sharply to you because
I always hear sharp words from you.
Your father—there is nothing else. That's your excuse—   525
the fact that I killed him. Yes, I myself. I
know it well; I won't deny the truth.
Justice took him, not I alone; you should
have been on her side, if you'd any sense.
This father, whom you always grieve for, was   530
the only Greek ruthless enough to sacrifice
your sister to the gods; he had not suffered any pain
when he created her like mine when I gave birth.
Come; explain this to me. For whose sake
did he sacrifice her? For the Greeks?   535
They had no right to put my child to death.
Did he kill her to help his brother Menelaus?
She was mine—so I was bound to punish him.
His brother had two children, and they should
have died instead of her, since their father   540
—and especially their mother—caused the Trojan War.

82

Did Hades feel a special lust to feast
upon my children more than hers?
Or did your all-destructive father lose his love
for my children, but still love Menelaus'?   545
Does that not show he was a reckless, worthless man?
I think he was, even if you do not agree; and if
the girl who died could speak, she'd say so too.
My conscience is at ease with what
I've done; if you think I'm wrong, make sure   550
your own opinion's right before you criticize.
ELECTRA: At any rate you can't say now that I abused
you first, and only then heard you reproach me;
if you'll allow me, I would like to set the record
straight about my father and my sister.   555
CLYTEMNESTRA: Most certainly; if you always began with words
like these, you would not have to fear reproach.
ELECTRA: Then I will speak. You say you killed my father.
Could there be a worse admission, whether he
deserved to die or not? I will say that you   560
did not kill him with Justice; that worthless man
you live with now pressed and seduced you into it.
Ask Artemis, goddess of hunting, whom she punished
when she sent a calm to keep the ships at Aulis.
Better—I'll tell you, since she can't be a witness.   565
The story I was told is that my father once, relaxing in
a sacred grove of hers, disturbed by his footfall
a dappled, antlered stag, and when he killed it
boasted, letting slip some foolish words.
Angered by this, the virgin goddess made   570
the Greeks stay there, until my father sacrificed
his daughter as her compensation for the animal.
That's why my sister died; the army had
no other way to go home or to sail to Troy.
He was compelled; he fought against it many times,   575
then most reluctantly he sacrificed her—not just for his brother.
However—to anticipate what you'll say—even if
he'd done this to help Menelaus, was it right
for you to kill him for it? By what law?

83

Watch out; if you lay down such laws you may   580
create both suffering and repentance for yourself.
If we all kill each other in revenge, you know
you'd be the first to die, if you get your deserts.
Take care you don't use an invalid plea.
If you can be so kind, please tell me why   585
you are now doing the most shameful act of all,
sleeping with the bloodstained man who once
helped you to end my father's life, and having
children with him, while you cast aside your former
offspring, though we're royal, and legitimate.   590
How can I approve? Or will you say that you
are also doing this in vengeance for your daughter?
If you do, you'll shame yourself. It would be an outrage
if you're married for her sake to enemies.
No! No one can reproach you, since you keep   595
on finding different ways of saying we
badmouth our mother. But I think you are
our slavemistress more than our mother.
I live in misery; you and
your lover always make me suffer.   600
You very nearly killed your son—
and Orestes lives wretchedly, in exile.
You often say I brought him up
to take vengeance on you. And know this well:
I would, if I'd been strong enough. Your heralds can   605
denounce me to the world as vicious,
far too free of tongue, or shameless;
but if I am like that, no one can say I've not
inherited my mother's character,
CHORUS: [My Queen, I see her words have left]
you breathing fury; I no longer see   610
you thinking carefully whether you're right.
CLYTEMNESTRA: Why should I have to think, confronted by this
    one,
who says such violent things about her mother;
she's a full-grown woman! Don't you think
she could do anything and feel no shame?   615

84

ELECTRA: No! Understand this well; I do feel shame,
even if you can't see it. I know I am
behaving crazily, and I demean myself.
I cannot help it; your hostility, and what
you've done, force me against my will;   620
shameful acts teach others they must act the same.
CLYTEMNESTRA: You little bitch, how dare you tell me what I
do and say makes you go on too much!
ELECTRA: The words all come from you, not me. You've done
the deed; and deeds find their own words.   625
CLYTEMNESTRA: By Artemis, you won't escape from punishment
for this defiance, when Aegisthus comes back home.
ELECTRA: Look here! You told me I could speak my mind;
but now you've lost your temper; you can't listen.
CLYTEMNESTRA: At least I let you get it off your chest;   630
won't you let me make offerings in peace?
ELECTRA: I will. Please do; make all your offerings. You'll
have no cause to blame me; I won't say a thing.
CLYTEMNESTRA: Come, servant, lift these offerings
of fruit, so I can raise my prayers to the god,   635
to free me from these dreams.
Phoebus, protector of the house, please hear
this prayer although it's secretive. I am not speaking
among friends—nor is it right to unfold all I want
into the light when she's near me;   640
she's hostile, and will use her busy tongue
to spread malicious rumours through the town.
Hear my secret thoughts, concealed in what I'll say.
The images I saw last night in those
elusive dreams—Apollo, god of light, if they   645
mean good to me, grant that they be fulfilled;
but if they don't, send them back to my enemies.
If someone's planning to deprive me of
my wealth by treachery, prevent them;
may I always live unharmed, and rule   650
this house and hold this royal sceptre,
living with the friends I live with now,
enjoying my prosperity with them

85

and with those of my children who do not hate me.
Lord Apollo, hear this prayer with favour,   655
give us everything the way we ask for it.
Although my other needs are all unspoken,
I expect you, as a god, to know them;
you are Zeus' son, and should see everything.

Sophocles' tragedy is explicitly about the return of Orestes to his home and the revenge that is taken, and the tragedy opens with that 'tipping point', with Orestes and Pylades standing on Argive soil, guided back there by the Old Man who had taken the child Orestes away from danger many years ago. We become aware of their plan to get into the palace by a pretence that Orestes has died, and they depart to invoke the aid of Agamemnon at his tomb. We are then confronted by Electra's continuing grief and mourning, to which the Argive Women played by the chorus attempt to apply an antidote or a corrective, rather than the consolation that Electra suggests they wish to bring.

As far as they are concerned, she is harming herself by pro-longing her grief, failing to recognize that her sufferings are not unique, showing an unjustified despair that reveals a lack of faith in Zeus, and bringing additional humiliation and misfortune on herself by her bad temper. This relatively unsparing critique comes in a sung and danced sequence (lines 121–250), in which Electra responds to the chorus, and it is followed by a dialogue between them (251–323). Here the chorus of Argive Women expresses more unqualified sympathy, and Electra details her experience, in the palace behind her, of Aegisthus and Clytemnestra.

Yet for all this, the action of the play is stimulated from another source entirely, which is a dream that Clytemnestra has just had which scares her badly. We have heard of her celebrations of the day on which Agamemnon was killed, the dedication of choral performances, and the monthly thanksgiving for her security she gives to the gods by sacrificing sheep (lines 277–81). Now Electra's sister, Chrysothemis, is sent from the palace urgently by Clytemnestra to deliver offerings and pour libations at Agamemnon's tomb, since the dream suggests a new threat coming from Agamemnon (417–27). The closely argued scene between Chrysothemis and Electra recalls that between Antigone and Ismene. But in this case Electra is successful in persuading her sister to substitute poor but heartfelt offerings from her for those of her mother, and to pray instead for Agamemnon's support for themselves and his son.

The final contribution to the immediate context of our scene comes from the choral song and dance (472–515), which celebrates in turn a growing confidence that revenge will occur and justice prevail, stimulated by Electra's ominous interpretation of the dream as an imminent threat to Clytemnestra and Aegisthus. Into our alert sense of crisis Clytemnestra now steps, herself intent on an offering she is to make in the playing space, with a chorus now more excited by the conviction of her guilt than at any time in the recent past. This offering, in common with those she had instructed for the tomb of Agamemnon, is part of a vital transaction for her of warding off any hostile implications of her recent dream. We have heard from Electra of Clytemnestra's screaming fits when anyone suggests that Orestes may be about to return home (293–99), and her tension matches Electra's excitement.

It has been made quite clear earlier (310–13) that it is the temporary absence of Aegisthus that has encouraged Electra to dare to come outside the palace, and Clytemnestra's first reaction is to her daughter's presence outside. As far as Clytemnestra and Aegisthus are concerned, Electra can only bring shame on her family by 'roving around outside' (516), and as I have said, this reflects a common prejudice about (particularly unmarried) women moving freely in public space (516–18). It is an irritation to Clytemnestra because Electra also obstructs the performance of the transaction on which she was intent. So Clytemnestra begins to change her purpose, taking the opportunity to correct the impression that she is certain Electra chooses to give to others, namely that her mother is arrogant, has no right to rule, and treats her daughter harshly. In this respect, Clytemnestra's judgment is thoroughly sound, because that is precisely what we and the chorus have been hearing from Electra.

Electra and the chorus must have moved away from the centre of the playing space, to allow room for Clytemnestra to appear from the palace with an attendant carrying the offerings, and to make some progress towards an altar. Clytemnestra can address the chorus while she appears to correct Electra, and she provides a justification for her actions and a condemnation of male ruthlessness that might well impress the young women of the chorus, but is unlikely to move Electra. This is a clever performance, because it takes the argument through in detailed steps, and can partly convict Electra as it may justify her mother, since Electra may be seen not to care about her dead sister Iphigenia, who might have condemned Agamemnon, could she speak (548). There were potential substitutes for Clytemnestra and Agamemnon's sacrificed daughter, since Menelaus, his brother, had daughters, and Menelaus and his wife Helen were far more directly responsible for the war (534–48).

Electra has kept silent, which creates a speech out of Clytemnestra's arguments, but Electra then enters a plea to be able to speak in turn (552–55), which Clytemnestra seems not to fear, since her daughter's tone is placatory (556–57). Yet this tone is disingenuous, as Clytemnestra will find out, because what Electra wants is the opportunity to accuse and convict her mother face to face in front of others, in public, an opportunity she is never normally given. What Clytemnestra now finds is that she is exposed and isolated in the playing space, deprived of a sympathetic or loyal chorus, rather against her expectations.

In her response Electra abuses her mother for being merely the victim of seduction by Aegisthus, and so not an agent herself, let alone an instrument of justice (558–62). She then proves herself incapable of constructing a convincing case for Agamemnon, revealing him to be carelessly impious, boastful, and ultimately weak (563–76). The only excuse she can offer for his sacrifice of her sister Iphigenia is that Agamemnon had displeased a goddess, Artemis, who was implacable. She also confuses herself with an argument about revenge that should lead her to abstain from it herself (577–84). Electra is no doubt buoyant in front of an audience of her peers, the young women of noble birth in the chorus, but she quickly descends from one final argument into abuse.

Clytemnestra should be ashamed to be sleeping with the

murderer of her husband and rejecting her own children by Agamemnon, something she cannot justify by reference to the sacrifice of her daughter (585–94). It is a precise and telling point, humiliating Clytemnestra in front of other women by degrading her sexual life and preferences, and it connects with Electra's opening gambit about Clytemnestra's dependence on Aegisthus. The rest is a climax of hostility, asserting how her mother treats her daughters like slaves, and revealing how the preservation of Orestes has been an enduring cause of suspicion and hostility. No denunciation of Electra by Clytemnestra can prove anything except that she is her mother's daughter in all her bad qualities (605–609).

Clytemnestra has now been frustrated in her second transactional purpose, to use this moment to justify herself publicly, and she has instead unwittingly submitted to her daughter's desire to abuse and humiliate her in public. As the chorus quickly observes (609–11), Clytemnestra has been provoked to anger, but she uses it to engage directly now with the chorus, challenging them to regard Electra as shameless (612–15). Electra disarms this accusation subtly, acknowledging as she has before to the chorus that her behaviour is demeaning, but repeating her barbed claim that she is reacting automatically to her mother's shameful acts (616–21). Clytemnestra lashes out at her, and ironically invokes Artemis, the goddess whose anger had resulted in the sacrifice of Iphigenia at Aulis, as she promises that Electra will suffer for this outspoken defiance when Aegisthus returns.

The scene concludes with Clytemnestra able to revert to her initial purpose and carry out her rite of offerings and prayers to the god Apollo at his altar in the playing-space. For her rite to be successful, she needs there to be no words of ill omen spoken, and Electra agrees to be silent and step aside (630–33). Yet Clytemnestra is alone in making this prayer, and Electra must be confident that the admission of her murderous actions will negate her mother's attempt to turn the dream's injurious effects away from her. Clytemnestra has to keep back some of what she would have included in her prayer to Apollo because she knows she is not amongst friends (637–43). So Sophocles shows us here an isolated woman, racked by fear of losing her wealth and prosperity, her power and prestige, and she leaves her other needs and wishes unspoken (657–60). Since she has just mentioned her wish to live peacefully with those of her children who do not hate her (654), we may suspect that her unspoken prayers are for Apollo to rid her of both Electra and Orestes (**Recording 3**). These prayers will, to Clytemnestra, seem to be confirmed by the immediate arrival of the Old Man, with news of the supposed death of Orestes.

Question and answer: Electra and Orestes, from Euripides' *Electra*

While the character played by a chorus in Sophocles' or Euripides' tragedies may be assumed to be aware of the action unless it is made clear that it is not, the extent to which it is involved by the individual characters varies considerably. We have seen this in the First Workshop, with the apparently interior monologue from Medea. That was a sequence that came quickly after the remarkable, public speech by Medea to the chorus and the subsequent dialogue scene with Creon, reviewed in this Second Workshop, in which public opinion is paramount. In fact, Euripides in particular seems to alternate between a traditional involvement of the chorus as a public presence and a fading of its role at moments of interaction between characters.

This dialogue between Orestes and Electra from Euripides' *Electra* provides a good opportunity to explore that issue. It is a challenging workshop piece, one that demands close attention to the rhythm of the script, as we shall see.

Euripides *Electra*—lines 215–99

ELECTRA: Oh, no. Women, I'm done. Our lament for the dead
    must wait.   215
Men I've not seen before, there, they've been hiding,
you can see them coming towards the house from near the altar.
Quick, run, they're criminals and we must get away!
You go along the path, and I'll run into the house.
ORESTES: Poor woman, stay there. I won't touch you, never
    fear.   220

ELECTRA: Phoebus Apollo, I kneel to you, don't let him kill me.

ORESTES: I don't hate you. Others I do, and I'd rather kill them.

ELECTRA: Go away, don't touch what you should not be touching.

ORESTES: I can't think of anyone that I've more right to touch.

ELECTRA: So that makes sense of your sword, and hiding by my
house?   225

ORESTES: If you'll just stay and listen, you'll say the same as me.

ELECTRA: I'm not moving. I'm completely in your power, either
way.

ORESTES: The reason I'm here is a message to you from your
brother.

ELECTRA: You dear man! Is he alive or dead? Tell me!

ORESTES: He's alive. First the good news—that's the way I
like it.   230

ELECTRA: May you live happily ever after, as a reward for those
sweet words.

ORESTES: And my gift to us both is to share that happiness
together.

ELECTRA: He must be miserable, a miserable life in exile. Where is
he?

ORESTES: He's tossed around from city to city, with no rights
anywhere.

ELECTRA: Not starving? Does he have enough to eat, day by
day?   235

ORESTES: No, he's not starving, but a man in exile is always
weak.

ELECTRA: But if you've come from him, what is your message?

ORESTES: He wants to know if you're alive, how life is treating
you.

ELECTRA: You can see for yourself. To start with, I'm all skin and
bone.

ORESTES: And worn down by grief. It's enough to make me
cry.   240

ELECTRA: And look at my head. My hair's shaved with a razor,
like a Scythian.

ORESTES: Your father's death gnaws at you; your brother's life
too, perhaps.

ELECTRA: Ah, yes! What could be dearer to me than those two?

ORESTES: Oh! And what do you think could be dearer to your brother than you?

ELECTRA: Dear to him at a distance. The man's not here. 245

ORESTES: So why do you live here, so far from the city?

ELECTRA: I was married off, a marriage like death, stranger.

ORESTES: That's dreadful news for your brother. To some Mycenean?

ELECTRA: Not to the kind of man my father hoped to give me.

ORESTES: Tell me. I'm listening, and I'll pass it on to your brother. 250

ELECTRA: I live miles from anywhere. This is his house.

ORESTES: It's the kind of place that would suit a ditcher or a farm-worker.

ELECTRA: He's poor. But he has good manners, and has respected me.

ORESTES: What does respect mean to your husband?

ELECTRA: He's never asserted himself, or come near my bed. 255

ORESTES: Some kind of religious chastity? Or are you not good enough for him?

ELECTRA: He wants to avoid insulting my family.

ORESTES: But why shouldn't he be pleased with such a good marriage?

ELECTRA: He thinks that the man who gave me away had no authority, stranger.

ORESTES: I'm with you now. He's afraid of Orestes and the law. 260

ELECTRA: Yes, that would worry him. But it's also because he knows restraint.

ORESTES: Oh! An excellent man by your description. He should be rewarded.

ELECTRA: For that to happen, the exile will have to come home.

ORESTES: Did your mother put up with this? You are her child.

ELECTRA: Women love the men in their lives, stranger, not their children. 265

ORESTES: What made Aegisthus insult you in this way?

ELECTRA: His plan was that I'd have feeble children with that kind of husband.

ORESTES: So you wouldn't have children who would take revenge?

ELECTRA: That was his plan. I hope he'll pay the penalty for it, to me.

ORESTES: Does your mother's husband know that you're a
virgin?   270

ELECTRA: No, he doesn't. We've said nothing, and kept it from him.

ORESTES: Next, these women. They're listening. Are they your friends?

ELECTRA: Such good friends that they will conceal perfectly anything we say.

ORESTES: So what should Orestes do about this, if he comes back to Argos?

ELECTRA: Can you ask me that? What a shameful question!
Isn't it the right time?   275

ORESTES: All right, so he comes. How should he kill your father's murderers?

ELECTRA: He would show the same ruthless determination as they did.

ORESTES: Would you be tough enough to kill your mother with him?

ELECTRA: Yes, with the same axe with which my father was killed.

ORESTES: Then I should tell him that all is sound as far as you're
concerned?   280

ELECTRA: I'd die happy if I'd added my mother's blood to the sacrifice.

ORESTES: Ah! I wish Orestes was near to us to hear that!

ELECTRA: But in fact, stranger, I wouldn't recognize him if I saw him.

ORESTES: That's hardly surprising. You were very young when you were separated.

ELECTRA: There's only one of the people loyal to me who'd
recognize him.   285

ORESTES: The man who people say stole him away and saved his life?

ELECTRA: That's him. An old man now. My father's minder when he was a boy.

ORESTES: After your father had died, was he given a tomb burial?

ELECTRA: His body was thrown out of the palace. That's what he
   got.
ORESTES: What did you say? That's a terrible thing. Excuse me,
   but awareness   290
of the sufferings of others bites deep. It's only human.
Pity's not something that you'll ever find in ignorant people,   294
but it's there in those who are thoughtful. And you can see   295
that being too thoughtful is a painful business.   296
Tell me everything. If I know it all, I can take the story   292
to your brother. It may be unpleasant, but he needs to hear it.   293
CHORUS: I can feel the same desire as he does to hear the story.
I live far away from the city, and I don't know about
the crimes that happen there. Now I'd like to find out.

The context for this dialogue is very much dependent on the
unusual setting, which is in front of a farmer's house, and the
opening of the play introduces us to the Farmer himself. He has
been chosen by Aegisthus as a husband for Electra, as a man of
sufficient poverty and insignificance to pose no threat to the royal
couple. He treats her with consideration, with one eye on the
possible return of Orestes to find his sister. So Electra's dejection
here takes material form in rural poverty and obscurity, but it by
chance coincides with Orestes' trajectory back to his birthright.

When the Farmer and Electra go off to their dawn labours,
Orestes and Pylades arrive; Orestes has found his father's tomb
and made offerings, and now he wants to locate his sister. The
two young men have to step aside when Electra returns from
drawing water, and they listen to Electra's lament and then to the
song she shares with the chorus of Argive countrywomen. Here
she refuses to join in a festival in borrowed clothes and offer
prayers to the gods, since the gods have done nothing to restore
Orestes and her, or to exact justice on their father's murderers.

So it is that Orestes has heard enough to know that this
woman is his sister, and that his search for her is at an end. He
comes forward with Pylades at this moment, and her frightened
outburst suggests to the chorus that they should run away down
a side passage into the space, while she runs into the house (218–
19). Although the language is not totally clear, it seems possible

that the men have been hiding by the side of the house/scene-building, and this then gives scope for an excited sequence of agitated physical action (220–27). Orestes has been holding his sword in his hand (225), which portrays his considerable anxiety in unknown territory, but which has also terrified Electra. She prays to Apollo, falling to her knees almost immediately (221), and he reaches out to her, a physical contact to which she objects (223–24). Since he will not go, as she wishes, she stands up and attempts to escape; it seems that he then restrains her, and she yields to his greater strength (226–27).

Apart from Electra's opening outcry to the Women of the chorus, who must be assumed to be held by a mixture of fear, curiosity, and an instinct to support Electra at a distance, this is a line-by-line exchange between the two characters, which strikingly continues right through our chosen sequence to achieve an extent that we have not encountered before. To say that the Greek technical term for this form of dialogue is *stichomythia* ('speech or conversation in lines') is of no great help, because the problem for the modern actor is not one of recognition of the form, but of how to sustain an extended dialogue of this kind. A short section of line-by-line offers no major difficulties, although it may be useful to register that this kind of script-composition works substantially by one line picking up on a word or idea in the last line, and turning it to make a different, contrasting or contradictory point. As we have seen before, the lines feed off each other, and this is recognizable and easy enough for modern performers in a short sequence; but it becomes rather daunting and dangerously artificial in a longer exchange.

What emerges in this dialogue is that it moves on in phases, rather as a monologue will do, and our understanding of these phases will be enhanced by an awareness of the larger and wider context of the dialogue and the scene. In this instance, we need to know that although Orestes wants to find his sister, he has also stated that he has come into the countryside away from the city of Argos so that he can quickly go abroad again if any one spies him (95–97). This Orestes is not, perhaps, the style of avenger that Electra would be hoping for, and it remains unclear what exactly he wants to find out before he commits to action.

So this scene, by the sheer chance of his stumbling upon her, should now prove to be a recognition scene between brother and sister, itself a vital and urgent transaction that would then lead into the planning and execution of revenge, and the siblings' restoration into their inheritance. The opening of the scene has merely been a flurry, in which he has hinted that he has real enemies to kill (222), but this first phase is ended with a striking deferral. Electra has given up and is now at his disposal, but Orestes chooses to announce that he is bringing a message from her brother (228).

This invention ushers in a second phase of the dialogue, which has its own, substituted urgency. Electra wants to know all that she can about her brother, that he is alive and surviving, and then wants to hear the message itself (229–37). Orestes has no difficulty in phrasing the inquiry (238), which roughly mirrors Electra's recent questions about him, but by refusing to declare himself he remains firmly at a distance. Electra speeds through visible aspects of her physical condition, and concludes with her grief for her father and her brother. In this third phase (238–45), Orestes plays with sympathy while shielded in an assumed identity, and is moved eventually to the point of crying aloud, asking Electra who she believes is dearer to her brother than her (244). Electra's reply to this is damning: her brother is absent, and she is dear to him at a distance (245).

Orestes has to change the subject, and in the subsequent phase of the dialogue he turns to the surroundings (246, 251–52), no doubt gesturing about him as he does so. In this phase, he leads the questioning forwards as a man who may pass judgment harshly, particularly when he discovers that Electra is married. Her husband is evidently poor, and he needs reassuring that the farmer is from a noble family and that he respects Electra (253 forwards). He presses his enquiries here, as we would say, searching for the farmer's motives in a rather patronizing tone, until he is brought up short by Electra's repeated reference to her brother's absence (263).

Orestes changes tack again, leading into the attitudes of Clytemnestra and Aegisthus to Electra's marriage, once again the interrogator, asking intimate questions that do not lead forward to revenge. The dialogue stutters as he turns to the chorus for the first time since scaring them, checking with Electra if they can be trusted (272–73), and at last he asks her what Orestes should do if he returns (274), initiating the penultimate phase. He is looking for ideas from her, but all he gains is grim and bloodthirsty resolution for the murders. So once again he stalls by renewing the concealment of his identity, which is secured by Electra's subsequent confirmation that she would not recognize her brother if she saw him (282–83).

The final, short phase of the dialogue concerns the one man who might recognize Orestes if he saw him, who was an attendant on Agamemnon when he was a child, and this prompts Orestes to raise questions about the tomb that he has already visited, to extend his procrastination even further. So he finally breaks from the drive of the line-by-line exchange, to indulge himself with a little speech (290–96) on the sensitivity of those who listen to the suffering of others, and to encourage from Electra a longer account of personal deprivation and insult to Agamemnon from the murderers.

It is clear from the comments of the Argive Women at the close of our section of script that they have been attentive, and are stirred by accounts of the ruling family. To an extent, we may imagine that Orestes is aware of this attention, and is being very cautious, both before and after his reference to them. Yet this is a very mild presence for a chorus, and the line-by-line exchange binds Electra and Orestes very closely together. The performance must work on the balance in rhythm between the short-term urgency of question and response within each phase, and the measured shift from phase to phase seen as building blocks in Orestes' deferral of the declaration of his identity, and of the task that inevitably awaits him.

Just as, in crude terms, a speech or monologue may be all too readily associated by us with the expression of 'character', so a dialogue may be susceptible to the kind of tired analysis that reductively sums up tragedy as 'conflict', and rests content with that. Now that is not to say that considering a tragic monologue as in part demonstrative of character, or tragic dialogue as expressive of some form of conflict is necessarily a waste of energy, or inherently misguided. But neither viewpoint—which is roughly what they are—is of much value without a fundamental assessment (a) of transactions and (b) of the public qualities lent by the presence of the tragic chorus.

By 'fundamental', I mean a process that should come first, and should also be expected to extend throughout the piece. These, in other words, are the terms of reference that should be brought by actors to any work on Greek tragic scenes. They should form as much a part of an actor's preparation for performance as any more general considerations of character in the embodiment of text. To those two terms of reference (a) and (b) I would add a third, which is (c) consideration of the implications of public space, carefully assessed scene by scene. As I said earlier, space is inevitably bound up with the crucial, public dimension brought by the chorus, and is even present forcibly when the chorus is not, as we have noticed in relation to the opening scene of *Antigone*.

Sanctuary and the predator: Andromache and Hermione, from Euripides' *Andromache*

It may be helpful to conclude this Second Workshop with a scene that looks on the surface to be satisfied with a display of contrasting characters and a primal conflict, but which is subject to all three considerations that I have adduced. It is yet another remarkable scene for two women actors, and comes from early in Euripides' play, *Andromache*.

Andromache—lines 147–272

HERMIONE: Around my head, a glittering, golden diadem;
from shoulder to toe, a dazzling length of embroidered robe.
Here I am. But the palace of Achilles, the palace of Peleus
did not furnish these first fruits of sacrifice for me.   150
Oh, no. It was Sparta, the land of Lacedaemon
and Menelaus my father who provided this trousseau,
part of a lavish dowry, to allow me the freedom to speak my
   mind.   153

But you, woman, are a slave, something picked up in battle.   155
What you want is to kick me out and take my place
in this palace. You have poisoned my husband against me,
I cannot get pregnant, there is nothing there, you did that.
We shouldn't be surprised; Asiatic women have a dreadful
   reputation
for this kind of thing. But I shall put a stop to it,   160
and this shrine of Thetis the Nereid won't help you at all,
neither will altar nor temple, because you are going to die.
Let's just suppose that a man or a god might be willing to save you:
in that case, it will be goodbye to the grand attitudes you've had up
   to now.
You're going to have to cringe and cower, fall at my feet.   165
I'll have you sweeping the floor of my house, your hand sprinkling
water drawn from the River Achelous in gold jugs of mine.
You will know your place on this earth. There's no Hector here,
no Priam, none of your gold. This is a Greek city.
You are a hopeless case. You have sunk to the point where   170
you have the nerve to sleep with the son of the man
who killed your own husband, and to have children
by him. That's just typical of all you foreigners.
Fathers and daughters, sons and mothers, sisters and
brothers rutting away, relatives of all kinds wading   175
through blood, and nothing to stop this lawless barbarity.
We don't want that kind of thing here. We know that it's
disgusting for one man to hold the reins of a pair of women,
and that anyone who wants to keep a respectable household
will look to his wife alone, and be content with married love.   180
CHORUS: Women are jealous creatures; it's the way their minds
   are made.
Sharing a husband makes them maddest of all.
ANDROMACHE: Oh dear . . .
The young can be a mortal danger to others, particularly
when someone combines both youth and injustice.   185
I'm afraid that, for you, the fact of my slavery will keep me
from saying what I have to say—in all justice;
and that again, if I win the argument, I shall pay for it.
After all, people who puff themselves up really don't like to hear

stronger arguments coming from those weaker than
   themselves.   190
What can I do? I cannot stay silent, and condemn myself.
Tell me, girl, what kind of flawless logic would have
persuaded me to deny you your conjugal rights?
That, for example, Sparta was a weaker city than Troy,
and that my own luck puts me above those who are free?   195
Perhaps I am proud of my body in its bloom of youth,
the size and strength of my city, my extended family—
so very proud that I want to displace you in your own home?
Or there again, that I want to displace you in having
children, who will be slaves, tied to my floating wreck.   200
No, what am I saying, people are bound to want to see
my children ruling as kings in Phthia if you have none yourself!
After all, the Greeks love me for Hector's sake.
It's not as if I was just any Trojan; I was royalty.
I haven't poisoned your husband against you.   205
Think about it: are you good to be with?
That's the only charm you need. Looks are not the answer,
woman, it's your temperament that matters; men like to be
   pleased.
But when you're provoked in the slightest, then it's Sparta
is a fine place, and Skyros doesn't count for anything.   210
You're a wealthy woman in a poor country; for you, Menelaus
is a better man than Achilles: that's why your husband hates you.
Even if she is married to a bad husband, a woman should
show him affection, not be contradicting him all the time.
So, you're married to a man who rules somewhere up   215
in Thrace, where everything is covered in snow, and men
go to bed and have sex with a string of women in turn, what then?
Would you kill them all? That would make you guilty
of subjecting all of us to the slur of being obsessed with sex.   219
My dearest Hector, to keep you happy I was prepared,   222
if Aphrodite tripped you up, to play along with those passionate
   affairs.
Many is the time that I had one of your bastards
pinned to my breast, just to avoid any bitterness between us.   225
That was the way that I brought my husband close to me,

by my temperament. As for you, you're so paranoid
you won't let so much as a drop of heavenly dew settle on yours.
Don't make it your ambition, woman, to surpass
your mother in your love of men. If they've got any sense,   230
children should not aim to repeat the bad behaviour of their
    mothers.
CHORUS: Mistress, I should like to encourage you, as far as
you find you can, to reach an understanding with her.
HERMIONE: So your assumption is that you're all reason and
    restraint, and I am not.
That gives you the right to lecture me, and answer me back.   235
ANDROMACHE: Well, yes, if I'm to go by what you just said.
HERMIONE: I hope your attitudes never cohabit with me, woman.
ANDROMACHE: You're just a girl, and what you say should make
    you blush.
HERMIONE: It's not just talk with you; you're doing what you can
    against me.
ANDROMACHE: Not that again! Can't you suffer in silence
    about your sex-life?   240
HERMIONE: What do you mean? Women everywhere care most
    about their sex-lives.
ANDROMACHE: That's fine if they're handling them well; if they're
    not, it isn't.
HERMIONE: Our civic life doesn't follow a barbarian model.
ANDROMACHE: What's shameful there is shameful here; there's
    no difference.
HERMIONE: Oh, clever, how very clever. But it won't stop you
    dying.   245
ANDROMACHE: Can't you see the statue of Thetis looking down
    at you?
HERMIONE: Yes, staring in hatred at your homeland, stained with
    Achilles's blood.
ANDROMACHE: I didn't kill him. It was your mother, Helen, who
    did.
HERMIONE: I see. You're not going to stop delving into my
    personal grief.
ANDROMACHE: All right, I shall say no more, and button up
    my lips.   250

HERMIONE: You can say one thing, which is the reason why I came out here.
ANDROMACHE: I'll say this, that you haven't got as much sense as you should.
HERMIONE: This precinct is sacred to the sea goddess. Will you leave it?
ANDROMACHE: If I am not to die. If I am, then I never shall.
HERMIONE: That decides it, then; I shan't wait for my husband to come back.   255
ANDROMACHE: But there's no way I'll give myself up to you before he does.
HERMIONE: I'm not going to consult your interests. I shall smoke you out!
ANDROMACHE: Light all the fires you like; the gods will observe it all.
HERMIONE: You'll be in agony from the wounds I shall cut in your flesh.
ANDROMACHE: Kill me. The goddess will come after you, for staining her altar with blood.   260
HERMIONE: You foreign creatures are tough and obstinate.
Will you outface death? Well, I have a way to get
you up from the sanctuary of your own free will, and soon.
I have bait that will catch you. But I shan't tell you
about it, I'll let the action speak for itself, and soon.   265
Sit there in your sanctuary. I'll get you up from there
before the son of Achilles, in whom you trust, gets back here,
and I'd do it even if you were sealed right round by melted lead.
ANDROMACHE: I do trust him. It's a dreadful thing that one of the gods
has provided remedies for us from all reptiles in the wild,   270
but no one has ever discovered a drug that works against
a woman, something far worse than snake or fire.

The personnel of this storyline are drawn from a version of the aftermath of the sack of Troy that centres on an area of Greece known as Thessaly, specifically the homeland of the leading Greek warrior Achilles and his dynasty, the region called Phthia. Briefly, Peleus married the sea-nymph Thetis and their issue was

Achilles, whose son was Neoptolemus: Achilles killed Hector at Troy, before falling himself, and his son Neoptolemus was fetched from home to achieve final the capture and sack of Troy. As one of his prizes of conquest, Neoptolemus was awarded the widow of Hector, Andromache, and he brought her back to Phthia, much as Agamemnon brought back Cassandra. Neoptolemus and Andromache have had a son, called Molossus, who is still young. Yet Neoptolemus is formally married to the daughter of Menelaus and Helen, Hermione, from Sparta.

The opening of the play reveals a complex of tensions, since it soon becomes apparent from Andromache's monologue that she is a suppliant at the shrine of Thetis (lines 43–44), which is a construction that contains both a statue and an altar, to which references are made later. This shrine itself is located outside the palace of Neoptolemus (43), but indeed the whole local region is known as an area dedicated to Thetis (19–20). The shrine will keep her safe, she believes, from the combined hostility of Hermione and her father Menelaus, who has arrived in Phthia and is now in the palace (39–41). Her own first thoughts are for Thebe, an Asiatic city from which she was led with a magnificent dowry to be the bride of Hector at Troy. She herself has now sent her son away for safety, to an undisclosed location (47–48), and crucially Neoptolemus is absent, on a mission to Delphi, to give an apology to Apollo: it is his absence that has made her vulnerable, removing his natural protection from her.

As if to emphasize her tenuous hold on life and her inability to control its circumstances, this fraught situation is immediately made more agonizing by news brought from the palace by an old Trojan slave that Menelaus has left to capture her son. All Andromache can do now is to send the slave after Peleus, the grandfather of Neoptolemus and the husband of Thetis, repeating her requests to him to come to the palace and provide some security. Yet this shock is amplified by the attitudes of the chorus of local women, who arrive in the space apparently to warn Andromache to leave the sacred ground of the shrine of Thetis and to avoid touching the altar. This assertion of the inviolable sanctity of the space goes along with strictures on the need for Andromache to recognize her status as a slave, a foreigner and non-Greek, who is owned by Hermione. Hermione is now part of the dynasty that rules Phthia and has their allegiance: even if they do feel sympathy for Andromache, the women of the chorus cannot afford to show it.

The space contains the action, and our sense of it not only places Andromache in a fragile position with a tenuous hold on sanctuary, but also suggests that Hermione may still be a figure who has been joined to the local dynasty, rather than being of its essence. As Hermione appears from the palace, she does so to a chorus whose allegiance she may have through fear, but whose sympathy she may not have. The public presence here of the chorus is not a constraint, but it sharpens our sense of insecurity in the leading characters, of how the local environment may eventually close around them to frustrate their actions through adverse judgment. As things stand, the chorus at present lacks a significant figure who would have the authority to unite in her/himself sympathy, allegiance and the power to act in the interests of Phthia and the dynasty. It will only find these figures as the play evolves and comes to its conclusion.

The transactional qualities of the scene between Hermione and Andromache are immensely strong. Andromache is committed to her hold on sanctuary, although it is now unclear to her how this will protect her son. To maintain sanctuary allows her the time, possibly, to substitute her child's grandfather Peleus for Neoptolemus as a protective figure in the household, and a viable restraint on Hermione and her father, Menelaus. Yet time is a gamble, and as the scene reveals Andromache cannot be sure of any of her possible protectors. For Hermione, the aim is to remove Andromache from sanctuary, and it seems that for the moment Hermione is willing to advance some kinds of persuasion: she has, in short, come out to talk to Andromache. Included in this purpose is seizing the opportunity to condemn Andromache ruthlessly in the eyes of the chorus, which may make future violence against her a little less unpalatable to them.

Yet Hermione lacks the finer arts of persuasion, and her grand appearance, flaunting finery and jewels, slaps her Spartan background in the face of the women of Phthia. According to her, the existence of this trousseau permits her independence from the household of Peleus and Achilles, as if in modern terms she had a private income or economic autonomy, and so she can say what she likes (147–53). Inept though it may seem, this assertive display is part of her assertion of the right to act independently as well, and so does serve her purpose of preparing the ground for action against Andromache without the prior approval of Neoptolemus.

But it also slams across to the chorus of Phthian Women and the audience the issue of status. Andromache is a slave (154), a non-entity in Greek terms, who has no rights and can be subjected to any kind of punishment. If she has committed a crime or misdemeanour then she is subject to whatever may be designed for her, and Hermione insists that Andromache is a witch, who has poisoned her husband against her and actually aims to supplant her in the palace (155–57). The evidence is that Hermione is barren, and we should recall that 'evidence' of this kind has been quite sufficient to condemn witches in more modern eras. It is, of course, meant to be emotive and prejudicial (158–59), and in such twisted logic it is inevitable that a person of that kind should not be allowed to claim the privilege of sanctuary (159–61).

In those circumstances, and with that kind of accusation supposedly justified, a slave might well expect to die (161). But Hermione makes an allowance for a chance intervention against the odds, which nonetheless leads back to issues of status: Andromache must accept her position, submit and perform the roles of a slave, serve Hermione, forget Troy and her own dowry, realize where she is now (163–68). Part of the point of Hermione's blunt insistence is to assert that Andromache should expect no protector, that her own husband and father-in-law are dead (168–69), a significant if slightly hopeful allusion to Andromache's expectations of Neoptolemus and Peleus, who here stands in for a father-in-law. What condemns Andromache utterly, as Hermione hopes, is that she is not only a slave and a foreigner with no rights, but that she has sunk to the level of lending her body to the son of the man who killed her husband (170–73). So we may now summon up our prejudices, and admit how disgusting the sexual practices and internecine violence of foreigners are (173–76), as Euripides teases out the irony of a taunt that would apply best to the horrors of Greek myth. But, for Hermione, the overwhelming prejudice backs up her moral demand for the standard Greek custom of monogamy (177–80), of which Andromache is in flagrant breach.

Whatever the reaction that Hermione may have hoped to inspire, the response of the chorus is flattening, commenting solely on the reaction of a wife to the jealousy she feels. But for Andromache, there is nothing to be gained by staying silent. She does pick up on the constant assertion of her slavery, and just begins to angle for a fair hearing, the extreme chance of justice inclining just enough towards her to help her (183–91). This is a highly rhetorical gambit, the kind of prelude that a speaker (the Greek for this is *rhetor*) in a law court at Athens might introduce to begin to lever favour or indulgence towards him before he has made an argument. It suggests that Andromache is to speak in a crafted manner, to offer reasoned artifice rather than emotive prejudice, and so to attempt to swing opinion at large rather than a hostile individual. It will also prove to be a far more polished attempt in that respect than that of Electra in the scene from Sophocles that we looked at above.

Andromache adopts the position that if there is no coherent motive for an action then the action cannot have taken place, which is an interesting argument that we might regard as flawed. Her method is heavily ironical, and the ironical questions must not be missed or passed over by a modern actor, and interpreted as statements to be taken at face value. To make that completely clear, Andromache is saying that Troy is actually an unlucky city, she herself is past her prime in looks, and her city and her family no longer exist so cannot bring her repute. She then carries on into similar observations on children in the light of her own inherent unpopularity with Greeks (192–205).

The second phase of her speech turns to Hermione herself, to adduce the proper cause for the alienation of her husband. It is a mixture of observation and advice, coming from an older woman to a younger, and it moves subtly into the theme of jealousy. Andromache first adopts Hermione's deployment of prejudice against foreigners and their nasty ways, to bring pressure on Hermione to mitigate her jealousy and her supposed obsession with sex (215–19). Andromache's second example is herself, in a flashback that vividly conjures up her dead husband Hector, and shows her in her loyally married role in direct contrast to the abject and subversive picture Hermione just drew of her. The reference to being willing even to nurse his illegitimate children is a subtle prompt about her own illegitimate son Molossus (222–27). But her final comments are blunt, and delivered with an eye for the pressure of public opinion: no one is more notorious amongst Greeks for sexual misconduct and her obsession with sex than Hermione's mother, Helen, who is universally despised and condemned. So Andromache urges Hermione to step back now, and demonstrate her independence by moderate and tolerant behaviour.

The reaction of the chorus (232–33) indicates that Andromache has been successful in prosecuting her case, and Hermione's first response indicates in turn that she is aware of this effect (234), although she disputes the right of Andromache to deliver it (235). Yet from here the script heads into a line-by-line exchange, where any point or topic must be picked up by the other speaker and spun back, as we have seen. This is not only a quick and tightly connected form of scripting, but also one that does not lend itself easily to reasoned argument, since it dispenses with that kind of development or exposition.

The first exchanges resume topics that have already been introduced—age, sex, Greek and foreign—but a new note is introduced by Andromache as she feels things slipping away. She appeals indirectly to the statue of Thetis in the sanctuary (246) immediately after Hermione threatens her with death (245). But in response to this, Hermione revives local revulsion at Andromache's occupation of the sanctuary in a rejection of any bid for protection from the goddess (252–53). At the same time, Hermione underlines her purpose in coming out of the palace to speak to Andromache, which was to get her to leave the sanctuary (251–53). So the result of Andromache's refusal is the threat from Hermione of fire, which would avoid the sacrilege of human force applied in a sacred place (257). But even with the additional threat of physical wounding, Andromache remains insistent on the indignation of the gods (258–60).

The tempo of insult on insult, threat on top of threat has led to a climax, and Hermione steps back, as if she knows that she holds what we would call the trump card, and that she will have the pleasure of seeing Andromache leave sanctuary of her own free will. While the immediate transaction has been extravagantly unsuccessful, it concludes with an announcement that confidently predicts its ultimate success. At the same time, Hermione's sense of urgency negates the value of Andromache's purpose in staying where she is, since all will be achieved before Neoptolemus returns, and there is and will be no point of appeal, to him or to the gods.

This scene depends on the creation of a sense of sanctity in a given area of the playing space, and the degree to which Hermione may be seen to respect it, at least in so far as it offers a foreign, virtually adulterous slave protection. That it is a sacred space, and that its sanctity is both watchful and active, is adequately proved not only by the arrival of unexpected help for Andromache when all seems lost, but by the ultimate and authoritative appearance of Thetis herself. While on the human scale Hermione may be contemptuous, and Andromache may be fearful and at an extreme of vulnerability, there is that low hum emanating from the sacred space that keeps her meter of confidence just flickering above zero (**Recording 4**).

Feedback and rounding off

I think it is essential that the Workshops should aim to culminate in presentations, so long as there is a good understanding that showcasing and full production values are an obstruction to insight. Some actors will say that they find it very difficult to 'hold back' from full performance. But those are emotive terms that reveal a problem about preparation which may make the actors who stick to them unsuitable for a workshop environment. The fact is that there are no pre-existent, modern production values that incorporate the organic qualities of Greek tragedy, and so sliding into them will be a quick route out of learning. The assimilation of Greek tragic scripts to a combination of modern assumptions about production is not something that requires an extended workshop process: it can be done by almost any competent actor or director at any point anywhere in the world, with very little preparation.

Feedback conducted on the right terms is also essential for the learning process. For the First Workshop, I suggested that there should be two main criteria: the extent to which the progress of argument through phases is made apparent, and the degree to which a sense of transaction(s) is communicated. For feedback on presentations in the Second Workshop, I would suggest adding to those two. What we need to see in connection with each scene is the degree to which the presence of the chorus brings a public dimension to the transactions and the progress of argument. To that end, we should expect the leading actors in each scene to involve other workshop participants as members of a chorus who may be addressed or involved. A distinction may be made here in the space between those who are seen to be chorus members, and those who remain as audience. In the presentations that I have offered online, the choral presence is no more than indicative, but it may be far more active than that in the Workshops themselves, and some additional comments on that will be made in the 'Last Thoughts' that conclude the book.

If the presence of the chorus as an extra dimension to the performance of the leading actors forms the third criterion, then the fourth must be the evocation of a sense of space. Space must be used to express transactions and their course effectively, and to register appeals to the public presence of the chorus and the audience. Yet considerations of space extend well beyond those pragmatic issues, and participants should be encouraged to discuss space from every possible aspect, much as I have suggested in my reviews of scenes above. There are no possible prescriptions for the evocation in performance of the different kinds of space which these characters inhabit. But, as I have stated, an awareness of this dimension must form part of the resources of any actor who wishes to communicate anything other than the quaintness of Greek tragedy to an audience.

I shall also attach here a list I give to Workshop participants of questions that may be asked of scripts and scenes, questions that may help them identify a transaction or think their way into space, at least as a start.

What is the situation in the play at this moment?

What was the 'tipping point' that set the tragedy in motion?

Why are the characters there?

Is the location significant?

What kinds of 'space' are involved? What is the relationship of each character to those spaces?

Is one character arriving, and the other in place already?

What is the relationship of each character to the chorus?

How public is this exchange? How important is public opinion?

What are the expectations of each character initially?

What kinds of emotion or motive are involved, and why?

Is one character demanding something of the other, or attempting to persuade someone of something or to do something?

So what kinds of transaction are involved?

How does the exchange start, and does it proceed in stages?

What is the outcome of this exchange? What is its effect on the evolving action of the tragedy? Does this tell us something about the nature of the transaction(s)?

It is amazing how many questions would be answered with greater resonance if participants looked over the context and the whole play repeatedly, as I hope they would in a rehearsal and production process: a workshop should be no less demanding. I sometimes have to prompt actors to look out for and look over any other scenes in the play involving exchanges between these characters to gain further insight, and this prompting should not truly be necessary.

THIRD WORKSHOP

Three-actor Scenes

Greek tragedies can be played with three actors and however many performers may be selected to form a chorus. It is even possible to have a recorded chorus, aurally or on screen, and no doubt some directors have chosen to create a spoken and character-based text by removing the chorus altogether. With three actors, doubling (tripling and quadrupling in some cases) is essential, and actors enter the world of their ancient counterparts. There may be a value in this for modern actors, one that is not purely determined by economics. Being obliged to dispense with one character to assume another may just possibly prompt a different kind of insight in the modern actor into how 'characters' were understood in antiquity.

They were undoubtedly created through variation in the voice, since this is almost functionally necessary—e.g. an actor plays a man and then a young girl in succession—and will almost certainly have been created through physical differentiation. Both of these variable capacities would have depended on the individual performer, his inclination, assumptions gathered from his background or training, observation of others, direction from playwrights/composers over the years, responses from audiences.

Doubling is interesting, although the skills required in doing it are not part of this series of Workshops, since production values and issues are not considered here. But it is worth observing that the same actor played both Phaedra and Theseus in Euripides' *Hippolytus*, in succession, and that most schemes of doubling for tragedy can be worked out by fixing on any lead roles that play all through, and then working forward from the start of the play with the other two actors, distributing the roles pragmatically. In these Workshops, the only skills considered are those of the speaking voice and spatial movement and interaction; but ancient actors were often required to sing and dance, sometimes solo, and also in conjunction with a singing and dancing chorus.

If you ever think life is hard as a performer, reflect on an ancient actor singing to a large, open-air audience while dancing and wearing a full-head mask, and remember how raucous and unsparing an open-air, mass audience can be. There must also have been very many bad or sub-standard performances of tragedy, which is all the more reason to get it right now. The material may not have been given that transcendent, primal, earth-moving, original performance we can easily assume must have taken place in that astounding, democratic theatre: the enactment may have been achingly bad, and disappointing. There really is everything to play for, in the studio where you are, now.

With three actors, many characters can be created, and many characters introduced to one another. Even in tragedies from the middle of the fifth century, as I have mentioned, a tragedy may be plotted via a sequence of dialogue and monologue scenes. Euripides' *Medea* is a one example that operates with two-actor scenes, although it still probably requires the standard issue of three actors. In an opening scene a male slave and a female slave, the Nurse, are in front of the audience while Medea is wailing from inside the scene–building, hidden but probably still an actor not an extra. In fact, the roles in this tragedy probably should be divided between three actors in the normal way, with one playing Medea, a second playing Jason (and one of the slaves), and the third playing Creon and then Aegeus (and the other slave, and the slave who acts as a messenger). So in this tragedy we have the following scenes, omitting exchanges with the chorus:

M slave and F slave (Nurse), with voice of Medea

Medea and Creon

Medea and Jason

Medea and Aegeus

Medea and Jason

Medea and M slave

Medea and Messenger

Medea and Jason

We also have the boys—played by silent extras—at crucial times, and one of those scenes will be included in the final Workshop.

An awareness of how a tragedy may progress through two-actor scenes, and through doubling/tripling/quadrupling, is helpful in assessing the value of three-actor scenes. Tragedies may have plenty of work for three actors without the playwrights/composers seeing the need to make a scene dependent on the interaction of three characters. To make this more evident, let's think about Sophocles' *Antigone*, a tragedy from approximately the same period in the middle of the fifth century as Euripides' *Medea*. In *Antigone*, many scenes unfold with two actors: the opening scene, reviewed in the Second Workshop, between Antigone and Ismene; the subsequent scene, between Creon and the Guard; later scenes between Creon and his son Haemon, Creon and Antigone, and Creon and Tiresias, also reviewed in the Second Workshop, and the penultimate scene between Creon's wife Eurydice and a Messenger.

The exception to this mode of composition is a scene in which the Guard brings on Antigone to Creon (lines 384–581). After providing a narrative of Antigone's actions rather like a messenger (407), the Guard is quickly dismissed by Creon and sent about his business (444–45), before Creon attempts to interrogate and incriminate Antigone in front of the chorus. So the central part of the scene is conducted by two actors (446–525), much as the opening had been, since Antigone had remained silent until just before the Guard's dismissal. To that extent, the presence of three actors has not resulted in full, spoken interaction between them, with dialogue remaining the operative mode of discourse. But Sophocles chooses to break this mould by introducing Ismene, summoned from the palace by Creon, and the final part of the scene involves all three actors in an integrated exchange, three voices raised in reciprocal incomprehension (531–81). And here, by the way, is my example of the doubling of a man and a young girl, with one of the actors playing the Guard and then Ismene.

So three-actor scenes have a close relationship to dialogue and to two-actor scenes, and it is always helpful to look carefully at how they are composed and constructed, since they are often dependent on two-actor forms to which the third actor/character brings a remarkable variation. In this Workshop I shall bring forward a small number as proposals for exploration, and there will be one or two more included in the Fourth Workshop, on acting with properties. Just as there is no standard pattern to three-actor scenes, there is no standard 'effect' that is contrived by them. They all prove to be very different indeed, and they are interesting because they show interaction between the actors at its most complex. For those reasons, they may demonstrate the art of composition for speaking actors at its most inventive, as it extends dramatic and theatrical possibilities into previously untried effects.

Three equals two plus one: Athene, Odysseus and Ajax in Sophocles' *Ajax*

One of the more striking three-actor scenes certainly seems to be aimed at spectacular effects. Here is the opening of Sophocles tragedy *Ajax*.

Ajax—lines 1–133

ATHENA: Son of Laertes! I have always seen you hunt
to seize some quick advantage over enemies;
and now I see you at the seashore house

of Ajax, where he has the last position on the flank.
Doglike you've hunted down and measured out   5
his new-imprinted tracks, to find out if
he is inside or not. Your course has brought
you to your goal, keen-scented like a Spartan hound.
The man has just gone back inside; sweat drips
down from his face and from his murderous hands.   10
But you no longer need to try to peer inside
this tent; just tell me why you search
so eagerly. I'm wise, and you can learn from me.
ODYSSEUS: Athena's voice—dearest to me of all the gods—
how easily I hear your call, although you are   15
invisible to me, and seize it to my soul,
just like a trumpet with its mouth of bronze!
You are quite right; I'm hunting on the track
of my old enemy, Ajax the famous shield-bearer.
I have been tracking him, and no one else, for a long time.   20
This night he has accomplished something unbelievable
against us—if indeed he is the man (we know
nothing for certain, we are wandering in the dark);
I volunteered to take the burden of the search.
We recently discovered all our livestock   25
dead—slaughtered by human hand
together with their guards.
Now, everyone believes that Ajax did this deed;
one of our scouts saw him alone,
leaping across the plain with a new-blooded sword,   30
and told me where; I rushed at once
onto his trail, and sometimes I am sure, but then
I'm thrown off course, and don't know where he is.
You came just when I need you; your hand
always steered my path—and always will.   35
ATHENA: Odysseus, I know; I came some time ago,
eager to guard the path and help your chase.
ODYSSEUS: Dear mistress, is there any point in my hard work?
ATHENA: Yes; Ajax did those things.
ODYSSEUS: Why did he act so crazily?   40
ATHENA: Anger about Achilles' armour weighed him down.

ODYSSEUS: Why did he turn in fury on the flocks?
ATHENA: He thought his hand was stained with blood by killing
   you.
ODYSSEUS: What? This plan was aimed against the Greeks?
ATHENA: He would have done it too, if I'd been careless.   45
ODYSSEUS: How could he get such daring and such confidence?
ATHENA: He went against you by himself, at night, and stealthily.
ODYSSEUS: Did he come near us? Did he reach his goal?
ATHENA: He reached the doors of our two generals' tents.
ODYSSEUS: How was his hand, so eager for the slaughter,
   stayed?   50
ATHENA: I stop him from achieving that irreparable joy;
I cast upon his eyes delusions which he could not overcome,
and turn aside his fury to your flocks, the undivided
spoils, mixed together, which the cowherds guarded.
He fell upon the beasts, and hacked horned animals to death,   55
cleaving them in a circle round him; sometimes he believed
he had the sons of Atreus and was killing them himself,
then that he was attacking all the other generals in turn.
And while he stalked in maddened frenzy I
encouraged him, and cast him in a net of suffering.   60
At last he rested from his work;
he tied up all the cattle that were still alive with ropes
and brought the whole herd back here to his tent,
as if he'd captured men, and not just animals with horns.
Now he has tied them up and tortures them in there.   65
I'm going to show this madness to you openly,
so you can tell it out aloud to all the Greeks.
Be brave, and wait to see the man; you won't
be hurt. I will deflect the piercing vision
of his eyes, so he won't see your face.   70
You there—tying your captives' hands
behind their backs—I summon you to come to me.
Ajax, I'm calling you; come here, out from your house!
ODYSSEUS: Athena, what are you doing? Do not call him out.
ATHENA: Be quiet, or you will be called a coward.   75
ODYSSEUS: Please don't do it; he is quite enough staying inside.
ATHENA: What could happen? Was he not a man before?

ODYSSEUS: Yes, my enemy both then and now.
ATHENA: The sweetest of all laughter is to laugh at enemies.
ODYSSEUS: It is enough for me if he stays in his house.   80
ATHENA: Are you afraid to see a madman in full view?
ODYSSEUS: If he were sane, I would not shrink in fear.
ATHENA: He will not see you now, though you'll be near to him.
ODYSSEUS: How can that happen, if he sees with the same sight?
ATHENA: I will put darkness on his eyes, although they are so
   bright.   85
ODYSSEUS: Everything can happen when a god contrives.
ATHENA: So stand in silence; stay exactly where you are.
ODYSSEUS: I'll stay—but I wish I was somewhere else!
ATHENA: Ajax, I call you out a second time;
why do you slight your closest ally, me?   90
AJAX: Athena, welcome; daughter born of Zeus, welcome!
I'm glad you're here; I'll see that you are crowned
with golden offerings in thanks for my successful hunt.
ATHENA: Well said. But tell me this; did you
dye your sword red in the Greek camp?   95
AJAX: That I can boast; I won't deny the fact.
ATHENA: Did you raise your armed hand against the sons of
   Atreus?
AJAX: Yes; they will never disrespect Ajax again.
ATHENA: They're dead—that's what you mean.
AJAX: They're dead—now let them take my weapons from
   me!   100
ATHENA: Good; what about Laertes' son?
What have you done to him? Did he escape?
AJAX: You ask me where that cursed fox has gone?
ATHENA: I do. I mean your enemy, Odysseus.
AJAX: He sits inside, mistress—the prisoner who gives me   105
the greatest joy; I do not want him dead just yet.
ATHENA: What will you do first? What great profit do you seek?
AJAX: First I will bind him to a pillar of my tent—
ATHENA: How will you torment that poor man?
AJAX: I'll whip his back until it is all red before he dies.   110
ATHENA: Do not torture the poor man quite so much.
AJAX: In other things, Athena, I tell you you can have your way;

117

but he will pay this penalty and nothing else.
ATHENA: All right—since you can do this, and it pleases you,
go on, do not restrain yourself from any of your plan.   115
AJAX: I will get back to work. I only tell you this;
be always on my side just as you are today.
ATHENA: Odysseus, do you see the great strength of the gods?
Could you find anyone who was more careful than
this man, or better at responding to a situation's needs?   120
ODYSSEUS: I know of no one else. I pity him
as he is now, although he is my enemy, because
he has been bound fast to a terrible downfall.
In this I think no more of him than of myself.
I see that all of us who live are nothing else   125
but phantoms, empty shadow.
ATHENA: Now you have seen this, you must never speak
a word of arrogance against the gods,
and do not swell with pride because you're greater
than another in your strength of hand or depth of wealth.   130
One day can weigh down everything a human being is and has
or lift it up again; the gods love prudent men
and hate those who are not.

In working on three-actor scenes, activating a sense of space is paramount. This crucial dimension formed part of the essential requirements in the Second Workshop, and by this stage it should be reasonably well developed in participants, if feedback as well as active preparation has been perceptive and encouraging. Space is a vital ingredient because the kind of space into which Greek tragic scripts are cast is not like the kind(s) of space with which we are familiar from modern and contemporary theatre practice. Like so many other aspects of the skills-base that is needed for preparing these scripts, it has to be reshaped or reconstructed, and the greatest threat is that instinctive response 'Oh yes, I know that already'—to which the answer should be 'No you don't', not unless you are somehow reincarnated from practising your craft in the ancient Greek theatre.

We may readily reset Greek texts in modern studio spaces, and dispense with the vocal power needed for performing in the open air to vast numbers, and with the full extent of the open space of the ancient theatres. Yet the relations between people, and the transactions those people conduct, are expressed in space, and scenes with three actors require a simple sense of 'enough room' in all the participants for the work to progress. Characters in almost all instances need to move about the space actively in their interactions in these scenes, and it will be no good to be restricted when aiming to release that quality in the work of preparation. So even if you have managed to work successfully in relatively confined circumstances up to this point, now is the time to locate that space—outdoor or indoor—with a sense of 'room' in it.

To animate that space, the rudiments of an analysis are necessary, and in this opening of Ajax we need to understand that this is the seashore (or the land directly behind it) at Troy, where the Greek army has for years been encamped. The play takes place in an open space, in front of (or around) the military tent of the leading Greek warrior, Ajax. Practically, it is the scene-building that represents that tent, and it is understood to have a door centrally placed in it. That door holds a surprise, because it has the capacity to project a platform which can carry bodies, and also a living person, and perhaps other items. This is one of the few mechanical devices of the ancient Greek theatre, and it is known in suitably straightforward language as 'the thing that wheels out', the *ekkuklema*. It probably first appears to our view in Aeschylus' *Oresteia*, and while the audience is familiar with its existence, when it will be used will always remain unpredictable.

What we see at the beginning of this play is the figure of a man tracking marks in the sand or the dust through the open space, and he follows a line that leads him towards the door in the scene-building. This we as readers know from the admiring description of his actions (1–12) given by a second figure whom the original audience will have instantly recognized, since images of her were iconic in Athens: she will inevitably wear a helmet and carry a spear, and perhaps be wrapped in the cloak or shawl known as the aegis. While the description is very detailed, and includes the observation that the man, Odysseus (for he is the 'son of Laertes') is actually trying to peer into the scene-building through the door (11–12), it is also describing actions that have taken place before these words are spoken. So the sequence of events is the man's silent progress across the space to the door, his nosiness at and around the door, and his interruption by the voice that then, to his astonishment and alarm, describes exactly what he has just been doing.

This is rather intriguing, since anyone spying out the ground does not appreciate the idea of being spotted, and will probably have been careful to check in advance whether anyone else is about. It is all the more so when one knows that this man is Odysseus, who is notorious amongst the Greeks of myth for being careful and wily. By any standards, this voice that he hears is alarming, since he has been discovered. But his opening words reveal to us some further actions that he must have been going through while Athena was speaking to him, because it is only her voice that is apparent to him (14–17)—though she is, of course, visible to the spectators. So he will have registered shock, alarm and surprise, but also a dawning recognition of whose voice this is, since in myth Athena honours Odysseus with her presence and company and advice from time to time.

Sophocles is here offering his audience an amusing and intriguing two-actor scene, without a chorus, another version of the secrecy that we found in the opening scene of his *Antigone*, yet with the open and otherwise empty space fraught with meaning and threat. We know there is threat very quickly, not just because the man is showing extreme caution, and is probably armed, but because the scene-building is identified as the tent of Ajax, his enemy (1–4, 18–20). What the invisibility of Athena offers this scene is not just the opening surprise and amusement, but the opportunity for the actor playing Athena to move around, away from and up close to Odysseus as the character may divinely fancy, so he is never quite sure of where he is addressing his words. This may be particularly true of his initial explanation (14–35), but it may also apply in the line-by-line exchange that follows (36–50). We hear of the slaughter of the army's livestock and their herdsmen during the night, and the suspicion that this was carried out by Ajax, who has been seen with a bloodied sword (21–31). Odysseus thinks he may have followed his trail successfully, but is not fully sure, and he will appreciate Athena's guidance.

Our dawning sense of a transaction is becoming clear: this is a pursuit of a man assumed on some evidence to be a criminal, which might lead to an identification and an interrogation, and presumably to some kind of military court of judgment. It is at present incomplete, and may be unsuccessful, and the transaction is changed by the addition of the presence of Athena, to whom Odysseus is willing to hand over responsibility for at least locating the supposed criminal. What the following line-by-line dialogue establishes is not so much his location as his guilt, with the excitement of the revelations growing as it becomes apparent that Athena has fortunately intervened to protect the Greek leadership from an insanely jealous man.

The provocation, which Sophocles assumes to be known to the audience, is that the arms and armour of the dead Achilles had been awarded by the Greek generals to Odysseus rather than to Ajax. While the initial reference to how near Ajax got to him and the other generals must be seen to scare Odysseus (47–48), the climax is the vivid description of Ajax's frenzy, how his fury was diverted by Athena away from the leading Greeks onto the livestock and their wretched guardians. The whole account becomes truly edgy as Athena indicates that this mad man is torturing livestock inside his tent at this very moment (61–65). The narrative, which has taken minds away towards the other Greek tents at night, now returns ominously to invest the scene-building behind Odysseus with live danger, and Athena's delight in her own role and her teasing invisibility will now take a new turn.

Athena has decided to provide Odysseus with living proof of the guilt of Ajax, and the state that he is in (66–67), since in ancient Greece a witness—one who has seen something with his own eyes—is the equivalent to many modern forms of documentary proof. This invisible goddess now promises to make Odysseus invisible in turn to Ajax, so that he can look on him without fear (68–70). She summons Ajax without waiting for a response from Odysseus, but before Ajax appears Sophocles allows time for a humorous exchange, in which Athena uses a set of almost taunting arguments to bring Odysseus round to her decision. Plainly Odysseus, faced with the imminent appearance of his most deadly enemy, would rather be anywhere else. But he is detained by Athena offering him the unmissable chance to laugh at that enemy, and to do so unseen. This promise he has to believe, we must assume, since Athena has been able to make herself invisible. But for this particular discussion to proceed with one of the participants, who is doubtful and fearful, currently unable to see the other, who is making the promise, is highly ironical.

The second summons from Athena brings on the third actor from the door of the scene-building, almost certainly carrying a whip and most plausibly still covered in blood. Ajax is convinced Athena is his ally in this operation (91–93, and particularly 116–17), as Athena has previously told us with some glee (59–60), and now we have Odysseus who cannot see Athena, and Ajax who can see Athena but cannot see Odysseus, who can see him. No one can know how this was performed, but if I were to say Ajax struts and Odysseus flinches then I would think few would disagree. Ajax has three points of reference: Athena to whom he boasts, the Greek camp where he thinks he has done vast damage, and the scene-building, which houses the poor beast that he takes to be Odysseus, and for which he has a precise plan of suffering. In our perspective, we would add a fourth, which would be the unseen Odysseus, who has been told by Athena to stand and 'stay exactly where you are' (87).

The proof has been given, the evidence shown to a key witness; Ajax goes inside, since he has work to do. The final dialogue between Athena and Odysseus depends on what they have just witnessed from the third actor. Even Odysseus pities his downfall since, as Athena points out, anyone can be cast down. This short transaction leads Odysseus to that pity, as well as accomplishing the bitter necessity of witness, and it also confirms the need to be calm, careful, and to avoid pride and arrogance. As one who has himself just been invisible to one who is downcast, mad and perhaps beyond help, Odysseus tellingly compares human beings to 'nothing else/ but phantoms, empty shadow' (125–26).

The script-construction of this scene, with its compelling,

magical qualities is relatively simple. There is an opening dialogue (lines 1–35) between A (Athena) and B (Odysseus), which compresses to a line-by-line exchange in two parts (36–50, and 74–88), before and after Athena gives her first summons to C (Ajax). This is followed by a line-by-line exchange between A and C, which is varied lightly by the inclusion of two- and three-line components at its beginning (89–95) and end (112–17). The scene concludes with another A and B dialogue (118–33). We might readily call this a framing device, which displays to us in its centre the evidence for the crucial transaction of witnessing, at the same time as it cruelly demonstrates human frailty, and the seemingly pitiless power of gods who must never be offended.

Electra, Orestes and the Old Man plotting and praying together in Euripides' *Electra*

This device of pairing characters in a three-actor scene is also used by Euripides, although to very different effect, in a tragedy that seems to have the playwright exploring the resources of scripting available to him. The dialogue between Electra and Orestes in Euripides' *Electra* was included in the Second Workshop, where its exclusively line-by-line construction was reviewed to highlight the subtle shifts and phases through which it passed. That exchange is then capped by a climactic monologue from Electra (300–38), driving home the message that Agamemnon remains unrevenged, and that her sole purpose in existing is to act as a call to her absent brother. Yet the intensity of this meeting, which is kept short of a recognition by the timidity and reluctance of Orestes, is framed by the presence of the Farmer, married to Electra.

This character has spoken to the audience at the opening of the tragedy to explain his position, and has urged Electra not to work so hard before leaving to do so himself. Immediately after Electra's monologue, he returns to the house to find two unknown men (Orestes and Pylades) in conversation with his wife. He starts from a position of tact and modesty, and is repaid by finding out from Electra that these are friends of Orestes; so he extends a welcome to them, and an invitation to step indoors. But

Electra is appalled at the thought of the meagre hospitality they can afford, and orders her husband to go and fetch her father's old slave. This man had brought up Agamemnon, and when Agamemnon was murdered by Aegisthus and Clytemnestra he had taken the baby Orestes away to safety. He is now a shepherd at a safe distance from the city, near the border of Argos with Sparta, and he can bring something good to eat, chosen from his flock.

So the play has already accustomed us to a character played by the third actor impinging, to a limited extent, on the intensity of the growing relations between Electra and this 'friend' of Orestes, whom we recognize through his earlier declaration of purpose to his companion Pylades. Pylades remains silent throughout (he is, contrastingly, very vocal in Euripides' *Orestes* and *Iphigenia in Tauris*), and is not included here in the cast for the three speaking actors. The third actor promptly returns as the Old Man after a danced song from the chorus (432–86), which leads inexorably towards a vision of the just death of Helen, as a parallel, it seems, to the anticipated revenge to be taken on her sister, Clytemnestra. The third actor will have changed his mask and his costume, and we might assume he will vary his voice and physical manner from the middle-aged Farmer to this Old Man, to achieve a strong and definitive contrast.

In the scene that follows, the Old Man brings about a recognition of the boy he had saved, although his news about offerings at Agamemnon's grave and how the identity of the donor could be established are initially dismissed by Electra. But whether Orestes likes it or not, he is finally recognized by a scar on his forehead in a brilliantly scripted line-by-line exchange. This scene has the Old Man leading off with a greeting; a puzzled exchange between Orestes and Electra about the Old Man's behaviour; growing excitement in an exchange between the Old Man and Electra, with Orestes silent, which leads to the Old Man pointing at the scar painted on Orestes' mask; and then an exchange and embrace exclusively between Electra and Orestes, dividing lines between them, once Orestes has been irrevocably identified. The chorus celebrates briefly in a danced song, and our sequence takes up from there:

Euripides *Electra*—lines 596–698

ORESTES: Well, then. Holding you close to me is a sweet
pleasure; we shall do this again at a later date.
As for you, old man, you turned up at the right moment,
so tell me how I can take revenge on my father's murderer,
and my mother, his partner in a marriage that offends the gods. 600
Will I find anyone in Argos who is on my side?
Or are we completely bankrupt, of friends and of luck?
Can I approach anyone for help? Should I go at night, or by day?
Where is the road that leads straight to my enemies?
OLD MAN: My boy, while your luck is out no one's your friend. 605
Chance would be a fine thing, you can be sure,
if someone shared in the bad times as well as the good.
Those who were your friends see you completely ruined,
without a hope left. So listen now to what I say:
if you want to get your father's palace back, and your city,   610
trust in luck and your own right hand. They're what you've got.
ORESTES: Yes; so what should we do to get where we want to be?
OLD MAN: You've got to kill the son of Thyestes and your mother.
ORESTES: That's the garland I came to win. But how do I do it?
OLD MAN: You couldn't get inside the walls even if you wanted
   to.   615
ORESTES: He's lined up his bodyguards, strong arms holding
   spears?
OLD MAN: You've got it. He's scared of you, and sleeps lightly.
ORESTES: Well, then, it's over to you, old man. What's your advice?
OLD MAN: All right, listen to my idea. Something just occurred to
   me.
ORESTES: I hope I follow what you're saying, and what you're
   saying's good.   620
OLD MAN: I saw Aegisthus while I was on my way here.
ORESTES: Those are welcome words. Whereabouts was he?
OLD MAN: In the fields near here, where the horses are pastured.
ORESTES: I see a glimmer of hope out of nowhere. What was he
   up to?
OLD MAN: It looked to me like he was setting up a feast for the
   Nymphs.   625

ORESTES: For the welfare of his children, or an expected baby?

OLD MAN: I can't say; but he had the gear with him to sacrifice a bull.

ORESTES: How many men with him? Was he on his own, or with servants?

OLD MAN: He had no Argives with him, just a group of palace servants.

ORESTES: So there's no one who'd recognize me when he saw me, old man?   630

OLD MAN: No, they're just servants, who've never seen you.

ORESTES: But if I was to be successful, they'd be on my side?

OLD MAN: That's the way slaves are, and that's handy for you.

ORESTES: But how on earth am I going to get close to him?

OLD MAN: He'll be sacrificing the bull: walk past where he'll spot you.   635

ORESTES: It sounds like his fields are right next to the road.

OLD MAN: Once he sees you, he'll call you over to join in the feast.

ORESTES: God willing, I'll bring a bitter taste to his banquet.

OLD MAN: You'll have to work out what to do next, as things fall out.

ORESTES: That's a fair point. Where is my mother?   640

OLD MAN: In Argos. Don't worry, she'll be joining him for the feast.

ORESTES: But why didn't she set out at the same time as her husband?

OLD MAN: The citizens blame her, and she's scared. So she stayed behind.

ORESTES: I understand that. She knows the city doesn't trust her.

OLD MAN: That's right. Everyone hates a woman who offends the gods.   645

ORESTES: So how do I do it? Kill her and him at the same time?

ELECTRA: I shall be the one to set up the killing of my mother.

ORESTES: Well, in that case I'm sure I'll be lucky on my side of things.

ELECTRA: This old man—there are two of us, but he can help us both.

OLD MAN: Yes, that's fine. But how will you find a way of killing your mother?   650

ELECTRA: Go and tell her I've been laid up in childbirth—it's a boy.   652

OLD MAN: Is the story that you gave birth some time ago, or just recently?

ELECTRA: Ten days ago. That's the period of purity after childbirth.

OLD MAN: Yes, but I don't see how this helps you to kill your mother.   655

ELECTRA: She will come here once she hears I'm recovering from labour and birth.

OLD MAN: You reckon? What makes you think she cares for you, child?

ELECTRA: She will. And she will cry about my son's low status.

OLD MAN: Perhaps. But bring the plan back to where you left it.

ELECTRA: That's simple. If she comes, it's obvious she'll die.   660

OLD MAN: Well then, let's say she comes right up to the door of your house?

ELECTRA: Then surely it's a small step from there to Hades.

OLD MAN: If I could only see that happen, I'd gladly die.

ELECTRA: But first you must show him where to go, old man.

OLD MAN: To the place where Aegisthus right now is sacrificing to the gods?   665

ELECTRA: Then go on to meet my mother and tell her my story.

OLD MAN: It will seem like my words are coming straight out of your mouth.

ELECTRA: Time for action from you. The first killing is allotted to you.

ORESTES: I'll leave right now, if someone will be my guide.

OLD MAN: Of course. I'm more than willing to take you along the road.   670

ORESTES: Zeus the patriarch, who scatters my enemies . . .

ELECTRA: . . . have pity on us; what we have suffered is pitiable.

OLD MAN: Yes, pity them, who were born your descendants.

ORESTES: Hera, sovereign of the altars of Mycenae . . .

ELECTRA: . . . grant us victory, if what we pray for is just.   675

OLD MAN: Yes, grant their father justice and vengeance.

ORESTES: And you, father, whom godless actions forced below the earth . . .

ELECTRA: . . . and lady Earth, I summon your help with my beating
hands . . .

OLD MAN: . . . these are your dear children: protect them, protect
them!

ORESTES: Summon all your allies amongst the dead, and bring
them with you . . .   680

ELECTRA: . . . all those who fought with you and killed the Trojans
in battle . . .

OLD MAN: . . . and all who detest the ungodly, stained with
pollution.   683

ORESTES: What you suffered at our mother's hands was appalling.
Do you hear us?   682

ELECTRA: Father hears all that we say, I am sure. You must go
now.   684

OLD MAN: All, I'm sure. So what's left is that you must be a
man.   693

ELECTRA: You, women, must be like a beacon to me, and let
your cries   694

flare up for success in this struggle. I shall stand guard,   695
balancing a sword in my hand, ready for the outcome.
If I am defeated, I shall never pay the penalty
to my enemies, or let them abuse my body.

Orestes demonstrates that he is completely bereft of ideas (596–
604), now that he has no choice but to act or to plan to act, and the
Old Man confirms that he is right out there, on his own, without
any friends (605–11). The scene then unfolds as a set of line-by-
line exchanges between the characters in succession, a variation
on the straight dialogue version of this mode that we saw in the
scene between Orestes and Electra. The general aim of the linked
exchanges is to achieve a satisfactory plan that will encompass
the killing, in revenge, of both Aegisthus and Clytemnestra.
To be satisfactory, the plan must look as though it will succeed
before either Orestes or Electra is killed in turn, or prevented
from carrying out their intentions. That is about as far as it goes,
and so the transaction is to conjure up enough ideas to make this
feasible, rather than to consider what comes afterwards.

In the first phase of the exchange, the Old Man confirms to

Orestes that Aegisthus is well-guarded in the city itself (615–17). This calls up an impromptu thought (618–20), which is that Aegisthus could be tackled while he is in the open, as he is right now, making a sacrifice and preparing a feast (621–27). This leads to a further thought, which again is about the level of protection: in answer to Orestes' question the Old Man replies that Aegisthus just has some personal slaves with him, rather than (free) Argive citizens. Not only will these slaves not recognize Orestes, but as slaves they will not put up much resistance, and will readily go along with the victor, if that is Orestes (628–33). Orestes now needs to know how to time his approach and attack, and once again the Old Man acts as a mentor, or personal advisor. He not only knows the lie of the land, but also that Aegisthus is likely to play the patron, and ask Orestes as a visitor to join in the feast (634–37).

The exchange between the Old Man and Orestes now gets drawn towards the problem of killing Orestes' mother, and there is an odd complication here as it proves to be the case that she has not gone out with Aegisthus, but does intend to join him later for the feast. This part of the exchange leads Orestes to the point where he has to face up to the idea of killing both Aegisthus and his mother together (646). But here he is sharply interrupted by Electra, who insists that she will 'arrange' the killing of their mother herself (647). This firm claim by his sister sees Orestes bow out of a potential dialogue with her (648), apparently in relief, as the sharp mind of the Old Man is now engaged by Electra.

Under his interrogation, she is willing to think through her plan to the point where she has drawn her mother to her with the false announcement of the birth of a son. This is precisely the humiliating and disabling outcome that Aegisthus had had in mind in marrying her to a poor Farmer, avoiding the dangers that would stem from the male offspring of marriage to an aristocrat. Electra is sure that her mother will come to visit her, although the Old Man is less so, and she has no idea how she will handle things next (662). All Electra has to do now is to resume the arrangements with the Old Man, those for Orestes and for herself, and then she suddenly turns back to Orestes himself, with an instruction to make the first move (668). As soon as the moment for action is acknowledged, all three actors swing the line-by-line exchange into a coordinated, spoken invocation of gods and of Agamemnon, who has his home beneath the earth. The attribution of speakers and the order of lines here are not certain. I have adopted one of a number of possibilities, with Orestes leading off the invocatory appeal to Zeus for help, followed by Electra and then by the Old Man, and with this sequence repeated until Electra breaks out of the prayer to conclude with a grim vision of defeat.

In the A, B, C pattern that I have adopted, Orestes as the heir to Agamemnon's legacy in the ruling dynasty of Argos, and the returning, male avenger leads the invocation of the gods, whose support is essential to this questionable act of violence. So he appeals to Zeus in his capacities as the deity who endorses patriarchy and who also may give victory in a struggle (671), and subsequently appeals to Hera (674). This invocation is necessary since Hera is the patron goddess of Argos and the region embracing Mycenae, and may also be believed to endorse marriage rather than adultery. His third appeal is to his father himself, below the earth (677), who should come to their aid with an army of the dead (680), a formidable reinforcement of their purpose.

Orestes' lead in all these cases would be seconded by Electra, who gives an intention to the appeal, asking Zeus to pity them (and consequently lend them his help, 672) and Hera to give them victory, if their cause is just (675). She adds an invocation of Gaia, Earth, in support of Orestes' appeal to his father in the underworld (678), and specifies that Agamemnon's army of the dead should be those who killed Trojans (681). For his part, the Old Man echoes words or phrases from Electra, constantly drawing attention to the idea of the children of the father who needs to be avenged, who themselves need support and protection (673, 676, 679). The important conclusion to this sequence is an appeal to their father to be heard, led by Orestes (683), and the assertion by Electra and the Old Man that their appeals have surely been heard, with a final call to Orestes to cross the boundary between adolescence and manhood.

In picking up a word or phrase, or an idea, from the previous speaker, this sequence develops a standard feature of line-by-line exchanges into a ritualized formula which has a distinctively religious quality. One might well expect an appeal to Zeus to be made by opening the arms and looking up to the sky, and an appeal to the dead and to Gaia to be made by kneeling, in order to bring hands and arms into play on the ground. If that were the case, then the trio of performers would also arrange themselves, perhaps to face 'out' while standing and 'in' while kneeling. They would then have to rise from their final position as Electra addresses the chorus, who would surely have been surrounding the actors and supporting their appeals, or simply following their lead physically. At the close, Orestes and the Old Man will be detached in some way from the grouping of Electra and the chorus, who are linked to the scene-building, and the two male characters will be ready to depart together, which will be along a side passage out of the playing space.

What Euripides does here is to create a spoken version of what might easily be a danced song, using and ingeniously adapting the resource of line-by-line exchanges. By this means, he is in fact avoiding a need to echo the extraordinarily elaborate sung and danced sequence between Orestes, Electra and the chorus in *Libation Bearers*, the second play in Aeschylus' *Oresteia* trilogy, which has the same function as this. Our sense of the 'catching' quality of each line upon the last, and of the forward impulse of this kind of exchange, should feed into our work on the earlier part of the scene, in which urgency and agitation should register strongly in interaction and movement in the playing space.

At the same time, we should be aware that the third party is an active listener, and potentially a point of appeal or corroboration, or indeed of avoidance, since we may believe that this Orestes is nervous of the pressure from his sister for a decisive avenger, for the kind of direct and unreflecting action to which he seems unsuited. We may also believe that Electra is impatient for a role in the action, and so seizes her chance when it is presented (647 and forwards), or that she senses at this point that her brother may be incapable of a resolute act of violence against their mother. What is most interesting is that the Old Man is the certainty that anchors this scene. He welcomes the moment and the young man who has stepped into it, even if in the wisdom of his wrinkled mask he holds back from having the ultimate, blow-by-blow game-plan for each separate killing that he knows will be necessary. Agamemnon's childhood male nurse proves that age, time and loyalty can nurture both recognition between brother and sister and subsequent, long-awaited revenge.

Although it is not scripted, the involvement of the chorus of Argive Women in this scene is palpable. At its close, the Women are left to dance and sing about the origin of the feud in the dynasty of Mycenae and Argos (699–746), and to read a moral out loud as if to Clytemnestra (743–46). They are in the playing space alone when they claim to hear a shout (747), and their excitement not only summons Electra out from the house but initiates an almost frantic dialogue with Electra (750–60), who herself quickly plunges into despair. When the Messenger arrives at the house shouting out for victory, it is the chorus that he addresses as 'victory celebrants' (761). The Argive Women of the chorus have been implacable towards Clytemnestra before, at the conclusion of their previous danced song (432–86, conclusion at 479–86), and correspondingly ecstatic at the recognition and return of the man who, with divine help, will assure them of a victory in which they themselves feel involved (585–95). They will follow the evolution of the plotting between the three characters in our scene with excitement, fascination and commitment.

Deianira, Lichas, and another Old Man: pinning down the liar in Sophocles' *Young Women of Trachis*

If a vindictive chorus lies at one end of the spectrum, then a sympathetic chorus might be thought to be at the other; yet each may well be as strongly tied to a leading character. In Euripides' *Electra*, the chorus has a clear dynastic loyalty to Agamemnon's line, and advises Electra (initially addressed as 'daughter of Agamemnon', 167) that prayers to the gods rather than lamenting will secure the desired result (193—97). They came to see her in order to invite her to a festival in honour of the patron god of Argos, Hera, and to encourage her to maintain her respect for the gods, and in their own way are as fixed on the one, murderous outcome as she is herself.

Like the members of the chorus in *Electra*, the chorus providing companionship for Deianira in *Young Women of Trachis* seems to be of unmarried, youthful girls or young women. While the term 'maidens' is well out-of-date, it does capture the issue of status precisely, since the lack of marriage is itself a status in ancient Greece. That status permitted involvement in certain festivals (and exclusion from other rites) in Greek society, and brought groups of teenage girls together as choruses to sing and dance at festivals. This aspect of Greek culture offered a model for the theatrical representation (by young men) of choruses of young women in tragedy. These choruses were understood to be one side of a threshold, and while Euripides' Electra ironically remains that side herself although she has the perceived status of a married woman, Deianira is separated from her comforting companions by a world that has been and remains harsh. Sophocles' chorus in *Young Women of Trachis* wants to understand her predicament, but cannot completely, and they fall silent soon after the suicide of Deianira, and in the presence of her enraged and dying husband, Heracles.

While the chorus of *Young Women of Trachis* is sympathetic to Deianira (102–11), the young women have always believed that Zeus would never prove to be 'mindless of his children' (140), and so they are mildly critical of Deianira's fears for Heracles, the son of Zeus (122–40). Like Deianira, they feel unqualified joy at the news of the return of Heracles, victorious from battle, and they sing and dance a short, celebratory paean, invoking Apollo and his sister Artemis alongside the ecstatic god, Dionysus (205–24). Their optimism in this song ignores any ominous implications of the oracles of which we have heard, and is intended to affect our reaction to the sight of a group of female captives. These are seen initially in the terms in which they are introduced by the Old Man, who first brings the good news, as nothing more than an offering to the gods indicative of the victory won by Heracles (182–83, with later confirmation from Lichas, 244–45).

Success is indeed the first theme brought in by Lichas the herald, whose office is to convey news and offerings, and to encourage by carefully chosen narrative an appropriate response. Lichas takes as his second theme that all has been enacted by Zeus (250–51), and although he weaves Zeus into his account, there is clearer evidence for Zeus's anger with Heracles than for Zeus's support for his actions (274–80). Yet Heracles is currently conducting (187–89) a sacrifice to Zeus, as if his actions in sacking the city of Oechalia and enslaving its population were endorsed, and the silent, enslaved women are seen by Lichas to have lost their freedom as a result of the slander voiced against Heracles by their king (281–86).

Young Women of Trachis—lines 293–496

DEIANIRA: I would be completely justified in rejoicing at the news
of this great achievement of my husband. That is true.
I should be. My feelings must keep pace with events.   295
Nevertheless, anyone who considers things carefully
may well worry about success. It can end.
In fact, friends, as I look at these unfortunate women,
I am struck by a terrible pity. They are without homes,
and have lost their fathers. They are exiles in a foreign   300
land. They may perhaps have been the daughters of free men,
once. Now they are living the life of a slave.
Oh Zeus, who decides the issue of battles, may I
never see you coming at my children in this way,
not at any time. If you do, may I die first.   305
When I look at these women, these are my fears.
You are a girl, and bitterly unhappy. Who are you?
Unmarried, or a mother? To look at you, I would
think that was beyond your experience. A noble face.
Lichas, whose child is this girl? Tell me.   310
Who is her mother, and who is her father? Looking
at all these women here, I pitied her most of all;
she alone shows a keen sense of what has happened.
LICHAS: How should I know? Why do you ask me about it?
She's possibly from one of the leading families there.   315
DEIANIRA: From the ruling family? Is she a child of Eurytus?

LICHAS: I have no idea. I didn't bother with many questions.
DEIANIRA: But didn't you pick up her name from one of those
  with her?
LICHAS: No. I certainly did not. I did my job in silence.
DEIANIRA: Tell me yourself, poor girl, woman to woman. It's   320
a really dreadful thing not to know who you are.
LICHAS: If she comes out with anything, I can assure you it
will be a complete breach of precedent. She has
not said a word the whole time. Not a whisper.
Just the pain of tears giving birth to more tears,   325
the poor girl, at the weight of this calamity, from
the moment she left her homeland to the winds. She
feels her loss badly. But we must have sympathy.
DEIANIRA: Let's leave her alone, then. Let her go on into the
  house
like that, as she prefers. As things stand, she has enough   330
sorrow to contend with. I should not wish to add
to her burden myself. In fact, let us all make a
move towards the palace. You have to get on
with your journey, and I have to organize things indoors.
OLD MAN: Just stay here a moment first, on your own,
  without   335
these people. That way you'll discover who the new arrivals are,
and find out things you should know, and haven't been told.
For I'm in possession of the full facts, in every respect.
DEIANIRA: What is this? Why are you keeping me back?
OLD MAN: Stand still, and listen. After all, what I had   340
to say to you earlier was worth while. This will be too.
DEIANIRA: Shall I call all of them back here again? Or
do you want to speak just to me and these women here?
OLD MAN: To you and these women. Nothing barred. Let that lot
  go.
DEIANIRA: Well, they have gone now. Proceed with your story. 345
OLD MAN: Nothing of what this man just said was spoken
in accordance with the straight truth. Either he's lying now,
or he was dishonest in the report he gave before.
DEIANIRA: What do you mean? Tell me precisely what you have
in mind. I don't understand what you said to me.   350

OLD MAN: I was there, along with many other potential witnesses,
and myself heard this man say that it was for the
sake of the girl you've seen that Heracles captured Eurytus
and the towering city of Oechalia. That the only god involved
in this campaign was Love, who used his magic on him.   355
Events in Lydia, hard labour as a slave for Omphale,
Iphitus hurled to his death: these had nothing to do with it.
Now he tells it another way, shoving Love out of the story.
Heracles tried to persuade the father to give him the girl,
to have illicit sex with her. When that failed   360
he prepared a petty grudge, and with that excuse
marched against her fatherland and sacked   362
the city. And now, as you can see, he is on his way   365
back home, sending her on in advance, not carelessly,
lady, nor as a slave. Don't look forward to that.
It's hardly likely, if he's all aflame with passion.
Mistress, it seemed the right course to reveal everything
to you, everything I happen to have heard from him.   370
A crowd of Trachinians heard all of this just the same
as I did, at the same time, with him in the middle,
enough to convict him. What I've said cannot
be pleasant to hear. I'm sorry. But it's the truth.
DEIANIRA: Pleasant? I'm devastated. Where am I in all of this?   375
What kind of hidden trouble have I taken
under my roof? I can't bear it. Nameless, is she?
The man who brought her here swore to that.
A girl whose rank shines from her face, her whole body.
OLD MAN: As for her family; her father was Eurytus, and she   380
used to be called Iole. As for him; he was content
to say nothing of her parents. He didn't bother with questions.
CHORUS: Bad men should die. If not all of them, then
at least those who disgrace themselves with treachery.
DEIANIRA: Women, what should I do? The truth is that I   385
have been hit very hard by what I have heard,
CHORUS: Go and find out from the man himself. If you are
willing to press your questions, you may get clear answers.
DEIANIRA: That is reasonable advice. I am on my way.
OLD MAN: Shall I wait here? Or what would you like me to do?   390

DEIANIRA: Stay there. Here is the man himself, making his way
from the house of his own accord. No need for a summons.
LICHAS: What should I say to Heracles, lady, on arrival?
Tell me. As you can see, I'm starting on my journey.
DEIANIRA: You took a long time in getting here, and now
you're   395
rushing off, before we've had time to renew our conversation.
LICHAS: Well, if there's anything you want to ask, I'm still here.
DEIANIRA: Will you give me my due—the certainty of truth?
LICHAS: May Zeus be my witness, as far as I know it myself.
DEIANIRA: Who, then, is the woman you brought here with
you?   400
LICHAS: A Euboean. I cannot tell you who her parents are.
OLD MAN: You there, look at me. Who do you think you're talking
to?
LICHAS: And what do you mean by asking me such a question?
OLD MAN: Have the courage to answer me when I ask. If you're
wise.
LICHAS: I am speaking to Deianira, a powerful woman,   405
daughter of Oeneus, spouse of Heracles, and—unless
my eyes happen to be deceiving me—my mistress.
OLD MAN: That's exactly what I wanted to hear from you.
You say she is your mistress?
LICHAS: That's correct.
OLD MAN: Is that so? Then what punishment would you think
correct   410
if you were found to be incorrect in your conduct to her?
LICHAS: What do you mean, incorrect? What game are you
playing?
OLD MAN: Nothing. No game. You're the one who's doing that.
LICHAS: I'm going. I was a fool to listen to you so long.
OLD MAN: No, not before you give the answers to a few
questions.   415
LICHAS: Ask away, then, anything you like. You're not the silent
type.
OLD MAN: That prisoner-of-war, whom you escorted into the
house:
you know who I mean?

LICHAS: I do. Why do you ask?
OLD MAN: You claim not to know who she is. But didn't you
say that this woman was Iole, the daughter of Eurytus?   420
LICHAS: To whom? In what company? Who is your witness?
Who will come forward and say he heard that from me?
OLD MAN: A good many citizens. A great crowd of Trachinians
heard you say it, as you stood in the middle of them.
LICHAS: Yes.
They said they heard me. But it's one thing to say   425
what you think you heard, another to be satisfactorily exact.
OLD MAN: What they think they heard! Did you not declare on
    oath
that you were bringing her back as a spouse for Heracles?
LICHAS: As a spouse? I say that? By the gods,
dear lady, tell me who on earth this stranger thinks he is.   430
OLD MAN: One who heard from you himself of a whole city
destroyed by his passion for her. That no Lydian woman
was the cause of it, but his sudden love for the girl.
LICHAS: Mistress, this man should be encouraged to leave. There is
no sense in chattering with a man who is sick.   435
DEIANIRA: By Zeus who hurls his lightning down on the heads
of the valleys of Mount Oeta, do not lie to me!
You are not speaking to a woman of no character,
nor to one who is ignorant of what human beings are like,
that they do not take pleasure in the same things for ever.   440
Whoever takes his stand in the ring against Love, gets
to grips with him like a boxer, undoubtedly has no sense.
Love rules over any of the gods he chooses, and
over me. So why not over other women like me?
If my husband has been caught by this sickness   445
I should certainly be mad to find fault with him,
or with this woman, who cannot be held jointly responsible
for anything shameful, nor for any harm done to me.
That is not the case. But if you have learned to lie
from Heracles, then you have learned a disgraceful lesson.   450
If this is the result of self-education, you will
be seen to be worthless when you would like to be good.
Come, tell me the whole truth. For a free man

to be known as a liar is a disaster and a disgrace.
You cannot possibly hope to get away with it: 455
you were heard by a crowd, and they will tell me.
Are you afraid? Why be frightened unnecessarily,
when it is not knowing which would cause me pain?
What can be terrible in knowing? Do you think Heracles
has not bedded many other women? Don't I know?   460
And not one of them yet has had a bad word
from me, or been abused. Nor will this girl, even
if he is melted by the heat of his passion for her.
I pitied her as soon as I saw her, because
her beauty had destroyed her life. The poor girl.   465
A terrible fate to be the unwilling cause of the destruction
and enslavement of your fatherland. But let all
of that blow away with the wind. Prove worthless to anyone
else, but never tell me any lies. Those are my orders.
CHORUS: Be persuaded by good advice. This woman will see   470
that you don't regret it later, and you'll have my thanks.
LICHAS: Well, my dear mistress, since it is plain to me that you
     expect
people to be no more than human, and are reasonable,
I shall tell you the whole truth and conceal nothing.
Things are just as this man has described them.   475
At some point a terrible longing for this girl
shot through Heracles, and on her account he sacked
Oechalia, the city of her fathers, and destroyed it.
For his part—and this must be declared—he never
denied any of this, nor told me to conceal it.   480
But, mistress, I myself was afraid that I would
hurt your feelings if I told you what you have heard.
The fault was mine, if you count it as a fault.
But now, since you do know the full story,
for his sake and for your own, equally for both,   485
tolerate the woman, and keep firmly
to the words that you have used about her.
In every other struggle Heracles has been pre-eminent,
but he has been utterly defeated by his love for her.
DEIANIRA: I already had it in mind to do what you say,   490

and will not take on a pointless fight with the gods,
succumbing to sickness myself. Let's go into the house,
and I can give you my instructions on what to say.
You must take gifts with you, an appropriate response
to the gifts you have brought. It would be wrong for you   495
to leave empty-handed, when you came in lavish company.

Deianira's response to the account by Lichas and to the spectacle
of the captive women is to complicate the idea of success with
'a terrible pity' (298). This emotion makes her put herself and
her children in their place, their security subject to the hazard of
battle, and so once again to Zeus 'who decides the issue of battles'
(303). These reflections bring her away from the celebratory
context sustained by the chorus (191–92) and by Lichas towards
the group of women, who begin to take individual form in front
of her. This is most true of one who seems to feel her position
more painfully than the others, a sign for Deianira of superior
class. Deianira interrogates Lichas about her, but is blocked by
his repeated professions of ignorance (314–19), and so she turns
to the young captive herself, conscious that she ought to be made
aware of her name and her parentage (320–21).

Yet Lichas intervenes again immediately, insisting that the
young woman has not spoken a word throughout the journey,
and pleading for an indulgence from the sympathy that he knows
Deianira feels. This complex set of subordinate transactions then
concludes with a return to the initial purpose, which was to
bring the captives for safekeeping into the house after the initial
welcome had been made. The permission to proceed is given by
Deianira (329–30, and 332–33), since the next transactions are
for Lichas to return to Heracles, and for Deianira to arrange the
disposal of the captives as offerings to the gods, indeed to prepare for the return of Heracles himself (333–34).

At this point, the playing-space becomes very busy, and we
need to account for its original, generous dimensions in understanding how the action interweaves. At the prompt from
Deianira, which will be at 'let us all make a/ move towards into
the palace' (332–33), Lichas must make his way to the side of
the captives and begin to shepherd them into the scene-building.

While Deianira herself may pause to let them proceed first, her attention is caught by the Old Man, who has stayed silent and to one side during the exchange between Lichas and Deianira. He tells her to stay behind, and his words puzzle her (335–38); it seems that he is quite adamant in his attempts to keep her behind, although the restraint can hardly be physical: it is perhaps rather more like obstruction of her path (339–40). All the while the group, ushered by Lichas and probably by extras as soldiers, is drawing close to and then filing into the scene-building. Some of them are still in view for some time—'Shall I call all of them back here again?' (342)—but eventually they all enter the scene building, and Deianira and the Old Man are left alone with the chorus, whom the Old Man trusts (344–45).

The Old Man now launches into his alternative account of the situation, which is a narrative that fixes itself on to his first, brief announcement at the same time as it contradicts what we have just heard from Lichas. It becomes evident that the Old Man himself was economical with the truth when he first arrived in haste, hoping for reward, with the headline news that Heracles was alive and coming home in victory. He had heard much more from Lichas himself, and he now risks a great deal by being the messenger who brings bad news rather than good. We might speculate that he may have expected Lichas to carry the burden of telling Deianira what, as a herald, he was willing to tell a crowd of Trachinians standing around him in the summer pasture (188–91, and 193–99). But the Old Man's decision is that it is more risky to be complicit in concealing the bitter truth than to be outspoken now so that Lichas can be challenged face to face (346–48, and 369–74).

What is revealed is that the silent girl is a victim of rape by Heracles, that he destroyed a city in order to get her when she was refused to him by her father, and that he has now sent her on in advance to be his concubine in the house. While Zeus had featured as the god involved in the account by Lichas, presiding over a general sense of judgment on those involved and providing just outcomes, the Old Man displaces the father of the gods (and of Heracles himself) with the wilful, entrancing Eros, or Love. The effect is that the uncertainty over Heracles' well-being, and over the import of the oracles at this tipping-point of time, is replaced by the extreme disturbance wreaked by sexual passion. Deianira is 'devastated', what we might call reeling from the shock, and the chorus has to intervene (383–84, and 387–88) to bring elements of stability. But before Deianira can conjure an initiative out of her confusion, Lichas emerges from the scene-building; and since Lichas has come out, rather than Deianira gone in, the Old Man has remained in place. The sense is that no one knows what will come next.

Initially, and as one would expect, the exchange takes place between Deianira and Lichas. Lichas wants to complete his business, to take any greeting from his mistress to her husband, in keeping with his role as a herald. But above all he wants to leave, since he has managed to convey the captives to the house successfully and lodge them inside. Deianira has one immediate aim, which is to get Lichas to confirm what she has just heard, specifically to confirm the identity of the young woman whom she had picked out from the crowd, since that is the keystone to the whole tale. In reply, Lichas may be almost indignant in his repetition of the lie he made before, that he knows no more than her nationality (401). The brazen quality of that disobedience brings in the Old Man, and our sense here is of almost a triangle, with each capable of looking at the other; or perhaps, in an alternative vision, of Lichas suspended in the middle between two interrogators.

Certainly, the Old Man swings in and confronts the herald, no doubt his social superior but one who can be reminded by an inferior of his duty. The dialogue here is crisp and pedantic, pushing at what is proper and 'correct'; but Lichas proves to be impatient and is determined that his intention to step out on his return journey to Heracles will not be impeded. It seems that he is obstructed, apparently a characteristic of the Old Man's obstinacy (414–15), and we must conclude that Lichas is confident of his ability to deflect or parry awkward questions from this non-entity (416). What the Old Man can do is to quote Lichas himself, and to adduce witnesses to those words by the score, something that Lichas tries to dismiss with a sophistry, claiming the predictability of misreport (425–26). But the Old

Man ups the stakes by asserting that Lichas declared the erotic facts on oath, a serious commitment for anyone and certainly for a herald (427–28). The open statement of what he has been concealing is too much for Lichas, who has to appeal to Deianira to dismiss the intruder, and implicitly to trust their relationship and the account he himself has presented to her (434–35). There is a strong class prejudice here: Lichas should be believed because of his status, and someone of lesser status who presumes to contradict him should be regarded as out of his mind ('sick', 435).

The tempo and the emotion have risen to this point, and Deianira's outburst leads into a speech that comes as a surprise, since it has not been anticipated by her previous forms of dialogue with these male characters. She opens with an oath (436–37) to balance or reflect the oath that Lichas is alleged to have given to the crowd (427–28), recalling the theme of truth-telling, and reintroducing the god (Zeus) to whom Lichas abundantly referred in his less-than-truthful tale told to her. What Deianira wants is to hear the facts from Lichas himself, since he alone knows as an eye-witness what they are; so far she has only an allegation, even if she is strongly inclined to believe it. To know the truth will resolve her mind, and will set in motion an appropriate response, as the action of the play will reveal.

In the first instance, Deianira's bid to persuade Lichas relies on convincing him that she is a reasonable woman, with an acceptance of human nature, one who will not struggle with a god (in this case, Love), and who will not blame those who are overthrown by divine power. This approach implies that Lichas is concealing the truth because he has a view of women's nature that would regard them as unreasonable in these situations, unable to control their emotions or to understand human (male in this case) sexual frailty. It is a frank but dignified speech, which moves from an expression of anger and frustration at Lichas stalling into a persuasive tone that concludes with a stab at his self-respect. If, in lying, he thinks he is being obedient to Heracles, he is nonetheless demeaning himself; if he has made the decision himself, then he is declaring himself to be worthless (449–52). The moral is that he cannot win either way, and that lying should be beneath his dignity.

By rights, this should be enough to loosen his tongue, but it does not. A speech of this kind must always hesitate between the sense of a culture in which people are skilled at constructing argument, and the uncertainty of how much argument will be enough or where the train of thought will lead. While Deianira is, like Clytemnestra, a woman who deals with men as a head of household substituting for her absent husband, here she is extemporizing. She does not have a speech prepared for the occasion, as Creon does in the monologue from *Antigone* in the First Workshop, and she has exhausted the possibilities of dialogue and interrogatory exchange. What she chooses to say reveals that she has considered to an extent what may persuade this man in this unexpected situation, but she has very little time to compose it. In this as in so many other aspects Greek tragedy is dealing in urgency, and unpreparedness. Characters are living and speaking on their wits, and even Creon had very little time to make his decision and then assess how he should present it to his council and his citizens.

So Deianira continues, and she seizes on the knowledge that Lichas spoke to the crowd to back him into a corner. His disgrace will be confirmed, soon enough, not by one man who may be dismissed but by a general public (453–56), and that is ignominy. She also then picks up on his apprehension, beginning to understand openly what has moved him to lie. Once again, it is his view of women and how they react that is the motivating force. It is not just that he would have to face her anger at the news, but that he would fear that she would maltreat Iole, leading to a bitter and possibly violent confrontation with Heracles. That lies behind his reluctance to cause her pain, and she tries to reassure him on all these counts, referring to her past experience of Heracles' infidelities and to her track record of tolerance. To do this effectively she ends on her pity for the young woman Iole, a recent action which Lichas himself had witnessed and which may therefore carry more weight than allusions to the past.

During the course of the speech, Deianira will have been able to appeal to the chorus in her self-justification as a wife, just as she has briefly alluded to the Old Man and his story. She is marshalling the weight of those present, and those imminently so in the crowd of Trachinian witnesses, against this isolated figure and his self-respect and reputation, and a final comment from the young women (470–71) cracks his resolve. Yet while Lichas, once he breaks into speech, may feel he is only confirming what she already knows and has no choice now but to do so (474–78), he remains apprehensive. He has to rely on what she has said about herself and her self-control, her understanding of human nature (472–73); but he is keen to clear Heracles of her suspicion (449–50) that he was instructed to keep the truth from her, and to take all the blame on himself. To do this he picks up on her words, her idea that he was afraid to hurt her feelings (481–82), but he remains extremely concerned that she should abide by those words, and exercise tolerance towards Iole, and so towards Heracles himself (484–89). Yet this would mean, effectively, to accept that he has introduced a concubine into the house to live alongside the wife.

Ultimately, Lichas believes that his transaction was successful, and Deianira is prompt to reassure him of that (490–92), without stating the bald facts of what the arrangement in the house will now be. Both seem to be acknowledging the need, as humans, to bow to the power of the gods, but the gods may still be at work. Sophocles covers this with a concluding statement that on the surface looks formally transactional: Lichas will be given words to say to Heracles, as he had requested, and also appropriate gifts to take back, that will balance those he brought. This sense of the reciprocal gift is a prominent feature of Greek and other cultures, but in this case the words carry an ominous irony. After all, what would be 'an appropriate response' in the circumstances? The answer is a robe imbued with a searing poison, taken by Deianira to be an ointment conveying a love-charm, by which she wants to win back Heracles' love. But Lichas will not know that until just before his head hits the rocks, as he is hurled down to his death by Heracles in a spasm of his agony (763–82).

In the recording (**Recording 5**), neither the chorus (there is just one, indicative figure) nor the group of captive women is present, and this reduces the play of sympathy to just the contact between Deianira and the silent Iole. But the recording is helpful in conveying a sense of the fluid use of a wide space, and of the structure of the scene, in which pity, a sudden sense of desolation, and a variety of forms of confrontation find their place.

Menelaus and Helen, an Old Woman, and an Old Slave: dealing with the unexpected in Euripides' *Helen*

As actors and directors—and in the same way as audiences do—we take tragedy seriously, even at times (and mostly then for the worst) solemnly, although I can readily forgive a performer who is at first solemn about working on tragedy. Yet we are aware that Shakespeare regularly lightens his tragedies with comic moments or characters, and the more Greek tragedies we encounter the more we may be surprised at the tone of some of them. There are indeed early, mildly humorous cameos from Aeschylus and Sophocles, with the Nurse in *Libation Bearers* and the Guard (in flashes, at least) in *Antigone* respectively. Here there may be a sense that the lower classes cannot quite maintain the gravity of any situation, or perhaps perceive it as fully as a free or dynastic character would do. But many of Euripides' plays offer a new tone that seems to be differently intended, as if the playwright was moving tragedy across to more unconventional territory.

So what matters for performers and practitioners is to maintain an open mind, to be willing to move with the material to a relationship with the audience that is powerful but not necessarily grave, that employs tragic pathos but may avoid tragic desolation. These challenges are posed effectively by a sequence from Euripides' *Helen*, in which three actors are used to create four characters. The script works through monologue, dialogue and three-actor interaction, and the unusual, temporary absence of a chorus that has entered the scene-building, to achieve its effects. The sequence forms a prelude to and then part of the scene in which a thoroughly innocent Helen is reunited with Menelaus, much to everyone's surprise.

There are many reasons why this sequence should form part of the Third Workshop. Although, strictly speaking, it only deploys three actors together right at the end, it leads up to that moment in an intriguing set of distinctive scenes. At the moment of recognition between Menelaus and Helen there is a long song and dance, which also briefly involves the chorus, and the chorus has an earlier short song when it reappears from the scene-building along with Helen. Although in production terms these would be important components, I have passed them by in the translated script with an indication only, since it is perfectly possible to work constructively on the spoken sequence without them. I have also not attached the preliminary speech from Menelaus, which might well be included were there enough time for work on it as a monologue. It should not be allowed here to take vital time away from work on the essential qualities of the interactive scenes that follow; but its contextual value for that work should nonetheless be appreciated.

Menelaus arrives in the playing-space just after Helen and the chorus have entered the scene-building in their determination to consult the king's sister, Theonoe, whose name means 'divine thought', and who has heavenly-inspired knowledge of the present and the future (lines 13–14). What Helen wants to know is whether her husband Menelaus is alive or dead, and Euripides sends the chorus off with her to clear the playing-space for the arrival of Menelaus.

What Euripides wants is for Menelaus to reflect on his harsh fate alone, without the possibility of conversing with a chorus, and he also wants him to have to knock on the door to acquire any information. This is odd and interesting, and places the performer in the situation of those characters who provide a prologue to a play, speaking reflectively, but also in a kind of open address in the hearing of the audience. It would also allow for the performer actually to address his thoughts to the audience, or parts of it in turn, since he is introducing himself as a familiar and famous character, but one who may at this instant be unrecognizable, since he is now a castaway, shipwrecked on a shore close to the palace, and in rags.

He has no idea where he is, or whose is the imposing residence he sees in front of him. But his assumption is that he can appeal for help and sustenance, and the fact that he has come himself to do so suggests that he will be relying on his status. In the broader context, by this point in the action we know a great deal more: namely that this is Egypt, and that contrary to our standard assumptions Helen did not go to Troy, but was kept here, and a phantom sent in her place. She was originally protected by the king of Egypt, Proteus, but when he died and was buried right outside his palace, his son Theoclymenus took a fancy to Helen (always in trouble, wherever she is). To escape his unwanted attentions, Helen came outside and took sanctuary at the tomb of his father, where she awaits news of her husband. All this she tells us at the opening of the play, as she introduces herself and the locale. The tipping point of the play comes with the arrival of a refugee Greek, Teucer, who brings news of the sack of Troy and the hazardous return of the Greek warriors. Helen warns him of the vicious hostility of Theoclymenus to all Greeks, but is also stirred by his depressing report that Menelaus is lost at sea, presumed dead.

So these are the tensions, marked out for Helen if not yet for Menelaus in the playing-space, with her need to keep herself safe at the tomb of Proteus in front of the palace. She has the support of the chorus, who are Greek women captured by Egyptians, and who are aware of how much her reputation has suffered unjustly. For his part, Menelaus believes he has his wife back down at the seashore, recaptured in Troy and safely stowed after the ship-wreck in a cave (424–27).

Although the door in the scene-building is much used in tragedy, banging on it and being confronted by a truculent slave is far more something that we might expect in comedy. Aeschylus has a good door-scene in *Libation-Bearers* (652–718), the middle play of the *Oresteia*, when Orestes and Pylades tell a grumpy and truculent answering slave to fetch the masters of the household to them, a mistress or a man. Rather like Menelaus, they can draw on the traveller's standard plea for assistance, shelter from the night which is swiftly descending, but in their case they can also promise (or pretend, in fact) that they are bringing news. The passage is interesting in the present context, because Clytemnestra appears at the door to assure them immediately of warm baths and soft beds. This remarkable scene is rendered with dignity, ominous and deceitful as it may be, in Orestes' pretence of his own death in front of his mother, and her artful dissimulation of her full and very mixed feelings about that supposed death.

For Menelaus here in our sequence from *Helen*, the bang on the door does not bring all that he might want. A doorkeeper has two options, both fully transactional. Orestes and Pylades in *Libation Bearers* have the advantage of the first, which initiates a welcome and entry; here Menelaus is delivered the second of them, which is the opposite, in no uncertain terms, by a strident old woman. This is about as bad as it gets: he is told to stop decorating the threshold by a woman and a barbarian, and probably a slave, or a being that he would consider a slave.

It seems that old people (both male and female) in comedy can have a grotesque value, and we hear of obscene dances by old female characters in Greek comedy. The comedies that we know (which are contemporary with tragedies by Euripides and Sophocles) are by Aristophanes, and scenes involving grotesque old men and women characters can be found in his *Wasps* and *Women in Assembly* respectively, with knocking on the door and its reception prominent features in *Women in Assembly*. If you want to get a feel for a comic door-scene in which a high-status character gets abuse and a drubbing from a doorkeeper, and undergoes a set of bizarre experiences that keep him from entering, the god Dionysus in Aristophanes' *Frogs*, who is dressed as the tough-guy Heracles, will give you a good return for your time.

After a long delay on these contextual issues, here is the script.

Helen—lines 437–624

OLD WOMAN: Who's that at the door? Get away from the house!
Don't stand there making a nuisance of yourself at the
courtyard gate. The master won't just be annoyed: you're a
Greek, and you'll die. You're not allowed anywhere near here.   440
MENELAUS: You could put that to me in rather a different tone,
old woman, and I'd go along with it. Don't be so angry.
OLD WOMAN: Go away! You're a foreigner, and a Greek, and it's
my job to make sure no Greek comes within reach of this house.
MENELAUS: Hey, take your hands off me! Be calm, don't push! 445

OLD WOMAN: I will push; it's your fault. You won't listen to anything I say.

MENELAUS: Take this message in to your masters, that I'm here . . .

OLD WOMAN: If I did take that message in, we'd both suffer for it.

MENELAUS: I'm a shipwrecked foreigner; such people have a right to protection.

OLD WOMAN: Go away, right now, and find another house, not this one. 450

MENELAUS: No, I'm going to go inside, and you must listen to me.

OLD WOMAN: You're a nuisance. Get it? You'll be thrown out next, and it'll hurt.

MENELAUS: Ah, where now are the ranks of my glorious army?

OLD WOMAN: Well, you may have been something over there, but you're not much here.

MENELAUS: This is dishonour. Oh my guiding spirit, I don't deserve this! 455

OLD WOMAN: Why are your eyes wet with tears? Who is there to pity you?

MENELAUS: I was both lucky and happy in times that are now past.

OLD WOMAN: Why not run along now and give your tears to those who care?

MENELAUS: What land is this? Whose is this palace?

OLD WOMAN: This is the palace of Proteus; the land is Egypt. 460

MENELAUS: Egypt? Oh, what wretched luck! What a landfall to make!

OLD WOMAN: And what fault do you find with the sparkling waters of the Nile?

MENELAUS: No fault with that. It's my bad luck that upsets me.

OLD WOMAN: Many people are unlucky; you're not the only one, you know.

MENELAUS: So is the lord of the house that you named at home? 465

OLD WOMAN: This here is his tomb; it's his son who rules the country.

MENELAUS: And where is he, then? Is he in the house, or away?

OLD WOMAN: He's not in there. And he is utterly hostile to Greeks.

MENELAUS: Since I'm getting the benefit of that, may I know the
    reason?
OLD WOMAN: Helen is in the palace here, she who's daughter
    of Zeus.   470
MENELAUS: What are you saying? What's that you said? Tell me
    again.
OLD WOMAN: The daughter of Tyndareus, who once lived in
    Sparta.
MENELAUS: Where did she come from? What explanation can
    there be for this?
OLD WOMAN: She came here from the land of Lacedaemon.
MENELAUS: When? Surely my wife can't have been stolen from
    the cave?   475
OLD WOMAN: Before the Greeks went to Troy, my foreign friend.
But do get away from the house. As luck would have it,
there's a turn of events, the royal palace is in a right state.
You picked a really bad time to come. If the master gets hold of
    you,
your rights as a foreigner will be certain death.   480
I'm friendly to you Greeks, you see, for all the sharp words
I've spoken to you, which were for fear of the master.
MENELAUS: What shall I say? What I am hearing is a new
miserable situation to take over from the one I had before.
I have taken my wife away from Troy, brought her   485
here with me, and put her safely in a cave.
But then I find that there is some other woman
with the same name as my wife living in this palace.
She said that this woman was the daughter of Zeus.
Does that mean that there is a man living by the banks   490
of the Nile with the name of Zeus? There's only one in heaven.
And where else on earth is there a Sparta, except where
the current of the Eurotas flows through lovely reeds?
Is the name of Tyndareus famous for having a double?
Does some land somewhere bear the same name as
    Lacedaemon,   495
or as Troy? I simply do not know what I ought to say.
But it's fair to say, on the face of it, that many men
in many countries have the same names; it's true with cities,

and with women too. So there's nothing to wonder at.
And again, I'm not turning tail at a servant's scare-stories.   500
There is no man anywhere so barbarous in his mind
who will not give me sustenance once he hears my name.
The fire that consumed Troy is famous, and I who lit it,
Menelaus, can hardly be unknown in any part of the world.
I shall wait for the lord of the house. I have   505
two lines of escape. If he proves to be a complete savage,
I shall hide myself and make my way to the wreck.
But if he shows a softer side, I shall ask him
for what I need in my present dire circumstances.
My situation is bad, and this is the worst of it,   510
that although I'm a king myself I have to ask for
subsistence from other kings. Never mind; needs must.
There is nothing stronger than harsh necessity:
those aren't words of mine, but they're wise nonetheless.
[CHORUS: lines 515–27]
HELEN: I have heard something dear to my heart from Theonoe,
and I'm on my way back again to my place at this tomb.
Theonoe knows the whole truth. She says that my husband   530
is still living! He's alive, and sees the light of day!
He has sailed through countless straits, backwards
and forwards, worn out by his wanderings;
but he will come here when his sufferings are at an end.
One thing she didn't say: if he will be safe when he comes here. 535
I was so pleased when she told me he was alive that
I held back from asking her that straight out.
But she did say that he was on land somewhere nearby us here,
shipwrecked on the shore with only a handful of friends.
Oh, when will you get here? How I want you to come!   540
Oh no, who's that? This is some scheme of that
impious son of Proteus, an ambush, I'm sure of it.
Now I must run as fast as a foal, no, a bacchant
of the god and reach the tomb. He is a rough-looking
type, this fellow who is out to hunt and take me.   545
MENELAUS: What a terrible effort you're making, stretching out
    like that
to reach the tomb, to touch its footings or its charred pillars.

Hold on! What are you running from? Now that you show me what
you look like, I'm staggered. You've made me speechless.

HELEN: This is an outrage, women. This man is preventing us   550
from reaching the tomb. He wants to seize me, and
hand me over to the king for the marriage I've rejected.

MENELAUS: I'm not a kidnapper, and do not serve any evil cause.

HELEN: That's all very well, but your clothes are distinctly shabby.

MENELAUS: Please stand still. Don't be frightened. Stop running
around.   555

HELEN: There, I've reached this tomb at last, so I can stand still.

MENELAUS: Who are you? Whose face am I looking at it in your
face?

HELEN: And who are you? It's the same question for both of us.

MENELAUS: I have never seen anyone who looked so like her.

HELEN: Heavenly divinities! For it is divine to recognize those
close to you!   560

MENELAUS: Are you a woman of this country, or a Greek?

HELEN: I'm a Greek. But now I want to know where you come
from.

MENELAUS: I have never seen anyone so completely like Helen,
woman.

HELEN: And I anyone so like Menelaus. I'm lost for words.

MENELAUS: You have correctly identified a most unfortunate
man.   565

HELEN: At last, after so long, you've come, into the arms of your
wife!

MENELAUS: Wife? What do you mean, 'wife'? Don't touch my
clothes!

HELEN: I am the wife whom Tyndareus, my father, gave to you.

MENELAUS: Torch-bearing Hecate, send me benign visions, I beg
you!

HELEN: You're looking at me, not at some servant of Hecate at
the crossroads.   570

MENELAUS: But I am one man, and I'm not the husband of two
wives.

HELEN: What do you mean? Are you the master of another bed?

MENELAUS: She's hidden in the cave, the wife I'm bringing back
from Troy.

HELEN: But you cannot have any other wife apart from me.

MENELAUS: Maybe it's not my mind, but my sight that's going wrong. 575

HELEN: Don't you see your wife when you look at me? 576

MENELAUS: You do look like her; I shan't deny that at least. 579

HELEN: So whom would you believe rather than your own eyes? 580

MENELAUS: What's wrong for me is that I have another wife.

HELEN: But I didn't go to Troy; that was a phantom.

MENELAUS: And who precisely can fabricate living, human bodies?

HELEN: The gods shaped the air into that wife you have.

MENELAUS: Which of the gods moulded her? How can I believe this? 585

HELEN: It was Hera, making a substitute, so Paris didn't take me.

MENELAUS: How did this work? Were you here and in Troy at the same time?

HELEN: Your name can be in many places, but not your body.

MENELAUS: Let me go! I came here carrying enough grief.

HELEN: You're going to take that shadow wife and leave me, aren't you? 590

MENELAUS: Yes, goodbye and good luck, since you do look so like Helen.

HELEN: That's the end. I've found you, my husband, but can't keep you.

MENELAUS: I'm persuaded by the scale of what I went through over there, not by you.

HELEN: Oh no, pity me! Who could ever have been more miserable than me?

My dearest are deserting me, and I shall never get 595
close to Greeks again, nor to my own husband.

OLD SLAVE: Menelaus, there you are at last; I've been looking
for you everywhere, wandering all over this foreign country.
Your companions sent me, those who are still left.

MENELAUS: What is it? Don't say you've been stripped bare by foreigners? 600

OLD SLAVE: A miracle, if that's not too weak a word for what's happened.

MENELAUS: Tell me; if you feel that strongly, it must be something
   strange.
OLD SLAVE: What I have to say is that you've laboured so much all
   in vain.
MENELAUS: That's a familiar sad song, for pain that's past; what's
   your news?
OLD SLAVE: Your wife has gone, vanished into the air, floating 605
up into the sky. You can't see her now; she's in heaven.
She left the sacred cave where we were keeping her,
and gave a short speech: 'Wretched Phrygians, and
all you Greeks, you kept on dying for me on the banks
of the River Scamander, thinking that Paris had Helen.   610
But he did not have Helen; that was Hera's trick.
And now that I have stayed as long as I had to stay,
and played my part fully, I am away into the sky,
to my father. The unhappy daughter of Tyndareus has been
abused unfairly, for she is totally innocent.'   615
Oh, hello, daughter of Leda. So this is where you've been.
I was just announcing that you'd vanished into
the depths of outer space; I didn't know that you
had a winged body. I shan't allow you to make
fools of us again like this. You gave enough trouble   620
to your husband and the allies while you were at Troy.
MENELAUS: That is finally it. What she's been telling me has turned
   out
to be true. This is the day I have longed for, the day
that gave you back to me, to take into my arms!

While we might assume that the Old Woman is simply enacting
her option of removing an unwanted person from her master's
premises according to his stated preferences (439–40, and
443–44), we do find out later that her motives are rather more
complicated and benign. From Menelaus' perspective, the
transaction must now be—more mechanically and pragmatically
than he might have wished—to get past the doorkeeper, in
order to speak to a person of authority who will recognize his
own status without insulting him. In a slave-owning culture,
as ancient Greece was, getting past the front door and its slave

keeper must have been a familiar theme to almost all of the original audience, carrying a seat-shifting embarrassment and amusement. It may look contrived and theatrical to us, but it would have had a penetration that has now largely lost its edge of reality.

The Old Woman plainly has a vigorous physicality as well as a strident voice. Menelaus may have sacked Troy, but he is getting pushed away from the gates of this citadel, manhandled by an old woman who tells him off like a little boy, shaking her finger at him in between shoves (445). What he wants is to turn a doorkeeper into a messenger (447), to get past her by turning her function, but she is having none of it. Instead, she makes the reasonable point that he is not listening to her, and so is failing to perceive the danger (to Greeks) of which she is warning him. For his part, he cannot understand the situation, because in his Greek ethical code hospitality is due to a stranger, and as a shipwrecked man (and leader of others) he needs assistance (449). But she is not just obstructing his entry into the building; in his interest, she is instructing him to go elsewhere, since that code will not be respected here (448 and 450).

These two are very much at cross-purposes, failing in what they wish to achieve, and the result is a simple statement about force (452), a threat which (by comparison with comic scenes) would probably have to be executed by summoning other male slaves from the palace. This second phase then descends into pathos, and an ironic take on it from the Old Woman, who provokes him to see where he now is, in an alien land (454, 456, 458). Menelaus has lost his accustomed status, since the army that he led successfully has disintegrated, and he slipped to the nadir of dishonourable treatment (455). For some reason, he tortures himself further with the idea that he was 'both lucky and happy in times past' (457), and this must only refer to status and prestige, because this is a man who had to wage war for his estranged wife.

He is prepared to cry about it all, but the lack of sympathy from the Old Woman proves to be an antidote. He comes round, and the dialogue enters a third phase, as he realizes that he does not even know where on earth he is. Egypt is way off track as far as he is concerned, but the inquiry allows him to move back to his main objective, which is to locate and appeal to the master of the house. Oddly, he doesn't get given the king's name, but the crucial fact is his hostility to Greeks, and it is this which leads into the final phase of the dialogue, in which the astonishing revelation about Helen emerges (470–75). Yet nothing of what he hears explains why she should be here at the palace, since the Old Woman reverts to her dominant concern of getting him to realize that, as a Greek, he is a *persona non grata* and should get right away (476–82).

With that, we can assume that the Old Woman slams the door, and Menelaus is left on his own in the playing-space for the second time. His subsequent monologue falls into two distinct parts. In the first part (483–99), he wonders at the news he has just heard and tries to rationalize; in the second (500–14), he reflects seriously on the threat he has heard, and puts together a plan of action. In the first part, he has to convince himself in order to manage the shock, and not be distracted from the purpose that has brought him to the palace. So this is an internal debate, for which the presence of the door and threshold is temporarily less relevant. After all, he has just been refused entry, and so he will drift away from the scene-building, in the reverse of the gradual movement towards it in his opening monologue.

During the exchange with the Old Woman it is likely that he was physically jostled and shoved at least twice in the first phase (445, 451–52), close to the door itself, and that subsequently he released himself from that direct assault, into self-pity in the second phase, and then into the questioning mode in the third phase. In this subsequent monologue he now is better acquainted with his immediate environment, and even the tomb of Proteus may filter into his general awareness as he reflects on his intellectual problem. The major contrast is between his reference out and away from the playing-space to the cave on the beach where he believes his wife is stowed (485–86), and his more local awareness of the palace, where another woman lives with the same name (487–88). The binary qualities of this confusion expand into the possibility of a Greek god and an Egyptian man both called Zeus (490–91), of two Spartas, two men called Tyndareus, and two places called Lacedaemon and Troy (492–96). So the invitation is for the actor to use his two hands and arms to express this possible duplication, with references out of the playing space and towards the palace in relation to Helen, to the heavens and to the palace for the two parts of the name of Zeus, away with confidence towards home and vaguely towards any other location that might contain the doubles of Sparta, Tyndareus, Lacedaemon, Troy.

After this workout, in space and gesture, he is prepared to accept the possibility of double names, and so to dismiss his astonishment. That relief brings him to a renewed self-confidence in the second part of his monologue, and the ability to plan in balanced and different way. It is clear that he will not now batter futilely at the door, but will wait for the lord of the house outside, who as he has previously been informed (467–68) is away. Although his restored self-confidence assures him that one with his reputation cannot be badly treated (500–504), he is prepared to be cautious, turning his binary frame of mind to practical use with two options. Option one is that Menelaus, if he remains concealed, can see for himself if the man is savage, and simply run away (506–507); option two, if he looks softer, is that Menelaus will try to appeal to him (508–509). Each of these plans entails that he is now more undercover to begin with, which is the practical side of the realization that, despite being a king, he has to ask for rather than expect help (510–12).

So at the first sound of the choral song, coming as it does from the scene-building, accompanied by the reappearance of the chorus through the door into the playing-space, Menelaus has every inducement to hide. That may be away to the side, or possibly behind the tomb of Proteus in the centre of the space. Wherever he is, the chorus does not see him, nor does Helen, who when she does spot him (at 541) has to make a dash for the asylum of the tomb, which had remained firmly in her mind: as soon as she came out of the palace, she had mentioned it (528–29). Her account of the encouraging vision of Theonoe may repeat that of the chorus, but it is bound in some part to be addressed enthusiastically to them. The wording of the vision, in

Helen's narrative, is a strange mixture of a part that sounds like an oracle (530–34), and a part that is a more immediate vision (538–39), sandwiching between them a missing element about eventual safety, the future tense of the reassurance that he is at least alive now (535–37).

Her concluding and heartfelt wish to have Menelaus with her (540) is, of course, answered in a beautiful irony with the terrifying intrusion of the ruffian and derelict who confronts her (544–45), whom she suspects to be lying in an ambush planned by her tormentor, Theoclymenus (541–42). So she has to run with frantic speed and agility, to gain the protection of the tomb (543–44). But she seems only to be sure of being in contact with it (at 556) after an extended script-sequence. This must presumably either be a chase about the space, or more probably a set of movements in which Menelaus blocks Helen almost unwittingly, and tries to approach her, while she runs here and there to avoid him. If the chorus is also active at this point, partly sheltering her and partly agitated itself, then we can imagine a lively and mildly amusing scene.

The sight of Helen has a stunning effect on Menelaus, who remains incapable of seeing how disreputable he looks to others at present. At first he just seems to want to get this woman to stand still for a moment (546–48), but it is her figure that pulls him up in astonishment (548–49). Once again, he finds himself protesting, on this occasion that he is not kidnapper or a slavish criminal (553), only to hear from Helen that he certainly looks the part (554), a comment that suggests that the sheer panic of being kept from the tomb (550–51) has just begun to subside. It may be that there is a last dash to final safety after this (555–56).

Until this point, Helen has only seen in the person of Menelaus what she feared, and he has been left to wonder on his own. But their dialogue really begins as a coherent exchange, with reciprocal questions fired off as they stare in astonishment, both now liking what they see (557–58). They move forward in harmony, with physical recognition beginning to stir (559–60), followed in the Greek by a pun on 'Hellene' and 'Helen'. Hellene means 'Greek', and that is how I have translated it twice in these lines (561 and 562), since the unfamiliarity of the word 'Hellene' to us would make the pun forced: you may of course restore it if you think you can make it work. The two name each other, at least in the mode of comparison (563–64), as they edge towards full acknowledgement, but Helen does not face the obstacles to recognition that Menelaus does. She starts towards him, aiming to clasp him in her arms, or be clasped (566), but he is indignant, and detaches her from his clothing (567). For Helen, it is the astonishingly early fulfilment of the prophecy of Theonoe; but Menelaus has to appeal to the goddess Hecate to banish these alarming visions, and to replace them with those that are easier to take.

So the recognition stalls, as Helen reaches in vain for the authority of Tyndareus as father of the bride (568) and indignantly rejects her identification with spectres (570). The final phase of this stalemate has each recounting her and then his particular story, revealing just how mutually exclusive those stories are, so widening the gap between them, although Helen knows that the man she is seeing is her husband. For Helen, the shock of believing that Menelaus may have another wife (572) may detach her from proximity to Menelaus and send her towards the chorus for sympathy and support. While Menelaus does worry about his possibly senior moment and the state of his vision (575 forward), Helen is confirmed in her suspicions, but also immediately grasps the nature of the problem. Menelaus has been deceived by the phantom of which Helen is well aware, and she gently tries to bring him to see the truth (from 582 forwards).

But Menelaus remains a rationalizing man, and cannot believe this story. So she edges back towards him, in a kind of sympathy for his distress, but also desperately wanting his preconceptions suddenly to give way. With the distinction she draws, presumably emotionally, between a mere name and an actual physical person (588), she launches herself at him again, hoping that she has said enough in the course of persuasion. But Menelaus fends her off (589), because he is blocked by the massive reality of the horrendous expedition, the siege and the warfare, the obligations, the weight of history. It would seem that she almost pleads with him finally, as the dialogue seizes up, but he must have at least made a move to leave (590–91), although his final line should surely be delivered directly to her face, not over his shoulder (593), since he is making a point.

Helen's natural recourse will be to the chorus, who alone in the world might be inclined to pity her, and who also share her experience of exile (594–96). This might be the occasion for an extended speech from her, but Euripides chooses to halt Menelaus in the playing-space by bringing on what we might loosely call a 'messenger'. In fact, this man later proves to be an Old Slave, who was present at the wedding of Menelaus and Helen, who served Menelaus throughout the campaign at Troy, and was saved from the shipwreck. All of that emerges later in a more leisurely moment of recollection, but for the time being he is just relieved to have found Menelaus, since he has alarming news to bring from the cave. In fact, as we hear what this news is, we may see why this old and well-loved retainer was chosen by the sailors in the cave (659) to break it to their war-leader.

What is clear is that Old Slave avoids answering Menelaus' urgent question immediately, beating about the bush while hinting at the unfortunate truth of wasted struggle and hardship (600–604). He then launches into the shocking truth, and reinforces his description with the blunt assertion that she cannot be seen (606), at which point we might think of him using his longstanding relationship to restrain and calm Menelaus. While this moment is affecting, the little farewell speech of the phantom Helen that he impersonates carries not just a confirmation to Menelaus, but an amusing irony as it is delivered in front of the human Helen, whom as yet he has not noticed. So the impersonation has a dual aspect, enhancing for a Greek the sense of eye-witness and so potentially of verity, but also creating the comic paradigm of unwittingly acting out a person who is standing right next to you. All that remains is for the Old Slave to move slightly at its conclusion, or for Helen to move into his line of vision, since he swings immediately into an almost comic kind of recantation which then turns into a rebuke. So while he is facing her, and perhaps finally also looking at Menelaus, Helen and Menelaus are interacting silently. They cross in front of the Old Slave to embrace, just after Menelaus has relented, acknowledged his delusion, and permitted the recognition and reunion to take place (622–24).

What follows this moment is a long scene of ecstatic reunion (625–97), which is sung and probably danced, with the singing (and the dancing) coming primarily from Helen, intermixed with what may for the most part be spoken contributions from Menelaus. While it is joyful, it also reflects on the consequence of the delusion under which all have been labouring, on the innocence of Helen, and the losses suffered over time. The play then resumes its spoken texture, with a further exchange between the three actors.

Feedback and rounding off

The ultimate test of work on a three-actor scene must be that of the fluency and constancy of interaction between characters. So, for example, what the Old Slave says to Menelaus will engage Helen, who will be gradually gaining confidence and drawing out of her despair as his short narrative progresses. The news he brings is more than she might have hoped for, and she must be looking to catch the eye of Menelaus as the Old Slave reels out the full announcement made by the phantom as 'it' flew away. But, at the same time, she must be hanging on the Old Slave's words, so her interaction is with both male characters. Similarly, she is possibly with the chorus when the Old Slave first arrives, and her delight and her growing confidence will be communicated to them, releasing her once again from their supportive presence to move into the open space and approach her husband once more.

For his part, Menelaus must be utterly dismayed initially, thrown into reflections that make his recent life an almost unimaginable mockery. These reflections must isolate him, abruptly, from anyone in the playing-space. Yet he must—at the same time—be drawn and gradually fascinated by the extraordinary correspondence between the details that emerge in the phantom's speech and what he has just been told by Helen. So he will be looking at her as much as he is transfixed by what the Old Slave is saying, and he will be drawn out of his abject reflections into something that is alive and in front of him. Indeed, both he and Helen might be subject to an impulse to go to each other at the close of the report of the phantom's speech (615), but they are prevented by the greeting immediately given to Helen by the Old Slave. Here both have to be patient, and in a modern production it would be tempting to have them either smiling, or attempting to interrupt in frustration, as the Old Slave pursues his misapprehension.

Such interaction creates the fullness of three-actor scenes, and yet it is often the subject of resistance from performers. It may be excluded from their view of what Greek tragedy should be like, since it contradicts the statuesque and solemn assumptions about an ancient form of theatre that many performers like to feel they can accommodate in a mildly patronizing way. This is rather like treating your grandmother as a dear old lady who knows nothing about sex: it says more about you and your vanities than it does about your grandmother. Masks can be turned to one performer, and the head or upper body then moved to incline towards a second performer, so it is pointless to say that this kind of interaction is only possible with open faces in a studio.

Interaction between performers should ideally be integrated with the appropriate degree of interaction of characters with the chorus, which ranges from the acknowledgement of their support in principle and for what may be evolving, to a reliance on them at specific moments as a point of appeal; for an extra boost of sympathy; or as a group that is mercurially responsive to prompts to enthusiasm, excitement, and even dynastic triumphalism.

In other words, while we may have been able to get away with some stilted performance, at least in patches, in relation to monologues and dialogue, any remaining complacency should be knocked out of us by the demands of three-actor work. It is not unusual for insights drawn from it to be applied back to mono-logue and dialogue, and for those reasons it may be always be a good idea to allow that much more time for process in this Third Workshop.

In feedback, these considerations should form part of the criteria applied to presentations. So while the phrase 'degree of interaction between all three performers' might be useful here, it will also be helpful to add to feedback the degree to which a non-speaking character is involved at any moment, by the other characters and through her or his own attention. As with dialogue in the Second Workshop, and indeed at any stage from now on, the use of space by the performers should receive a demanding critical assessment. How is the space inscribed with significance by the performers and their interpretation of the scene, and how do they make sense of the transactions between three characters through their use of the space? If the environs are intensely hostile to one character, but not to another, or if the space is profoundly sacred, these are qualities that should be transmitted to us through the whole performance, and not just by some brief gag or mugging carried out by an actor as a passport to complacency in the rest of the scene.

Finally, it may be appropriate to introduce a criterion of pace and timing to the presentations in this Workshop. It is perhaps most evident with three-actor scenes that there are phases through which the script passes and by which it works, as the accent shifts (for example) from one pairing of speaking characters to another. The physical initiative may also pass visibly from one pairing to another, or the physical mode of movement adopted by performers may palpably change from one phase to another. By this time, the level of self-reflection and critique should be sufficient to begin to establish conviction about pace and timing in these contexts, and it is well worth bringing observations forward into the feedback, although it would be inadvisable to be dogmatic. All presentations generate their own rubric for consistency in these aspects of performance. Some may be poorly judged, and many may be inconsistent even in their own terms; but there is no absolute rule, and certainly no stick with which to beat others.

FOURTH WORKSHOP

Properties

One of the strongest attractions of Greek tragedy for performers is undoubtedly the perception that it has a purist emphasis on the skills of the actor, the same feature that also makes working on it daunting, since there is little to hide behind. Once a character is out in the open, she or he will have to remain actively involved until the actor either leaves to assume the role of another character, or has a temporary respite while a chorus sings and dances (or, in the case of most modern productions, recites) before continuing as the same character.

Yet there are some major qualifications to be made to this belief. As previous Workshops have made clear, there is the engagement with and by the chorus to complicate that purist vision, and inevitably the crucial aspect of interaction with other actors as characters. There is also the importance of the scene-building in many scenes: its contribution to the setting and the context, and its ominous qualities, the threat it may contain or which it poses to characters. The scene-building may have been defined by removable, decorated panels indicating locale. Colour and to a degree 'design' may also be reflected in the costumes. We know how much her rich costume matters to Hermione in the scene from *Andromache*, how much her plain or poor garments matter to Electra in Euripides' *Electra*. The complete pattern of costumes (including those of the chorus) in any tragedy has much to communicate about relative status, ethnicity, and gender.

We have also seen how significant an item of 'set' such as an altar, a tomb, or a small sanctuary in the playing-space may be, how it can be central to the conception of the action that the tragedy offers us as a place of refuge and asylum, or of worship offered to the gods. What is left to us, in this Fourth Workshop, is to factor in to a set of developing skills how Greek tragic scripts make use of objects as properties, how the tragedians use the significance they carry to bring substance and pathos to the transactional nature of specific moments in the development of the play.

The problem with properties in theatre practice is that actors tend rather naturally to think that they are more important than an object, and perhaps that they are doing it a favour by picking it up and waving it around for a period of time. The corollary of this attitude is that it ought to look good, particularly look good with them, and if it does not then it has not been well made, and they would rather do without it. 'Can't I mime it instead?' is the plea one can hear, and at times it is important to go through these phases in order to reach a better place. This is, of course, a slightly cruel parody, but it is not always that far from the truth.

These difficulties partly arise from the fact that as a culture we are not that used to handling and using material 'things' any more, compared even to no more than a century ago, and can feel a little awkward doing so. There was at that time, in most parts of the world, a continuing reliance on intermediate technology of all sorts, and plainly we can all think of cultures where this still applies. At the same time, 'things' have multiplied with industrial manufacture to such an extraordinary extent that they have lost their individual nature. In pre-industrial societies, objects were made with great labour and replaced with difficulty or expense. As a consequence, ownership or possession of a particular object was often a more intense relationship, from which release only came either in disaster or accident, or with an absolute discard, which would include that of giving it away. We may now replace almost anything we use or lose with little sense of the rupture of a specific attachment.

So what we need to restore is a sense of what objects may have meant to the ancient Greeks, or we shall not easily see how they thought they could use them tragically. There is no simple answer to this; but the study of vase paintings, of objects represented in sculptural reliefs or held by statuary is the only sound way to acquire a sense of what is involved. There are military objects (weapons and armour), tools of many different kinds, containers (pots, baskets, caskets and boxes), writing materials, sacred insignia (wreaths of wool, diadems, the prophet's staff), and indeed garments, which may be used as properties. Looking at how the human being relates to the object in these pictures and representations can be informative, since much is contained in a gesture, the way the hand holds something, the way the eye is focused on it.

We cannot be sure whether the objects that appear as theatrical properties were actual or virtual, whether they were found— brought in from everyday life—or made as representations. This is an intriguing issue, and it would be possible to debate the advantages of each course of action, but it will not really illuminate the tasks facing modern actors. In most instances, if not all, a modern performance will expect to make, or to simulate with a substitute or an equivalent item, and for the purposes of this Workshop thoughtful selection is bound to be the rule. There is no need for absolute imitation for most properties; but equally it is important that there is no significant element of distraction in the choice of representative object. It is also extremely important, in my view, that any object handles well.

While that is context, and very valuable, probably essential context, there is also a principle that can be applied to the work from the beginning, or preferably as a preparation. This principle is what I call 'establishing the autonomy of the object', and there are many exercises that can be put together simply as a preliminary with everyday modern objects. The task will be to introduce the chosen object to the audience as a focus for attention, as a defined item that has almost the same status as a human character, and which is displayed to the audience throughout the subsequent improvisation as an autonomous 'player' in the scene.

The aim is, simply enough, to displace the assumption that the object is 'owned' by the actor, that it is at his or her disposal, that it merely serves her or his purposes. The result should also be that in terms of space and physicality the object 'stands out' from the actor, is not crudely clasped and crushed to the body, put or cast aside in a place where it can be ignored by both actor and audience. Even more striking, of course, is the improvised scene in which the object is the *leading* character, where *its* story is what the audience is following, where the audience invests its hopes and apprehensions and relief in the object itself. So along with the autonomy of the object goes its integrity, which should never be forgotten by the actor, if the actor wants the object to perform to its full capability.

In the sequences that follow, this principle must be followed, and severely critiqued by other workshop members if the object becomes subordinated unnecessarily. This Fourth Workshop is about the value of properties, and their role, and work in it will be invalidated if that is forgotten. Workshop participants should not be afraid to explore every opportunity to establish the autonomy of the object as a property, and should remember to revive and sustain that autonomy throughout their scene.

Speech and writing: handling the letter in Euripides' *Iphigenia in Tauris*

I have chosen a piece from Euripides' *Iphigenia in Tauris* to start with, since as a three-actor sequence this follows on well from the last Workshop. This play-title is slightly misleading, since it should really be translated as 'Iphigenia among the Taurians', but it has become conventional. In the play the defining feature of the community of the Taurians, who resided in a region on the northern edge of the Black Sea, at the limits of Greek knowledge, is that it practises human sacrifice. The play is set in the precinct of the goddess Artemis of the Taurians, in front of her temple and by her altar, which is stained with the blood of unfortunate

Greek travellers. The priestess of these rites, who presides over
the ritual preliminaries but does not conduct the sacrifice itself,
is Iphigenia, who had herself been swept up at the point of sacrifice by her father Agamemnon and brought here by Artemis. Into
this fatal spot have been sent Orestes and Pylades, instructed by
Apollo to come here and seize the statue of Artemis, and bring it
back to Greece.

At the point at which our text begins, Orestes and Pylades
have been discovered, and brought as captives to Iphigenia at the
temple for sacrifice. Neither Iphigenia nor Orestes has as yet revealed their identity in a long exchange, in which Iphigenia has
shown a lively interest in what has happened to the Greeks, in
particular to her father and mother. That she misses her brother
has been made clear before this, and her sense of isolation is
not much mitigated by the presence of a sympathetic chorus of
girls or young women from Greece. What Iphigenia proposes is
that one of the two friends should take a letter from her back to
Greece, so evading sacrifice. While Iphigenia enters the temple
to fetch the letter, Pylades accepts that he will take it, despite his
protests that some back in Argos may regard him as a coward.

Iphigenia in Tauris—lines 723–802

ORESTES: That's enough; what Apollo said has hardly been of help
   to me.
Look, here's the woman coming out to us from the temple.
IPHIGENIA: (*to guards*) Leave us now, and go inside. Make
   everything   725
ready for the sacrifice. Help those in charge of it.
Strangers, you can see that I have here a folding
tablet of many leaves. But listen to what I want
to add to this. No one behaves the same in trouble
as when he breaks out of fear into confidence.   730
So I'm apprehensive. Whichever of you undertakes
to carry this tablet with him to Argos may, when
he's left here and got home, not bother with my letter.
ORESTES: What do you want to do? What precisely is your problem?

IPHIGENIA: Let him swear that he will carry this letter across the sea 735
to Argos and deliver it to those who are close to me, as I choose.
ORESTES: And will you give him the same kind of oath in exchange?
IPHIGENIA: What would you have me swear to do, or not to do? Tell me.
ORESTES: To get him alive out of this land of barbarians.
IPHIGENIA: That is fair enough. How else could he deliver the message? 740
ORESTES: Are you sure that the king will go along with this?
IPHIGENIA: Yes.
I shall persuade him, and I'll get into the ship myself.
ORESTES: (to PYLADES) Take the oath. (To IPHIGENIA) Dictate to him a solemn oath.
IPHIGENIA: What you must say is 'I shall give this tablet to your friends'.
PYLADES: I shall give this letter securely into the hands of your friends. 745
IPHIGENIA: And I shall see you safely beyond the dark rocks.
PYLADES: So which of the gods do you choose to sanctify your oath?
IPHIGENIA: Artemis, in whose temple I perform an honourable role.
PYLADES: And I shall choose the lord of heaven, almighty Zeus.
IPHIGENIA: What if you break your oath, and do me an injustice? 750
PYLADES: Then I should not get home. What if you don't see me off safely?
IPHIGENIA: May I never set foot alive in Argos again.
PYLADES: But listen, there's something we've left out.
IPHIGENIA: It can always be adopted, if it seems right.
PYLADES: Let me have this exemption. If there is a shipwreck, 755
and the tablet is lost with all the other
gear on board, and all I can save is myself,
then the oath cannot be allowed to hold firm.
IPHIGENIA: Let's cover all possibilities. You can guess what I'll do.
What's written down there in the leaves of that tablet— 760

I'll speak it aloud, so you can pass it all on to my friends!
That's complete security. If you can keep the letter safe,
what's written on it will speak its silent message.
But if the written message vanishes in the sea,
so long as you save your skin, you'll save my words.   765
PYLADES: You've expressed it well; it's in both of our interests.
Now you must let me know who in Argos I should take this
letter to, and the message I should hear from you and repeat.
IPHIGENIA: Take this message to Orestes, son of Agamemnon:
'She who was sacrificed at Aulis sends this message to you.   770
You may think she is dead, but Iphigenia is alive.'
ORESTES: Where is she? Are you saying she's come back from the
  dead?
IPHIGENIA: You're looking at her. But don't put me off my script.
'Bring me home from this land of barbarians and back
to Argos, before I die; release me from the goddess's   775
rites, in which I have the honour of sacrificing strangers.'
ORESTES: Pylades, what shall I say? What is going on here?
IPHIGENIA: 'If not, I shall bring a curse down on your house,
Orestes', just so you hear that name twice and can learn it.
ORESTES: Gods!
IPHIGENIA: Why do you call on the gods in my affairs?   780
ORESTES: It's nothing. Carry on. I had drifted off somewhere
  else.   781
IPHIGENIA: Say that 'The goddess Artemis substituted a deer   783
for me, which my father sacrificed, thinking that he
was using his sharp sword on me. She saved my life,   785
and settled me in this country.' This is my letter,
that is what is written down on these tablets.
PYLADES: You took a very fine oath yourself, and have bound
me by my oath with an easy obligation. I shall not
take long to fulfil the oath that I swore.   790
Look, here I am bringing the tablet and correctly
handing it over to you, Orestes; it's from your sister.
ORESTES: And I duly receive it. But I shall put this letter to one
side, and take my pleasure firstly in person, not in words.
Oh, my dearest sister, I am stunned to find you   795
against all my expectations actually in my arms!

What I have heard is incredible! I'm overjoyed!
CHORUS: Stranger, how dare you defile the servant of the
   goddess,
And lay hands on robes that none should touch?
ORESTES: You are my very own sister, child of the same   800
father Agamemnon. Don't turn away from me!
You never hoped to have him again, but I'm your brother!

As sacrificial offerings to the goddess, Orestes and Pylades have been guarded rather than bound, and these guards are now sent into the temple to get things ready for the rite (725–26). Iphigenia has emerged carrying the 'letter', which was probably represented as a wooden, folded frame with a wax interior surface into which letters have been incised with a stylus. The message for the letter was dictated by Iphigenia to a Greek captive, destined also for sacrifice, who pitied her isolation, and the conclusion is that unlike Phaedra in *Hippolytus* Iphigenia cannot write. It is important that the actor playing Iphigenia accepts the indications in the script (727–28) and displays the letter prominently, to establish what I have called the autonomy of the property here. It will be passed from one character to another, under precise conditions, and will eventually be discarded, and all these transactions need to be invested in the property itself.

The first phase of dialogue proceeds between Orestes and Iphigenia, and it explores her worries about a possible failure to carry out the task that is the condition for the release and liberty of one of the two friends (728–33). Iphigenia insists on an oath from this Greek stranger to conduct faithfully what he has agreed to do (735–36). Orestes in turn suggests that Iphigenia should swear an oath to send the individual out of the country, and to get the king Thoas to agree to this breach of precedent (737–42).

Orestes then instructs both Pylades and Iphigenia to swear their oaths, telling Iphigenia to begin the process by creating a verbal formula for her mission (743 and 744), one that Pylades will repeat (745). This becomes the second phase of dialogue, between Pylades and Iphigenia. Iphigenia reciprocates, as requested, with a commitment to send Pylades safely from the land of the Taurians (746). They now select their respective gods, Artemis as the presiding local deity and Zeus as the most powerful god for oaths, on the understanding that these gods will punish them if they fail in their commitments to each other (747–52).

What has happened to the letter? It seems likely that right at the beginning of these phases, Iphigenia hands the letter to Pylades, and we may find that the scene progresses best if it is held prominently by both of them during the exchange of oaths. When the oaths conclude (752), Iphigenia may release it, and only when she has does a further thought occur to Pylades, with the mind of Greek for subtle points of obligation. As he voices his concern about possible shipwreck, which might see the loss of the letter while he himself was saved (755–58), he may well hold up the letter as a responsibility he has now taken on, but one that is a perishable, material object. This is the third phase of dialogue, and it prompts Iphigenia to consider that the conveyance of the words rather than the object itself is the precious component of her bond (759–65).

Iphigenia clearly expects Pylades to be able to commit a number of sentences to memory at only one hearing, and we should not be altogether surprised at this. Objects carrying writing were relatively special cases, and vast amounts of business and personal communication were transacted orally. There are many indications that Greeks might expect—and be expected—to remember what someone said in considerable detail, and no doubt the precise wording rather than the general gist was at times committed to memory. So Iphigenia confirms that in this way she will have two means at her disposal, which should secure her purpose, and Pylades is also happier with this solution to his own worries (766–68).

Now it is always possible that Iphigenia reads from the letter. There are instances of reading ability without the ability to write, and these may have been far more common in a society where the physical act of writing may have been conducted by slaves or others for masters or patrons. Yet Iphigenia must have composed the words in the first instance herself, and she has every reason to remember them, since they express so much that matters to her. It seems far more likely that she speaks the words from memory while Pylades holds the letter. It also seems unlikely that he follows what she is saying in the letter itself, because the script does not appear to build that kind of interaction into the scene. The reason perhaps for this is that the dialogue now shifts to Iphigenia and the reaction of Orestes to what she is saying, at least in the opening parts of the recitation.

She starts with the astonishing facts that the message is for Orestes, that she herself is Iphigenia, and that she is alive (769–71), and it seems that Orestes only really registers the last of these strongly, judging from his question (772). Although Iphigenia immediately identifies herself (773) once again, she continues with her letter, which makes abundantly clear to the two friends that this priestess, in this sanctuary, in this barbarous land is Orestes' lost sister (774–76). So while Orestes and Pylades have the truth dawning on them, Iphigenia remains in the dark, carefully repeating the name of Orestes so they get it right (779), and indeed threatening Orestes with a curse if he fails to come and find her (778).

His exclamation, which calls on the gods, fits the moment of dawning recognition as he sees it, since they can make sure that this becomes what it promises to be and have their role in it suitably acknowledged (780). But since Iphigenia is not aware of anything like a recognition happening, she sees no place for invoking the gods to have a role in her affairs at this moment (780). She continues with the narrative in the letter about her father's actual innocence, how a deer was substituted for her for sacrifice at Aulis by Artemis, who brought her here.

Attention now shifts briefly to Pylades, who is delighted to find that he can discharge his sworn obligation to Iphigenia so easily, and so quickly (788–90). He holds up the letter in its physical form, and moves to Orestes in a parody of a long journey (791), handing it over to him in an elaborate and probably mock-formal gesture (791–92). Orestes promptly responds with an appropriate, transactional formula of receipt (793), but he passes from that play-acting to the sheer pleasure of reunion, addressing Iphigenia as his sister, and quickly aiming to clasp her in his arms (796–97). In so doing, he also quite clearly discards the letter, since he has someone living and breathing to hold instead

(793–94), and it may be that he pushes it back into the hands of Pylades.

He is prevented from grasping Iphigenia just as he would wish by an outcry of 'sacrilege' from the chorus (798–99), and we can see that she has turned away. But he subsequently passes tests of knowledge of the family tree, and is finally acknowledged by Iphigenia through his ability to recall other, envisaged objects. These include a tapestry that Iphigenia wove on her loom at Argos, with scenes from the historical family feud, the lock of hair that Iphigenia sent to her mother Clytemnestra, and the ancient spear hanging in her own bedroom at Argos. The accumulation of these absent properties finally serves as security for a joyous recognition between brother and sister.

The child holds his own cradle: recovering the past in Euripides' *Ion*

In *Iphigenia in Tauris* the property has no intrinsic emotive value, and as a physical object it may be erased and made to carry any significance assigned to it. Yet it serves effectively to convey the transactions and communications between characters. In a decisive sequence from Euripides' *Ion* there lies an immense contrast, since the objects are from the beginning extremely emotive, and are invested with even more significance as the scene progresses.

The plot of *Ion* is complicated, and indeed involves more than its fair share of 'plotting'. The play is set in the precinct of Apollo at Delphi, outside the front of his temple and so by the altar. The movement of the play is to adopt the young temple attendant Ion into the Athenian royal dynasty, led at this time by a man called Xuthus, who is married to Creousa, who have both come to Delphi to seek advice and help on the problem of the succession. When Xuthus first seizes on Ion for adoption, Creousa reacts with hostility, and attempts to have Ion poisoned. Once Ion finds out that Creousa is behind this plot, he pursues her, and she takes refuge at Apollo's altar. The chorus of Athenian women has accompanied Creousa to Delphi, and is extremely sympathetic to her.

Ion—lines 1369–1444

ION: Ah! See how the tears pour down from my eyes
as I let my mind turn to my mother. She was   1370
a bride in secret, and when I was born she smuggled me
away without holding me to her breast. A nameless orphan,
I led the life of a slave in the house of a god.
What I've had from the god is good, but I haven't
been lucky. I've been deprived of a mother's love   1375
and care, lost that time when I should have been
held in her arms, indulged, felt glad to be alive.
And she has had a wretched time too. As a mother,
she felt the same pain as me, in losing the joy a child would bring.
Even so, I shall take this wheeled cradle and dedicate   1380
it to the god, so I don't find out anything I might regret.
If the woman whose child I am happens to have been a slave,
it would be far worse to find her than to leave the secret
    undisturbed.
Apollo, I am making this a dedication at your temple.
But what am I doing? I am battling against his will,   1385
since he's kept safe for me what will identify my mother.
No, I must be brave enough to open it.
I cannot possibly expect to escape what fate has in store.
Here are sacred wreaths, covering the binding that guards
my most intimate possessions: what have you kept hidden for
    me?   1390
Look at this cradle, with its beautifully made wheels:
not a sign of ageing in any of the outer wrapping, and
not a trace of mould on the basket-work. That's god's work.
It's been a long time for this treasure between then and now.
CREOUSA: What am I looking at? Is this some kind of
    hallucination?   1395
ION: You, be quiet. I've had enough trouble out of you already.
CREOUSA: Don't threaten me. This is no time for me to be quiet.
For what I see there is the cradle in which I
abandoned you, my boy, my son, when you were a baby,
in the cave of Cecrops, in the Long Rocks at Athens.   1400
I shall leave this altar, even if I must die for it.

ION: Grab hold of her! The god's driven her mad. She's left
the safety of the altar and its images. Bind her arms.

CREOUSA: I don't care; kill me if you like, so long as I
get hold of this, and you, and what's hidden inside it.   1405

ION: This is outrageous! She's seizing me like some sleazy bailiff!

CREOUSA: That's not true! You're my dear boy, and I've found
you.

ION: Your dear boy! I suppose that's why you were planning to
murder me?

CREOUSA: You are my boy. Don't tell me that mothers don't love
their children.

ION: Stop twisting your web of deceit: I'm going to catch you
out.   1410

CREOUSA: Yes, please, let's get to that, my son. That's what I'm
after.

ION: Is this cradle empty, or does it have something in it?

CREOUSA: It has the clothes you were wrapped in when I
abandoned you.

ION: And can you put a name to them before you see them?

CREOUSA: If I can't tell you, then you can kill me. I promise.   1415

ION: Tell me, then. You've got quite a nerve. Formidable.

CREOUSA: Look in there. Something that I wove when I was just a
girl.

ION: Yes, but what exactly? Girls weave all sorts of things.

CREOUSA: It's unfinished, like something made while someone is
learning.

ION: Come on, what does it look like? You won't catch me out
like that.   1420

CREOUSA: Woven into the middle of it is a Gorgon, to start
with . . .

ION: Oh Zeus, is this fate breathing down my neck, hunting me
down?

CREOUSA: . . . and then on the fringes there are snakes, like
Athena's aegis.

ION: Look at this.
This piece of weaving that I've found is just like that.

CREOUSA: It's a long time since I was a girl, making that at the
loom.   1425

ION: Is there anything you can add, or is that your one bit of luck?
CREOUSA: A pair of shining snakes, crafted completely in gold,
the gift of Athena, who tells us to raise our children in them:
they are like those that Erichthonius had long ago.
ION: Yes, a gold item. But what's it for, how's it used? Tell me. 1430
CREOUSA: It's hung round the neck of a new-born baby, my child.
ION: They're in here. I'm longing to hear from you about the third
   thing.
CREOUSA: On that day, I laid a wreath of olive leaves on you,
from the first olive tree that grows on Athena's acropolis.
If it's there, it won't have lost its colour. It can't.   1435
It comes from an imperishable tree; it will still be fresh.
ION: My mother, my dearest, darling mother! I couldn't
be happier, you couldn't be happier, I'll kiss your cheek!
CREOUSA: My child, the light in your eyes is dearer to a mother
than the sun (the god will forgive me). You are in my arms.   1440
I never dared to hope I would find you. I thought
you were under the ground with Persephone and the dead below.
ION: The boy who died but who is not dead
is in your arms, my dearest mother, a living apparition.

The sequence selected here is plainly aimed at pathos and at
achieving an overwhelming emotional climax. But we should
also be aware that there has been a close and intense scene
already between Ion and Creousa, near the beginning of the play
(lines 246–451). In it, Creousa used the device of 'this happened
to a friend of mine' to reveal the rape by Apollo and the lost
child, since she wishes to ask Apollo directly what he has done
with the child. This approach is forbidden by Ion, but it leaves
him wondering about Apollo's conduct, and some parting
words from Creousa also leave him speculating briefly about
her possible connection to this alleged incident (425–32). For
her part, Creousa has heard from Ion during that scene how he
was conveyed to the temple as a baby, and brought up by the
Prophetess of Apollo in ignorance of his parentage.

So we might say that the ground has been prepared, and we
should sense that these characters have been given information
about each other that is disturbing and suggestive, granted their

awareness of their own past, but that this has been obscured by the headlong conflict into which they have both plunged.

We also know much more about the way in which Apollo and Creousa's baby was cradled and clad, since at the opening of the play the god Hermes talks of it in great detail. He was instructed by his brother Apollo to fetch the child from its resting place in a cave on the Athenian acropolis, where it had been laid by Creousa soon after its secret birth. We learn from him that the baby was left in a basketwork cradle, which was curved on its lid and its base, so that it might be rocked. At Delphi, Hermes left the lid open so that the baby might be seen and pitied, which indeed was the endearing effect on the relatively stern Prophetess. Round the baby's neck Creousa had placed a golden necklace of the entwined snakes of Erichthonius, a traditional Athenian royal symbol of protection for their babies, and she had wrapped him in a shawl she had woven herself.

Admittedly, we may have forgotten these details by the time of our scene, granted the hectic pace of the action and the homicidal intentions of both Creousa and Ion in turn. But the general effect on us is similar to that which we may sense for the characters, in that we have been previously prepared for this recognition scene, as we may recall that the two characters have been, through their earlier and very nearly revealing conversation. Yet the bridge that the cradle forms between son and mother has to be built in the scene, even if we already know that it exists once we see it in Ion's hands.

The cradle is in Ion's hands at the beginning of our sequence because his step-mother, the Prophetess of Apollo, has consigned it to his keeping. She has come urgently out of Apollo's temple to prevent him from driving Creousa from the altar, and she is inspired at this moment that he is due to leave Delphi to hand over the cradle to him. This done, she retires into the temple, leaving him to think about his natural mother, since the Prophetess has in many ways drawn attention to the mystery of her absence, and has herself relinquished Ion with an embrace on parting (1363). The material presence of the cradle in his own arms prompts Ion to reflect on mother and son, in two forms.

In the first, he is drawn to thinking of the deprivation of a mother's love and care that he suffered, in the physical terms of suckling and the warmth of contact contrasted to the nameless existence as a temple slave (1371–73, and 1375–77). In the second, he does consider his mother's feelings, tears starting to his eyes as he thinks of the drastic moment of separation from her child (1369–72), and then of her loss and loneliness in the long aftermath (1378–79). Yet it is the material presence of the cradle which he and we have prominently at the forefront of our attention.

He may well have been near the temple doors when he received it, and he may well wander a little while he is reflecting what to do with it. The thought that he might dedicate it to Apollo may send him back towards the temple, an act that would suppress anything (like discovering that his mother was a slave) that he would rather not find out (1380–84). But he does not proceed far with this impulse, resolving instead to open it and to accept that Apollo prompted the Prophetess to keep it so that he should see what it contained (1385–88). This is a vital step, since (metaphorically speaking) instead of being buried away the cradle will burst open, and he recognizes the fateful quality of this decision (1388).

Creousa is by the altar, and has been in the privileged position to hear the full exchange between Ion and the Prophetess, and to become fascinated by the sight of the cradle. From the outside it may appear to be no more than a specific 'model', which would be emotive enough in her troubled state. But it is also wrapped or bound, and these bindings (of leaf or wool, or both) will be rather more distinctive, especially since like the cradle they are unstained by time (1389–94). Once Ion draws attention to these, as he starts to unwrap it all, Creousa is inexorably drawn, and we would expect Ion now to be quite close to the altar.

He is uninterested in her reaction, since it is an intrusion into his own intense (and, as he believes, highly personal) experience at this moment, but she wants to look closely, since her experience is even more intense. He tells her dismissively to be silent, and she thrusts that idea back in his face, asserting that her life will not be silent, and that he cannot tell her what to do (1396–97). She sees two things at once: firstly the cradle, that it is the one in which she abandoned her baby, and then secondly that Ion who is holding it now must be her child (1398–1400). It is an astonishing and overwhelming moment of utterly clear perception, and on assured impulse she leaves the safety of the altar to approach both young man and cradle (1401).

Ion had come running into the precinct when he was chasing her, with armed men behind him. He was reacting to an attempt on his life, and he is of considerable status at Delphi, as guardian of the deposited gold of the sanctuary, as Hermes has informed us. So those men are within reach of the altar, a presence that also threatens the frightened and awestruck chorus, and Ion ruthlessly commands them to seize Creousa as she leaves the altar's protection (1401). He regards her statements as no more than part of the onset of a madness that Apollo has justifiably visited on her, that has made her leave sanctuary, and happily takes his chance to have her bound (1402–403). Yet despite this command, it seems that Creousa is indeed inspired by the god, since apparently she insists on pushing right past to grab Ion as he holds the cradle, which astonishes him (1404–406).

It may be that in this crush Creousa is seized and held, if not bound as was instructed (1403), almost as she insists on his identity as her son and he sarcastically mocks the idea. He cannot be taken back as reclaimed property until he himself is convinced that the objects he is holding can be securely identified, and so can undeniably identify him. This is a transactional step that they both see clearly and accept quickly (1410–11), which will be 'make or break' for what is, for Ion, a preposterous fantasy. By now, Creousa is absolutely certain, since the objects are imprinted on her memory: that which she can plainly see—the cradle—and those within, which she can vividly envisage.

Ion must at this point step away from her, carrying and con-cealing the cradle from her, but allowing himself the opportunity to pick through its contents. If we have good recall, we shall be enumerating them just like Creousa, since Hermes told us what they were, and this allows a subtle empathy between audience and character. Euripides spins this exchange out carefully and precisely, step by step, and Creousa insists that she will answer correctly on pain of death. So we start with whether or not the cradle is empty, proceed to clothing, then to the kind of clothing (juvenile and unfinished weaving, that of a learner), and finally to the pattern woven on it, which is revealed in two stages: the central, presumably protective motif of the Gorgon (1421), and then the border of snakes, connecting the baby with the power of the goddess Athene (1423).

Between these two stages, Ion cries out to Zeus that at this moment of precise identification he senses his destiny hunting him out (1422). He then apparently holds up the property, acknowledging and displaying to all witnesses the precise match (1424). Yet he still prefers the idea of luck or chance (1426) to that of destiny, and insists on the listing and identification of further properties, by asking the open question whether or not there is anything else in the cradle. On this occasion, Creousa describes the representation with great precision, but does not mention the artefact in or on which it is made (1427–29). Ion seizes on this with a careful question (1430), which is correctly answered (1431), and the second object is then displayed by him (1432). He himself asks for the description of the third property, which may be an indication that by now he is beginning to yield (1432), and he significantly uses the word for longing ('I'm longing to hear from you about the third thing'). By this point the line-by-line exchange had already opened out to accommodate Creousa's detailed description of the necklace in three lines (1427–29), and the climax comes in her four-line description of the wreath of imperishable olive leaves taken from Athena's tree on the acropolis of Athens (1433–36). On hearing this, Ion is overwhelmed by emotion, perhaps as he takes out and displays this third object.

Practically speaking, it may be a little painful to crush a sturdy, woven cradle in the impassioned and urgent embrace that clearly follows (1437–42), so it may be that Ion hands it to someone else. If the chorus has drawn around while the dialogue builds, gradually less threatened themselves and in support of Creousa during this vital transaction, then it may be that it is handed over to one of its members; perhaps less attractively, it may be thrust quickly at one of those men who came in pursuit with Ion. Yet they do stand as impartial witnesses, and they might be curious to look in at the contents as verification of a surely god-given reunion and restoration.

There are other possibilities. Ion may drop it on to the ground, but alternatively he may be by Apollo's altar and place it there, where it can be inspected by others during the long sequence of joy which is now danced and sung by the two actors. Unlike the letter/tablet in *Iphigenia in Tauris*, this is a set of objects that will be treasured later, and retain much of its reuniting value. It is important to realize that in many plays an altar (in *Andromache* it is a shrine, with a statue) is a highly significant property. Even when it is not being used as a place of asylum, as a sanctuary for a leading character, and so as a focus for much of the physical action, it may still haunt the play. The blood-stained altar in *Iphigenia in Tauris* and the 'knowing' altar of Apollo in *Oedipus the King* are two other striking examples.

The children as live properties in Euripides' *Medea*

In Greek tragic theatre, the extreme end of the spectrum of objects is arguably represented by silent human beings who are made into objects of another's passion. This we have already seen with the 'silent mask' of Iole in *Young Women of Trachis*, who almost completely fits our disturbing term of a woman treated 'like an object', and who is moved around by others according to their inclination. It seems from the narrative we are given in the play of the outrage at Oechalia that Iole is young, and elsewhere in Greek tragedy we find children used to evoke pathos. In many cases, these children are—like Iole—silent, which serves to confirm their often fatal status as objects to be manipulated in an adult world of will.

In Euripides' *Medea*, the children that we are going to consider here as 'live' properties are part of the world of the play from the outset. They are introduced into the backstory given by the Nurse at the opening of the play, and almost immediately then seen, as they run into the playing-space with the Old Slave who is their 'minder'. In fact, the two sons are at the heart of the bitter dispute that now exists between Jason and Medea, their father and mother. It is not so much that we are witnessing an ancient version of a custody battle, but that they prove to be pawns in the larger battle between the ruler of the city of Corinth and Medea.

We hear very early on that Creon has decided to banish the sons as well as their mother from Corinth (lines 67–73). This decision actually contradicts Jason's leading motive for marrying Creon's daughter, which is to improve the status of his sons, as he insists later (559–67) in an argument with Medea. The Old Slave has only heard a rumour, so he does not know the reasoning behind the decision. But the decision would suggest that Creon is not aligned with Jason's thinking, and would instead rather see Jason in a position to father with his daughter children who would have no older rival, male half-brothers.

From the outset, the Nurse fears for the children, and the accent is on the threat to them as the opening scene of the play concludes. The Nurse instructs the Old Slave to take the children into the house but to keep them well away from Medea, and she tells the children themselves to keep away from her, and not even to come within her sight. As Medea extends her cries from inside the house, she herself calls the boys accursed, and wishes them dead along with their father, that the whole family could be obliterated (111–14). The Nurse responds with apprehension just short of despair, pitying the children and fearing for their future at the mercy of a commanding rage such as that of Medea (115–21).

This is a fearful and a fearsome opening to the play, with the children stuck in an utterly vulnerable position at its heart. While Medea's personality then occupies most of the attention in front of an arriving chorus, the boys become a bargaining counter in the argument that Medea has with Creon, as we have earlier seen in the Second Workshop. She claims that she wishes to stay for just one day to make arrangements for them, but subsequently her mind fixates on methods of achieving revenge on the principals of this new marriage—Creon, his daughter, and Jason himself. This speech was approached, in the First Workshop, with a close eye on its reflective qualities, despite the constant presence of an almost colluding chorus.

Once Medea has secured her bolt-hole in Athens, by offering its king Aegeus the drugs that he craves to make him fertile,

Medea then declares two things to the chorus: the first is her intention to send a poisoned garment to Creon's daughter, and the second is to murder her own sons. She offers two reasons for this action: the first is that no one should be able to take her children from her, and the second is that this action will hurt Jason most. The boys are then brought out from the house to greet and embrace their father, who repeats to them his plan for their leading role in the city of Corinth alongside the children he may have with his new wife (914–21). Yet Jason is distracted by Medea's weeping, something that no matter how genuine it may be she still manages to turn to her purpose. She wants Jason to plead with his new wife to let the boys stay in Corinth, which will fit his plan but is against Creon's recent decision. To do that, she is going to have them take a gift to Creon's daughter. The boys, and Jason, and the Old Slave leave, with the boys unknowingly carrying the poisoned gift.

Keeping track of the evolution of intentions and decisions during the tragedy is difficult, but this is where our scene begins. Just before we see the Old Slave returning, the chorus of Corinthian Women sings and dances a deeply pessimistic song, in which they envisage the effects of the poisoned gifts and can see the fatal outcome for the children.

Medea—lines 1002–1080

OLD SLAVE: Lady, you're lucky; the royal bride has taken your gifts into her hands, welcomed them, and these boys have been granted a reprieve from exile; no hostility to them there.
What's this?
What's the matter? You've been successful. Why are you
   upset?   1005
MEDEA: Ah!
OLD SLAVE: That's not in tune with the message I have brought.
MEDEA: Ah, again and again!
OLD SLAVE: Is there something I don't know?
   I thought I was bringing
good news, but have I got that wrong? Is my message bad?   1010

185

MEDEA: A message is a message. I don't blame you for yours.
OLD SLAVE: So why are you looking at the ground, and crying?
MEDEA: There is much to make me do so, old man. The gods
and my own evil thoughts have contrived all this.
OLD SLAVE: Bear up; your children will surely bring you back
    from exile.   1015
MEDEA: Sadly for me, I shall bring down some others before that.
OLD SLAVE: You're not the only woman to be parted from her
    children.
Humans don't live forever, so we must take setbacks lightly.
MEDEA: Yes, I shall do that. Now go inside the house
and sort out what the children will be needing for the day.   1020
Children, children, you now have residence, a city
and a house to live in for the future. I am left out of it,
sadly, and so you will never have your mother with you.
I shall have to leave, to cross into another country as an exile
before I have had the delight of seeing you successful and
    happy,   1025
long before adorning your bed and your bride, your marriage bed,
and holding the wedding torches up high, at arms length.
I have willed this misery, my own stubbornness has willed it into
    being.
What was the point, children, in giving you an upbringing?
Why did I struggle and wear myself to skin and bone, why did I 1030
suffer the hard labour of childbirth, pointlessly?
And yet, sure enough, there was a time when I had great
hopes of you, that you'd look after me in my old age
and wrap me up in death beautifully, with your own hands,
something for others to envy. But now these sweet thoughts   1035
are completely dead. Without you, away from you, I shall
lead a painful, poor life, and I shall suffer.
But you will never see me, no longer look at your mother
with those dear eyes, turning away to another kind of life.
Oh no, no! Why are you looking at me with those eyes,
    children?   1040
Why are you smiling what must be your last smile?
Ah! What shall I do? I haven't the heart for it,
women, when I see my children's bright eyes!

I won't be able to do it. Forget about those decisions
I had made; I'll take my children away with me.   1045
If I harm them, I shall suffer double the pain myself
that I would inflict on their father. What forces me to do that?
No, I'm not that person. Forget about those decisions.
But wait, what has come over me? Do I want to become
a laughing stock, letting my enemies get away unpunished?   1050
I must bring myself to do it. What a coward I am,
to let soft talking affect my mind like that!
Off you go, children, into the house. If there is anyone
whom the law forbids to be present at my sacrifice,
let him look to that himself; I shan't hold back my hand.   1055
Ah, ah!
It is anger that drives me to do this. No, no, it must not!
Yes, suffer, but leave them alone, keep your hands off the children!
Let them live there with me, and soothe you to smiles.
No, by the avenging spirits who rise from the underworld and
    Hades,
I shall not allow my sons to be insulted   1060
by my enemies: that is never going to happen.   1061
There can be no doubt that it is all over; no one has escaped.   1064
You can be sure that the diadem is on her head, that the tyrant's
daughter is dying in her marriage dress; I can see that clearly.
As for me, I am going on a journey of total misery,
and I am sending these children down an even more miserable
    track.
So I want to speak to them. Give me your hand,
children, give your mother your right hands to kiss.   1070
Oh dear, dearest hand, dearest to me, dear lips,
your faces, children, the way you look, so well-bred,
you should be prosperous, but not here, over there—your father
has deprived you of what's here. Oh such sweet cheeks,
soft skin, lovely breath, life's pleasure.   1075
Go away, get away from me! I cannot bear to look
at your faces any longer, I am defeated by evil.
I do know that what I am going to do is evil,
but anger is the cause of the worst things that humans do.
It's too strong for any other decisions that I might take.   1080

Euripides chooses to divide the aftermath of the delivery of the gifts into two different parts. What we most expect is the arrival of news of the calamity that the poison has wrought on the wedding party. But that is delayed, and at first we hear what should be good news, in the opposite of the platitude that good news travels slowly, bad news fast. That Creon's daughter should offer a reprieve to the children, as requested, before she has put on the garment, should not be a great surprise; it represents, after all, no more than the effect that Medea herself felt a lavish gift would have on a young woman who is close to power.

Yet it is not an offer that has any substance, since in a very short time indeed the children will be accomplices to disfigurement at least and probably to murder. Had Medea truly wished to achieve this reprieve, it is all too clear that she could have sent the gift without the poison, even if we do grant that—in common with most tragic characters—she is operating with what we would call a ticking clock in her ears. The certainty of her real purpose confirms that the request for a reprieve for the boys passed through Jason was probably no more than a pretext for sending the gifts, which would otherwise have been suspect coming from her, as Jason seems to sense (959–63).

Medea has already been moved to tears by the stark contrast, in that preceding scene, between the paternal image of security given as Jason stands with them and the alternative that she has firmly in mind. What the announcement by the Old Slave does is to increase the pathos, nudging us as an audience to see what might have been, but allowing that impetus to crash headlong into Medea's tragic resolve. That resolve is announced by her tears, repeating those of the previous scene but now at a later and more fateful stage of developments, and by her veiled responses to the Old Slave's puzzlement.

Medea has pride, rage, purpose, and will, alongside acknowledged skills and verbal and intellectual ability, and she is three-quarters human. She is, in many respects except the last, a close counterpart to a figure such as Oedipus, and it is the mass of such a personality that makes the determination it has tragic. Less impulsive than Oedipus, Medea is in her isolation more reflective, and we might speculate that it is the divine element in her genetics (her grandfather is the sun-god) that keeps her well-away from self-destruction, to the great detriment of others.

The children are in this scene from the beginning, shepherded by the Old Slave whose task it is, primarily, to mind them in their passage from home to school and back, or from home to the gymnasium. What seems clear is that while he expects her to take them to her arms in joy at the good news, she remains standing apart, downcast, as he says (1005, and then 1012). It is noticeable not only that she is apparently motionless, crying out and in tears of grief, but also that she makes no mention of the children until she instructs him—on a standard, everyday pretext—to take them into the house (1019–20).

At first, the topic of exchange between Medea and the Old Slave is that of the news he brings of their reprieve, and then it is of the consequence, the gap between exile for her and relative civic integration for them (1015–18). What Medea slips in is a reference to bringing down others (1016), an obscure allusion either to the poisoning in progress or to her unchanged intention to kill the children. It is the Old Slave who builds the children back into this rather one-sided conversation, and who feels that age and perhaps his see-it-how-it-is status allow him to offer Medea comfort (1015), and then advice (1017–18). She dismisses him, to carry out the usual tasks on this unusual day.

The children are now the epicentre of the earthquake that is stemming upwards and outwards from Medea; they are not exactly the focus of the scene, but a constant point of reference. There can be no doubt that Euripides intended this scene to evoke pathos, whatever else we may find in its train of thought and feeling, and any modern performance will exploit that quality. I am thinking here of the expedient of having the children playing together and being interrupted, occasionally paying attention to their mother, since our sense of play and freedom is a symbolic contrast to the threat of death. This seems a very likely choice under modern direction, either for the young actors who might portray them, or for older actors who take on those parts in a workshop.

The first phase (1021–27) of Medea's monologue does seem addressed to the children, as if explaining to them what has just been decided, and the full implications of it. What this means is that the idea of separation is the primary topic, and this leads into what Medea seizes on as a vivid image of loss: the denial through exile of her presence at the weddings of her sons, of her involvement as a proud mother in the ritual preparations and celebrations (1025–27).

If the children seem to be addressed directly in this opening phase, perhaps closely, then what follows from Medea is a mixture of an abrupt self-apostrophe—itself a Greek term that means 'turning aside' or 'away' from the flow of dialogue—and a rhetorical address to the children. What I mean by 'rhetorical' is that although the children are addressed, it is obvious that they cannot answer the questions posed by Medea (1029–31), who is using them to put questions to herself. In fact, those questions are an appendage to the leading statement (1028), which is that Medea has brought this misery on herself, since she is stubbornly determined on her plan to kill the children. In that case, she says, I wasted my time and effort foolishly in birth and upbringing.

That impasse of thought leads on to a rejoinder, in a continuation of this strange mixture of reflective and rhetorical elements. The children continue to feature almost as topics in her flow of thought, their physical presence bringing to life aspects of her own hopes and experience. The rejoinder is that she did have a good reason for all the hard labour of childbirth and nurture, which was that the children would reciprocally care for her in her old age (1032–35). Yet the end of those hopes brings her back to the idea of separation, although she does not spell out the fatal kind of separation that she has in mind until the final hint of 'another kind of life' (1039).

It would seem that the mention of eyes (in 1039) brings her out of what might be termed a reverie. Her indirect address to herself via the children has extended into a meditative and reflective monologue, in which the physicality of the children is a stimulus to emotion and pain. It is worth observing how physically and materially evocative these first three phases of the speech have been, with hands, arms, and eyes in interplay with the person of the speaker, and objects conjured into view, such as the torches and the marriage bed and its ornamentation. But now eyes become more immediate than a figure of speech, as—in our contemporary cliché—we would say that the children's eyes unwittingly and innocently 'burn' into her consciousness.

So we would see Medea at this moment confronting the children and facing those eyes and those delighted smiles (1040–41). But she must surely turn away from them into another abrupt self-apostrophe (1042), which then diverts itself almost immediately into an address to the women of the chorus (1042–48). This we can easily understand, since the women are an obvious and readily available source of support for any inclination she might have to spare the children. The chorus had already opposed her stated intention when it first became explicit, after Medea had secured the promise of asylum from Aegeus (811–23, following her speech at 764–810), and here Medea is willing briefly to play a gambit with public opinion, and with herself.

Yet this flirtation with clemency is short-lived, and prompts a reaction. She will not let her enemies have the upper hand and laugh at her weakness, which they would call her cowardice (1049–52). These are resolutely Greek male terms of reference to which she whole-heartedly subscribes, and the reaction takes the form of an assertion of these values after another abrupt self-apostrophe (1049), which breaks the previous line of thought and mode of address. There is no pretence in this short phase of talking to anyone except herself, and it is followed by a natural consequence, which is that an order is given to the children to enter the house (1053). At this point, the chorus is also implicitly called to order, in a terrible perversion of a standard formula of ritual exclusion (1053–55). In normal circumstances, only those stained by pollution would be excluded from a pious sacrifice; here the stain of pollution lies on the sacrifice, and so most of humanity would be excluded.

At this point, Medea finds it possible to go beyond simple self-apostrophe, specifically to address and reprimand her own wilful anger, almost personifying it as a force that operates on 'her' (1056–57). So at one point anger is 'you', and then Medea becomes 'you' (1058). This is a relatively complex idea of self and motivation, and what I have translated as 'anger' I have then slightly coloured by the use of the word 'drives' in conjunction with it (instead of 'works', 'achieves', 'effects', which would be more literal versions of the verb used). The Greek noun is *thumos*, and it connotes an impassioned inclination or determination, so including the kind of anger that prompts an action.

What Medea—once again briefly, and here even more so— sees as the advantage of clemency, and of opposing her *thumos*, is the delight that the children will bring to her if they remain alive (1058). But the reaction to this warm thought is harsh, and in place of that plea comes an oath, calling on some of the darkest powers that can be summoned (1059). Medea declares to herself, in front of the chorus, that she will not allow her enemies the chance to insult her children (1060–61). Again, the principle of pride proves to be paramount, and she supports it with contingency, since by now the poison must have had effect (1064–66), and a secure future for the children in Corinth is out of the question.

She stabilizes her fluctuating resolve by pairing the misery that she will undergo and that facing the children, emphatically claiming 'total misery' for herself, and then offering 'more' for her children. It is not a convincing verbal strategy, nor is it a justification, but it is the best that she can do, a bizarre and grotesque version of 'this hurts me as much as (more than, in this case) it hurts you'. So she springs from reflection into direct contact with them, with physicality once again prominent. If these children are relatively small, the actor has either to bend down or to lift them up to kiss their mouths, which she seems to do (1071) after kissing their hands (1069–71).

It is hardly surprising that such an emotional indulgence in the sweet feelings of motherhood should trigger a reaction, which is that she cannot look them in the face again. What she finally expresses is an idea of a kind with that of Phaedra in *Hippolytus* (lines 380–83), on knowing what is good but not doing it. Here Medea acknowledges that her *thumos* is in charge (1079), and so she is led to evil: the sentiment will be expressed as the children walk into the scene-building. This they have presumably attempted to do earlier, at the order given to them by their mother (1053). We may choose to think that they have paused at her subsequent outcry, and so remain for her renewed approach to them (from 1067).

I would have chorus members closely involved in every phase of this scene, on the simple principle that if they are addressed directly by Medea at a certain point, then at any other point they may be expecting to be involved. The women have declared their opposition to the killing of the children just earlier, and from the first moment of the scene, when the Old Slave announces the reprieve, this is bound up in the train of Medea's thought. A good understanding of space would surely relate the children to chorus members in an uneven balance to the relation of the children to Medea. The presence of the chorus is that of a surrogate mother who cannot assert her rights against the will of the dominant natural mother. It would be unlikely that the children could respond to them much, caught as they are in the powerful aura of their mother.

It is also important to realize that self-apostrophe and a reflective monologue signal that many transactions will be internal, played out by the speaker on herself. This is not true of all; there are clearly minor transactions involving the children and the Old Slave, which are fundamentally instructions to enter the scene-building. In the exchange with the Old Slave, there is also a failed transaction alongside a successful communication: the Old Slave's message fails to bring relief, contrary to his expectations. In the first part of the monologue, Medea is reconciling herself, and supposedly the children, to the fact of separation. Yet there is a pretence here, a dissimulation of the real nature of that separation, which she obscures by her emphasis on her own exile. Medea then switches to a declaration to the chorus that she will take the children with her, into exile. But she reacts, condemning her own softness and cowardice and reasserting to herself her determination to punish her enemies.

At this point, the children are sent into the scene-building, as a sign of the fatal transaction to which she is now committed, after a ritual exclusion has been declared, with the chorus firmly in mind. The climactic transaction is with her own *thumos*, which she at first bans from touching her children, but to which she succumbs and accepts that she does so, in the revival of the ideas of insult and violent revenge. The ultimate step is then to embrace and perform what is a comprehensive farewell to her children.

For the recording (**Recording 6**), we chose to have the actor working without anyone else in the space, so what it reveals in particular is the way in which the presence of the children sears itself into the emotional consciousness of Medea as articulated in the monologue. In any workshop, the performer would need to have support in the physical presence of both children and chorus. Yet the recording in this form marks a significant difference from the material, objectified qualities of the properties in the next scene.

The missing father and the dead child in Euripides' *Trojan Women*

Children are inevitably objects of pathos when they come to harm, and the fate of Astyanax, the son of Hector and Andromache, who is crushed when he is hurled from the walls of Troy by the victorious Greeks, is as pitiful as any. Euripides' tragedy, *Trojan Women*, has this act close to the end of the play, which is about the winding-down of the military occupation at the site. The Trojan men are all dead, the women are enslaved, and the action of the tragedy traces the allocation of royal Trojan women to individual Greek commanders, and also feeds in atrocities. The sacrifice of one of Hecuba's daughters, Polyxena, at the tomb of Achilles is one of these, and the seizing and ritual murder of Astyanax another.

Through her son Hector, Hecuba is Astyanax's grandmother, and although we do see his mother Andromache, it is Hecuba who presides in defeat, and to whom the Greeks come to declare their intentions. Since Hecuba is regarded by the Trojan women (whether her daughters, her daughters-in-law, or others) as the leading dynastic woman and now the leading Trojan, the Greeks treat her in that manner too. The tragedy looks at the different responses to catastrophe by women younger than Hecuba: her daughter Cassandra, the celibate prophetess soon to be a concubine; her daughter-in-law Andromache, mourning her husband Hector, and seeing her child Astyanax taken from her;

and not least Helen, who has now to account for herself to both Trojan and Greek.

Trojan Women was the third and final tragedy in a trilogy of episodes in one myth. The first two tragedies are lost, but a fair bit is nevertheless known about the plot of the middle one, *Alexander*. It is clear that Euripides was hard on the Trojans as well as on the Greeks. Specifically, when a prophecy had declared that Paris (aka Alexander) would destroy his own city, he was exposed as a baby on the mountains, but had been saved and brought up by a shepherd, in what seems to be an adaptation of the Oedipus myth. When he came of age, he proved to be a victor at games held in his honour in the city, provoking hostility from Hecuba that her royal sons were being humiliated by a shepherd boy. She conspired to have him killed, but he was recognized by Cassandra and welcomed back to the dynasty, despite the import of the prophecy remaining unchanged. *Trojan Women* traces the outcome of that decision, and that is what makes it a full tragedy, since to a certain extent Hecuba is living the consequences of her own actions.

So while *Trojan Women* is indeed a victim drama, there are varying degrees of innocence and involvement in it, along with a great deal of emphasis on dynastic pride. One very clear message of this tragedy as the conclusion to the trilogy, and one which a democracy should have taken from it, is that in a Greek city (*polis*) all will suffer as the result of the decisions and motives of any elite. As with all ancient Greek tragedies, stemming as they do from democratic Athens, there is an open invitation to witness and judge the behaviour of mythical dynasts, and either to be drawn into sympathy with the pathos of their experience, or to use a sense of class difference ultimately to establish a safe distance from them. So in *Trojan Women* there is a clash between our standard expectation that we can distance ourselves from the suffering of dynasts, and the grim totality of the fate that grips Troy.

Women of Troy—lines 1156–1206

HECUBA: Place Hector's rounded shield upon the ground:
a grim sight, painful for me to look at.
You Greeks! You can better boast of your brawn than your brains.
What cause did you have to fear this child, and to contrive
this novel form of slaughter? Did you think that he might ever   1160
restore the ruins of Troy? You were nothing even then,
when Hector was carrying the battle before him,
and we were losing men from the thousands around him.
But with the city taken, the Phrygians all dead,
your fear of a baby grew so much . . . I cannot commend fear,   1165
in a man who suffers fear without subjecting it to reason.
My dearest boy, death came at you before you had a chance of
    anything.
Had you died in defence of your city, with your youth and
a marriage behind you, a tyrant living like a god,
you would have been blessed—if any of that brings blessings.   1170
But as it is, you enjoyed nothing of what your royal house held for
    you.
You saw it, understood intuitively that it was for you, but never
    knew it.
You wretched child, how pitifully the walls guarding your
    inheritance,
Apollo's fortress, have sliced through the curls on your head.
These curls, that your mother tended like a garden, day after   1175
day, the kisses she planted on them, where now the blood
flows from a wound grinning in the shattered bone: it would be vile
    to say more.
Your hands, you have in them still the sweet image of your father,
and yet they are laid out in front of me, flapping from their joints.
There is your darling mouth, oh so often boasting to me,   1180
lifeless now, how you deceived me when you fell into my dress,
'Granny', you'd say, 'I'll cut you curls and locks
of my hair, you just see I will, to put on your grave,
and I'll lead a bunch of my friends there, to sing and say
    goodbye.'
But you are not burying me: here the old bury the young.   1185

I have lost my children, lost my city, and I'm burying your pitiable
    corpse.
Aah, what of the kisses I showered on you, what of my care,
my nursing, my broken sleep, gone, gone! Tell me, what
would a poet write of you on your tomb?
'The Argives killed this child once upon a time   1190
in fear.' For the Greeks, an epitaph of shame.
But still, if you do not have your inheritance, you will have
your father's bronze-backed shield to be buried in.
A shield that protected Hector's arm, his lovely forearm.
He guarded you in turn, the best you could have, and you've lost
    him now.   1195
Touching to see how the leather strap bears the mark of his
    fingers,
where the sweat from his forehead has dripped on the rounded rim
of the shield as he laid it against his bearded chin:
Hector, my son, who took on the struggle of battle so very often.
Fetch and bring here what little we have in our present
    circumstances   1200
to dress this wretched corpse. The luck we have been given
does not stretch to adornment: what I have, you will have.
Anyone who flatters himself on the security of his success
is a fool. We are human, and it's in the nature of luck
to jump about here and there like a madman;   1205
nobody is just plain lucky, in and of himself.

I have mentioned the child, for obvious reasons, and in this
instance we may more immediately recognize the relationship
to the idea of a property that is handled by the actor than
perhaps was the case with Medea and her children. To kill
the last dynastic male of Troy, which is the symbolic status of
Astyanax, before the final razing of its city and its temples,
confirms absolute conquest and revenge. He is handed back and
forth between Greek and Trojan: taken alive by the Greek herald
Talthybius from his mother Andromache, returned as a corpse
by Talthybius to his grandmother Hecuba, and finally taken
again by Talthybius to be buried. Just before our monologue
opens, Talthybius has returned after washing the boy's body

in Scamander, the river of Troy, as an act of ritual purification before burial. Talthybius then leaves to prepare the grave itself.

These are all significant transactions, and they point to the fact that Hecuba and the women are being left with one part of the act of mourning—a lament on the receipt of a body, such as we see for Hector towards the close of Homer's *Iliad*—and another part of the act of burial, which is the clothing of the body after it has been ritually washed. What Euripides chooses to do is to let Hecuba articulate her sorrow largely in spoken verse, rather than in song, before she instructs the chorus—or other extras—to fetch what fine clothing they can find (1200–202). As the body is being clothed, just after this speech ends, song and lament are mixed with speech.

If these are the principal and highly recognizable transactions, and the body of Astyanax the principal 'property' of the scene, there is also a parallel and related transaction, subsidiary to it. This involves the shield of Hector, which we first see (568–76) in the collection of his armour on the wagon that is carrying Andromache and the living Astyanax to the ship of Neoptolemus, son of Achilles and leading conqueror of Troy, to whom Andromache has been awarded as a slave. When Talthybius returns with the child's body, he informs Hecuba that Andromache wished the boy to be buried in his father's shield, and so he brings the shield with him. It is not explicit that the body lies in the shield, and it could be that the two properties are brought together at some point. But it seems most probable, and I have assumed that the body is in the shield.

The shield is to double as a coffin for its owner's son, and it is finally itself given a wreath in the process of clothing the boy's body. Andromache wishes to part from it in this way because she does not want to be able to see it in her new owner's house in Greece, still less in her new, enforced bedroom, as will be the case. Plainly, for Andromache, the shield more than any other item of equipment symbolizes its owner Hector, her dead husband, and so he will in that symbolic way be buried with his son. The shield is indeed a property, and in this case also an object given a function for which it was not primarily intended, although we know that shields might be used to carry back dead

bodies of men killed in battle, from the famous Spartan phrase
'better to come home on your shield than without it'. Even the
ownership of it, as a property in that sense, is at issue, since
Andromache manages to deny a spoil of battle, inherited by
Neoptolemus from his father, who had killed Hector, to its new
owner, and instead reclaim it and unite it in the grave with its
original owner's son.

In this case, the property has been introduced to us before
it has been deployed, as part of an assemblage to which direct
reference is made (568–76), indicative of the collection of goods
and chattels which the conquering Neoptolemus has as his
portion of victory, and which includes at that moment both
Andromache and her son. Like them, this assemblage is placed
on a wagon (569) which is brought into the playing-space, and
from which both performers (the actor playing Andromache,
and the mute extra playing Astyanax) descend. So it is placed
centrally before us for a long time. Once Andromache moves
from lament into speech (from 610 forward), her concentration
on her role as a wife and so on her dead husband allows the
armour on the wagon to represent his passing away, his death
and absence, almost as an archetypal warrior.

In this way, the property is invested with significance, and
stamped in our minds with the emotive longing for Hector
that Andromache expresses. At the same time, in her reply to
Andromache in the same scene, Hecuba attempts to console her
and draw her away from an emphasis on the husband she has
lost to the future of her son Astyanax, standing there with her,
who may return to Troy to restore it, or have children who will
(701–705). Euripides introduces this emotional aspiration just at
the moment when Talthybius arrives to announce the removal
and murder of the boy. So both the shield and the boy have been
thoroughly invested with significance before they come to be
handled in the scene which we are working on.

It is also worth thinking at this moment briefly about costume
and clothing. It may seem self-evident that in the scene of utter
desolation which the play presents, at the conclusion of a heavily
military or war-zone trilogy, that the women are in symbolic
rags, perhaps themselves grimy, dishevelled, uncared-for. We

know they are now enslaved, and that they have lost everything. But this instinct about the application of symbolic dress may not be quite right. It is certainly clear from Electra in Euripides' play, as we have seen, that costume can be quite simply indicative, and there are many other instances that show that tragedy was willing to use costume to portray specific kinds of status. In this case, Hecuba refers sufficiently to having her hair shorn in mourning for her menfolk for us to envisage that aspect to her mask. But it is interesting that the women are still able to find some fine clothes for the body of Astyanax when asked to do so by Hecuba. It may be that the phrase 'left only with the clothes she was standing up in' gives us a better pointer here.

This may seem an unnecessary point of quibbling, and rather outside the strict brief of acting. But in this instance I think our sense of status is very important, since Hecuba has not quite lost her role as queen, and is still standing near or in her city. The tipping point for the action of the play is the assignation of the remaining Trojan women as slaves to specific masters, and it is their conclusive loss of status which is part of the dramatic subject. This tragedy represents the stripping away of the last vestiges of dynastic authority, not an extended indulgence of nostalgia for it, taken from a position when it is no more than a distant memory.

We see this at many points in the play, notably in the attitude and recurrent deference of the Greek herald Talthybius to Hecuba as the leading Trojan. But it is also strongly marked in the scene immediately preceding this, in which Menelaus appears with his soldiers to drag his errant wife Helen out of the scene-building in which she has been living with other Trojan women. He is supposedly there to exact vengeance on her, and the Greek army expects death. But the action of dragging her out curiously becomes something of a demonstration to the powerless Trojan women of his determination not to forgive. Hecuba first intrudes into his consciousness, and then oddly begs him to allow Helen to speak. It is with some deference to Hecuba that Menelaus allows this, and also allows Hecuba to speak after Helen to accuse her fully. The debate ends with Menelaus stating his agreement with the former Trojan queen, accepting her arguments and also accepting that they lead conclusively to Helen's execution. Yet he hesitates to carry it out here and now, and decides to defer the execution to a time after their return to Argos. As we know from the standard versions of the myth, this will never happen.

This scene also offers us another vision of costume and clothing, because Hecuba arraigns Helen for dressing herself up to come before her husband, and failing to cut her hair in submission. Helen will walk off to the ships unaffected by the disaster at Troy, and will retain her status while others suffer its drastic removal. Her fine costume offers us a glimpse of the luxury and life that Astyanax might have had, which is recalled when his body is clothed in similar finery after death.

Hecuba's first task is to take over temporary responsibility for the body from the Greeks, who have given it a ritual washing in the river. Talthybius has announced his own departure, since he has to supervise digging the grave, and it seems most likely that his men leave with him. They will return later, with Talthybius, to remove the body. In these circumstances, it seems inevitable that the body on the shield should be placed centrally, with the chorus at a respectful distance, and Hecuba able to stand away or approach the body.

Her first response is, perhaps surprisingly to us, rhetorical rather than intimate, and this should alert us to the issue of status. The return of a body of a child that has been ritually killed, or executed, by the enemy calls for a rejoinder and an accusation on behalf of the child's community and city, since the child is a dynast. At least, it appears so to Hecuba, and she cries out both to the Greeks and against them, as a surrounding but unseen presence. Her theme is their weakness, that makes them afraid of a child, but she also recalls to us as an audience her own futile and indeed fatal ambitions for Astyanax expressed as encouragement to Andromache (1160–61, recalling 701–705).

It is not an even or easy sequence of thought for us to follow, but her condemnation seems to be total, of their worthlessness when the battle was on and equally when it was over (1161–64). The emotive contrast is undoubtedly between grown men and a boy, and the adult male Trojans need to be conjured into mind as much as the Greeks, to leave the boy an isolated and unthreatening figure. Her conclusion apparently lays claim to the value of the control or restraint of emotion by reason (1165–66); but it is belied by her own extravagant hopes for the child, which would actually make the Greeks' fear grimly reasonable.

This address to the Greeks, with the boy as a topic of argument, may well be given at a distance from the body, partly spoken out to the surrounding and hidden army that dominates her fate and that of the dead body on the shield. It is expansive as well as rhetorical, and it is plausible to think of gesturing down to the boy while speaking notionally upwards and outwards and around to the Greeks. But it is, of course, also bound to take in the chorus, since Hecuba is performing for them, representing the pitiful objection that the conquered make to the victors.

The second phase of the speech acknowledges the boy's death, and is what people now tend to call the eulogy, which should be a summary of achievements and qualities of temperament and character. In this case, what has to be stated is the negation of the possibility of a eulogy. The child died too young, and this is understood in a series of negations. He should have progressed through the formal status of youth (between child and man) to marriage and then to military service, coming into possession of his inheritance as a dynast (1168–69). That inheritance actually obsesses Hecuba, presumably because continuity is the essence of dynasty (1171–72), and it is not just his life but the inheritance itself which has ended.

What is worse, it is the walls that were supposed to guard the inheritance that have actually killed the inheritor (1173–74), and it is this dreadful thought that brings Hecuba right to the child's head, which we reluctantly picture through her words. It is smashed, and she fingers the curls that lie over a gaping fracture, which she can only briefly describe before refusing to go further (1177). The child is nurtured by the mother like a garden (1175), an image of continuity in itself as of fruitfulness, and if the curls recall the mother, the child's hands recall his father (1178–79). This is an observation by a grandmother, and at the same time an evocation of the use to which those male hands are put in holding shields and grasping spears.

The tour of the corpse is becoming almost unbearably emotive, but Hecuba has the courage to face death—she has done it so many times—and to evoke life in its face. The child's mouth still allows it to speak through Hecuba's recall of its words to her (1180–84), and if this were like other scenes of narrative embodiment then it might encourage the actor to portray the child. What I mean by this is that certain kinds of narrative report in tragedy carry the direct, quoted speech of someone whose words and actions are being described. These reports are delivered to the chorus as much as to any other character(s) present. Most of these reports are describing someone who is absent; but bringing the dead child momentarily to life is not so very different.

What the child says refers to the curls to which Hecuba drew attention, but it leads also into another formal aspect of what the child should have lived to experience, which comprises the burial of—and the memorial rites for—his grandmother. That hair would have been cut for her (1182–83), as hers is now cut for him and for all the other brothers of his father, and Hecuba seems to be making him promise a chorus of young men singing in her honour at her tomb (1184). It is to be expected that any lament for a lost dear one would also turn into a lament for oneself, because one's own loss is a way of testifying to the importance of that person to you. So here that is tied to the perception about the old burying the young (1185), and Hecuba confirms the hammer-blow that this death represents to her, because her children have gone, and her city has gone: this is nothing left beyond this burial (1186). At this point, her control breaks, and she wails hopelessly of the wasted love, the wasted, watchful hours of care. The climax is the epitaph (1188–91), but it is nihilistic, and returns to her theme of the rule of fear: there is no comfort in the fact that it will bring the Greeks shame. That epitaph will never be engraved.

In the second, major phase of the speech Hecuba turns, through repetition of the theme of inheritance, to the shield itself, which until now has merely been the object in which the corpse has been laid. If men more often died in battle than in other circumstances, and if shields were brought home when they were not taken by the victorious enemy as trophies, it may be that wives did sentimentally see the imprint of their husbands in them. Alternatively, this is something that men could see themselves, gradually forming in this vital object, and Euripides is transferring that perception from regular military service and campaigning into a script for a mother. Perhaps we should understand a common, shared perception in a culture such as this.

But in any case we must see the shield as a prime example of the intense value placed on specific objects in the pre-modern eras. The feature of all military equipment is that it is your particular piece of an extensive set. In a hoplite (heavily-armoured) Greek fighting-line of the period during which these tragedies were performed, your shield covered the right and potentially unguarded side of your companion on your left, particularly unguarded when he was striking forward with his weapons. So the metaphor that a strong warrior's shield guards his country and not just himself has a strong hold in the awareness of each man who fights in line. You don't lose your shield, you don't trade it in that often, you don't sell it on e-bay: you keep it as long as you are alive, and I would imagine that you look with no little emotion on the dents that are made in it.

Hecuba's thought, after she has envisaged her son's lovely forearm, is that if the shield guards the man then the man also takes care to preserve the shield (1195), and we sense that she is also thinking that he was the best guard of the city itself and its inhabitants. The shield brings the man back to life, because it is made to be held, because the strap is grasped by fingers which over the years leave their mark, and because it is stained by a sign of life rather than death, which is sweat (1196–98). So the bearded father is there at the burial of his beardless son, and transmits to him what might have formed part of the boy's eulogy, his courage in battle (1199). It is a brief, but intense and utterly precise evocation of the physicality of a man we had seen in the second play of the trilogy, and whose character we will have judged.

Hecuba has now completed what she had to say, and the boy is a corpse. So she orders the clothing for his burial from the women around her (1200–201), who will fetch it from the scene-building. Once he is clothed, they will have to relinquish him again to the Greeks for the interment. In some ways, the burial clothing is the last possession that she has and of which she can dispose, and this prompts the commonplace sentiment that one should count no one successful until his life is finished. Only then can his good or bad fortune be judged, and Hecuba insists that no one is in control of his fortune, despite any illusions that some are consistently lucky people. So fortune is like inheritance, or life itself, in that despite appearances it can be lost, and does not belong to the person concerned. But this commonplace is given unexpected life by the striking image of fortune jumping about like a madman (1204–205), a recall of the desperate and disturbed response of her daughter Cassandra earlier in the play, as she faced existence as a slave and a concubine.

The actor in the recording of this scene (**Recording 7**) was given the benefit of a material indication of the body of Astyanax and the shield, but had no chorus with which to interact. Yet the centrality of the focus is paramount, and powerfully apparent from the recording, and that in itself is enough to be usefully indicative of phrasing within the monologue and control, even if a workshop might well explore other and additional qualities of the scene amongst the full resource of its members.

Fictional death and heartfelt mourning: the empty urn in Sophocles' *Electra*

I would regard Hecuba's speech from *Trojan Women* as the most powerful scene of its kind ever written, an outstanding example of what we would call tragic pathos, yet even so one whose full ironies are hidden from us in the loss of the two preceding tragedies, particularly in relation to Hecuba's questionable dynastic role in them. Both the child and the shield are emotive since they carry the meaning of death, and in Sophocles' *Electra* another, more humble property also has this function. It is a bronze urn, brought to the palace where Electra and her mother live with the usurper Aegisthus.

The tipping point at the beginning of Sophocles' play is the return of Orestes, at last, to his homeland, accompanied by

Pylades and advised by the Old Man who took him away from danger when he was a child. Orestes has been instructed by Apollo at Delphi to take revenge by killing his father's murderers himself, and not in a military action. The urn forms part of a plan to get into the palace without being recognized, and the plan is that the Old Man will first bring news of the death of Orestes in a chariot race. He will be followed a little later by Orestes and Pylades as two strangers tasked with bringing the ashes of Orestes back home in an urn; this will gain them entry to the palace from an unsuspecting and relieved Clytemnestra. It is interesting that this central feature of Sophocles' plot is actually developed from a feature of Aeschylus' *Libation Bearers*, a lie that Orestes offers to Clytemnestra to mask his true identity.

The situation in Sophocles' tragedy which reaches this tipping point is the constant mourning of Electra, and we find that in the temporary absence of Aegisthus she has come outside, and is joined by a sympathetic but corrective chorus of local women. She comes quickly into conflict with her sister Chrysothemis, who has been sent out by her mother to make propitiatory offerings at their father's grave. This introduces the other important element of propulsion in the action, which is the dream that Clytemnestra had last night (417–27), another element of the plot derived from the middle play of Aeschylus' trilogy. This dream is clearly threatening to her continued rule with Aegisthus, and she is very disturbed by it. Electra persuades Chrysothemis to discard the offerings, and to substitute a lock of her own hair and the belt of her garment. She must pray to their father to help them against their enemies and support their brother Orestes, since Electra senses that the dream must have something to do with him.

So here we have a major shift in the nature of the ritual, manipulated as a transaction by Electra to take advantage of what she thinks must be a favourable moment. In fact, Clytemnestra herself emerges from the scene building intending to make offerings at the altar to Apollo in front of the house, to ward off any bad consequences stemming from the dream. Before she can complete her offerings she is confronted by Electra, who is urged on by the opportunity to convict her mother in front of a group of women, and by the threat to eject her from the palace and imprison her, of which her sister Chrysothemis had earlier informed her (378–91). But our sense of Electra's increasing excitement and confidence and Clytemnestra's fear is broken by the arrival of the Old Man with his story of the accidental death of Orestes. At its conclusion Clytemnestra must be relieved as she takes the Old Man inside, while Electra has been cast back into total despondency, and collapses by the scene building's door.

It is important to trace all the elements of the roller-coaster ride of emotions that the female characters have in the first parts of this tragedy, and the significance of the transactions in which they are involved. This aspect of the play is the counterpoise to the male deceit about the death of Orestes, which links together a set of false transactions, which start with the announcement of the death and its proper reception by the relatives. Rather than seeing Electra in a steady state of mourning, we should see her as at this time extremely volatile. She is able to express those emotions because she is, unusually, outside and has a group of women who are willing to engage with her state of feeling. But this strand of the plot takes a further twist when Chrysothemis returns from the grave.

Chrysothemis is now excited by what she has seen at her father's grave, and is intent on persuading her sister that she was right, and that the new offerings she has found have been left by none other than Orestes. This, of course, encounters the hammer blow of the news of Orestes' death, and Chrysothemis is then subjected to Electra's plan that the sisters should themselves now take on the task of vengeance. Here we see echoes of Sophocles' own earlier scene between Antigone and Ismene, and Chrysothemis duly takes Ismene's part and some of her arguments, leaving Electra resolute and hardened against her. The Argive Women played by the chorus sing in praise of Electra, and it is at this point that our scene begins.

Sophocles *Electra*—lines 1098–1229

ORESTES: Women, have we been directed right, and are we travelling straight to where we want?

CHORUS: What are you looking for? Why are you here?   1100

ORESTES: I have been asking all the way for where Aegisthus lives.

CHORUS: They guided you correctly; you are there.

ORESTES: Could one of you go in and tell them that two men have come whom they'll be glad to see?

CHORUS: She should, if you want the nearest relative to herald you.   1105

ORESTES: Then go, woman, and tell the people inside that some men from Phocis want to see Aegisthus.

ELECTRA: Oh no! Don't tell me you have brought clear evidence to prove the rumour that we heard?

ORESTES: I don't know what you've heard; old Strophius   1110 has ordered me to bring some news about Orestes.

ELECTRA: What news? Fear's creeping into me.

ORESTES: We've come bringing some few remains of him in this small urn. As you can see, he's dead.

ELECTRA: I am destroyed. That's it, now all too clear; my   1115 grief is here before my eyes—and small enough to touch.

ORESTES: If you have cause to weep about Orestes' fate, know that this urn contains his body.

ELECTRA: Stranger, by the gods, if he's inside the urn please let me hold it in my hands;   1120
I want to weep and share my sorrow with
these ashes for myself and my whole family.

ORESTES: Bring it, and give it to her; whoever
she may be, she does not ask in hatred.
She's a friend, or a blood-relative.   1125

ELECTRA: Oh last memorial of Orestes, dearest
of all men to me! I sent you out with such
great hopes—and this is how I take you back.
Now I embrace you in my hands—and you are nothing;
when I sent you out, you were a radiant boy.   1130
I wish that I had left this life,
before I sent you to a foreign land, with these
two hands abducting you and saving you from death;
I wish you'd died that very day, so I could give
you your due place in our ancestral tomb.   1135

Instead you fell in agony away from home,
an exile in another place, far from your sister.
So, I'm suffering; with my loving hands
I could not wash your body as I should have, or pick up
the miserable remains after the raging fire.   1140
You suffered also; foreign hands attended you
and brought you back, a tiny weight inside a tiny urn.
I'm desperate with grief; the upbringing I once
gave you was useless—that sweet, loving work
I often did for you. I know your mother   1145
never loved you more than I.
I was the sister whom you always called for, since
no nurse looked after you; I did.
Now everything has vanished in one day
with your death. You have gone like   1150
a hurricane, and taken everything. My father has departed:
I am dead, because of you; death's taken you;
our enemies are laughing. That mother who is not
a mother will go mad with joy—whom you so often sent
me secret words about, to say you'd come yourself   1155
to take revenge. A daemon of ill fortune stole
all this from you and me, when he sent you
to me like this; not your most precious flesh, but
just a piece of dust, the useless shadow of a man.
Oh!   1160
This wretched body!
Oh! The dreadful
path you trod, my dearest, has destroyed me;
my own brother, you've destroyed me.
So you must take me with you in this little box,   1165
nothing to nothing; I will live below
with you for ever. When you were alive
I shared in everything with you; so now I want
to die, and not wait to be buried after you.
Death is the one release from pain and suffering.   1170
CHORUS: Electra, be more practical! Your father was a mortal;
Orestes was mortal too. Don't grieve so much;
all of us must suffer this.

ORESTES: Oh god, what shall I say? I'm lost
for words. I have no power of speech.   1175
ELECTRA: Why are you hurting? Why do you say that?
ORESTES: Are you the famous, beautiful Elektra?
ELECTRA: Yes; but I have lost my looks.
ORESTES: Poor woman, you have suffered terribly.
ELECTRA: Stranger, you surely do not grieve for me?   1180
ORESTES: Look at this body, wasted by godless abuse!
ELECTRA: You really are concerned about my suffering.
ORESTES: They have neglected you—ill-fated, and unmarried.
ELECTRA: Stranger, why d'you look at me so sadly?
ORESTES: I did not realize the depth of my misfortune.   1185
ELECTRA: What has been said to make you feel like that?
ORESTES: I see you etched by many sufferings.
ELECTRA: You only see a little of my misery.
ORESTES: What worse could there be than what I can see?
ELECTRA: I have to live with them—the murderers.   1190
ORESTES: Whose murderers? Where does all this pain come from?
ELECTRA: My father's murderers; I'm forced to be their slave.
ORESTES: Who forces you to that necessity?
ELECTRA: My so-called mother; but she doesn't act like one!
ORESTES: What does she do? Beat you? Humiliate you all the
  time?   1195
ELECTRA: She beats, humiliates and torments me.
ORESTES: Is there no one to help you, and prevent her?
ELECTRA: No. You've brought in ashes my one hope of help.
ORESTES: Poor woman, as I look I pity you.
ELECTRA: Then you're the only person who has ever pitied
  me.   1200
ORESTES: Perhaps I am the only person hurt by what you suffer.
ELECTRA: You aren't a distant relative of mine?
ORESTES: I would tell you, if we can trust these women.
ELECTRA: Yes, we can; they are my loyal friends.
ORESTES: To learn the whole truth, you must first let go that
  urn.   1205
ELECTRA: Stranger, I beg you, don't make me.
ORESTES: Trust me, and you will not be wrong.
ELECTRA: No! Please! I beg you. It is dear to me; don't take it.

ORESTES: I will not let you keep it.
ELECTRA: Orestes, we're
both lost in misery, if I can't bury you!   1210
ORESTES: Be careful what you say; you are not right to grieve.
ELECTRA: What? Not right to grieve for my dead brother?
ORESTES: You must not speak like that of him.
ELECTRA: The dead man now rejects me too?
ORESTES: No one rejects you; this urn's not for you.   1215
ELECTRA: Yes, if Orestes' body is now in my hands.
ORESTES: It's not Orestes' body—just a story, so they think it is.
ELECTRA: Where is that poor boy buried?
ORESTES: Nowhere; living people do not need a grave.
ELECTRA: What do you mean?
ORESTES: I am not telling lies.   1220
ELECTRA: He is alive?
ORESTES: If I'm alive.
ELECTRA: Then you are he?
ORESTES: Here is our father's
signet-ring; look, and make sure I tell the truth.
ELECTRA: Oh day of joy!
ORESTES: Yes, it is.
ELECTRA: Orestes, are you here?
ORESTES: Yes, I am.   1225
ELECTRA: I am embracing you.
ORESTES: Now and forever.
ELECTRA: Dearest friends, women of Argos,
look! This is Orestes, 'dead' by trickery -
and now by trickery he has come back to life,
CHORUS: Dear girl, we see; and in my happiness   1230
at your good fortune tears creep from my eyes.

Orestes and Pylades arrive at the palace from a side passage into the playing space, and the performers are disposed in it so that they encounter members of the chorus first. In the strict sequence for bearers of this kind of news, they have to identify and reach the right place first (1098–1102), and then find the right people. It is interesting that Orestes does not react when he is straightaway introduced to 'the nearest relative' (1105). There is no reason why he should have been anticipating meeting Electra first, or outside at all. But he does not let it interrupt his plan of action, abruptly telling her to go inside and announce their arrival (1106–107). The words he uses point to Aegisthus as the person to whom they wish to give their message, as the male head of household apart from his political position as king, and this is interestingly another echo from *Libation Bearers*.

He cannot, however, get past Electra and get on as he might wish. She insists on knowing, and she starts from looking apprehensively at the object they have brought, the 'clear evidence' (1108–109). We need to be aware that his transaction is stalling here, since there is no point in the family knowing about their false story and being in possession of the urn if the urn has not got Orestes and Pylades into the palace. Instead, the urn becomes a focus for Electra's dread, which both he and Pylades see, and it exercises a fascination for her (1112–18). Her request to hold the urn (1119–22) puts him on the spot, since it is a vital passport for them both which they will need to get back from her, and because her state of feeling is likely to cause them a considerable delay. He tells his attendants to hand over the urn to her, using the plural (1123), by which we know that some attendants are indeed there; in a workshop there is no harm in dispensing with these and having Pylades carry the urn, since we hear no more about them.

We have before now in the play seen two sets of offerings, those carried by Chrysothemis (or by an attendant along with her) and those brought out by an attendant for Clytemnestra. These are the objects which we have been shown, some at least in the hands of Chrysothemis because the script says so (326–27), others plainly not, since an attendant raises the offerings for Clytemnestra at the altar of Apollo. It is quite possible that Chrysothemis gave the offerings to someone (a chorus member, an attendant?) while she was talking animatedly to her sister, if only for the convenience of the actor. But in our scene, once Electra has got hold of the urn, will there be any reason for her to let it go? There is a sequence at the end of the scene where Orestes attempts to persuade her to release it, and it may be helpful to look at that first.

That sequence is started, as the line-by-line exchange

continues, by Orestes saying that he pities Electra (1199). She is struck by that, and when he adds that he is perhaps the only person hurt by what has happened to her, we are moving into the transaction of recognition, since she asks if he might be a relative of hers (1202). That it is a transaction is marked by Orestes now checking, for the first time, if the women of the chorus are loyal and can be trusted. His preliminary condition is that Electra must release the urn from her possession (1205), presumably because he believes that he can then tell her that he is not dead. This is almost logical—she must let one belief go in order to accept its contrary—but it is not much good emotionally. The sequence then is that she objects with an appeal to the gods (1206); he insists; she then objects with a supplicatory appeal to his bearded chin (1208); he bluntly states in a half-line that he won't allow her to keep it (1209); and she says that she will be wretched if she is deprived of the right to bury him (1209–10). This is not only just what he might have feared—he does still need the urn—but also is ill-omened, since mention of his burial or death by someone as dear to him as her does carry that unwanted quality (1211). Orestes spins it out as Electra remains upset and confused (1212–15), and so Electra still believes she has his ashes in her hands (1216). She is at first able to discard the idea that this urn holds his ashes, then able to discard the idea that he is buried anywhere (1217–20).

From that point, things move very quickly, a prompt that we can take from the flow of half-lines. It may be that she puts the urn aside, because she will need to embrace her brother fully, which for any performer at any time is difficult with an urn in your hands. We know or can deduce that Greek performers are often able to hand material objects over to others, or take them from others (attendants who may be otherwise invisible in the script) at a crucial moment. It is also quite clearly important that for both characters the urn is now seen to be an empty vessel, and that the man is truly substituted for it in her perception and her arms. She will go on to dance and sing, and while Electra in Euripides' tragedy does just that with what is meant to be a water-jar on her head, it would create a bizarre spectacle to have Electra dance with the urn here. But before we leave this end of the sequence, we should note that the transaction of recognition is achieved by the display by Orestes of their father's signet ring (1223), and the witnessing of the identification of Orestes by the women of the chorus (1227–31).

So it will be at the discretion of performers and director how many of the opportunities for the urn to be taken and snatched back by Orestes and Electra in this short section of script are realized. Actions of this kind will not disrupt the meaning, and what matters is that the urn retains its significance for both characters for as long as possible, and that as an audience we register that as much as possible. The object is inscribed with meaning by characters and performers, and it should continue to communicate that inscription of meaning to an audience for as long as it is needed.

So the technical question remains of how a performer will choose to use the urn in the central part of the scene, during the spoken grief of Electra, and how much she will relate it to her movements. At one end of the spectrum the urn would not be released at all, since it could be released only at the end of the scene. This offers the performer the range of arms, and the use of her hands, and the almost inevitable consequence that the urn is consistently treated like the physical body of Orestes in a shrunken form, clasped, grasped, held tightly, whatever the synonyms we might choose, and also addressed, presumably at arms' length. We may even feel convinced that this is how the performers in antiquity would have acted this script, and there is no good reason to believe that that conviction is wrong in this instance.

At the other end of the spectrum, the urn might be passed about like a parcel, in an agitated performance that constantly draws attention to it, and which frees the performer to express a relationship to it at a distance. You might well underestimate the qualities of that realization until you have tried it in a workshop, in the round, with other performers as a chorus and an audience. What releasing the urn does is to put full emphasis on the performer's relationship to it, which is demonstrated over space. In other words, the performer has all her resources fully available, and in addition this kind of performance suggests to a modern audience very strongly the high degree of apprehension that Electra must feel about this object. We know that she wants to have it; but we also may need to know how disturbing she finds it and its supposed contents. One should beware of metaphors in the theatre, but it is as if it were radioactive, and that it will bring her own death with it, as far as she knows at the time.

My belief is that any performer faced by this scene would do best to explore both ends of the spectrum, with help from others, and much of the ground in between. Similarly, we must remember that the actors playing Orestes and Pylades are crucially engaged in this, Orestes by the sight of his sister whom he is putting through torment, and Pylades by his concern for the execution of their planned action. The chorus has proved itself to be sympathetic, and has told Electra to moderate her mourning. Its members too must now be highly sensitive to the extent and depth of her grief.

In that context, I can direct attention to the recording that we have, which cannot reproduce all the different kinds of work that would be constructive. As in the case of all our recordings, it is simply indicative of how the script may be realized, and you will see that it is set approximately in the middle of the spectrum that I have mentioned. So although in this instance very much will depend on the work that is done and its variety, I shall offer some brief guidelines to aspects of the script, notably of the central monologue of grief.

It is relatively clear on a reading that the monologue has two major phases to it, the first looking back, the second introducing their mother, with a conclusion that concentrates on how Electra herself is destroyed. The problem for Electra is that what she has is not the body itself. Many of the stages of the reception and preparation of the dead have already taken place. What is probably left to her, although it would undoubtedly be restricted or denied by Aegisthus and her mother, is the actual interment, which she mentions in her desperate desire not to release the urn at the end of the scene (1209–10). Yet she does have a formula for greeting and formally receiving the vessel as itself a memorial of Orestes, and she links reception with the moment of farewell when he left so many years ago (1126–28).

This leads her to consider not just the contrast in expectation between then and now (1129–30), but also how, had he died earlier, she would then have been able to conduct all the appropriate rites herself. She is referring here to the fact that she managed to save him from her father's murderers by entrusting him to the Old Man (1132–33). She also wishes, as an alternative which only stands up in the logic of emotions, that she herself had died then, before she sent him away into exile. So these are drastic wishes, and they show how deeply she would value being able to carry out the rites herself, and how sharply she feels being deprived of that role. She is also drawing attention to distance, and how that has not only been a reality of long exile but also then becomes the basic cause of her inability to serve him in death (1136–37). Specifically, she could not wash his body with her loving hands, or pick up the remains from the fire to place in the urn, so foreign hands have done these things instead (1138–42).

We would probably say that there is a transition accomplished between the two phases of the monologue in the declaration that Electra had been responsible for nursing Orestes (1143–45), because this evokes thoughts of their mother. We might expect there to have been a wet-nurse to provide him with milk when he was a baby in a household of this rank, and indeed we see this figure briefly in Aeschylus' *Libation Bearers*. Electra puts the emphasis on her own role, and the failure of her mother to do any of the caring or the hard work, and insists that she always answered her brother's cries (1143–48). Her own desolate position now thrusts itself into her consciousness, since there is no longer father or brother, with the implication being that there never has been a mother, who is perversely one of the enemies who are laughing (1149–53).

This grotesque, funereal family picture groups Orestes, Agamemnon and Electra herself as the dead, since, as we would say, her hopes and prospects of a life worth living have died with him. But instead of mourning for them all, her mother will go mad with joy (1153–54), and in the final section of the monologue Electra seeks to merge herself with Orestes, in death and even in the urn itself. This partly returns to the theme of the missing stages of preparation for cremation. Electra here wants to miss out those stages for herself, to negate her existence without delay, to share with him as ashes in the urn, as she shared with him in life.

Electra's immersion in grief, which surpasses what is due to an inevitably mortal man, triggers once again the sympathetic warnings of the chorus (1171–73), but they receive no reply from Electra. Instead, Orestes is finally moved to speech by the deception that he has practised on Electra, and it may be that we asked to believe that he has only through this lament come to realize that this 'nearest relative' is in fact his sister. The ensuing dialogue seems to have the effect firstly of recalling Electra gradually to an awareness of her surroundings, and then of encouraging her to detail her sufferings (approximately 1174–85, and 1186–96). For his part, Orestes concentrates from the beginning on her physical state, and this proves to be the outward sign of what she calls her slavery (1192). Electra insists that she is actually subject to the physical abuse a slave might expect, and from her own mother, although this damning assertion stems from a prompting question by Orestes (1195–96). At this point, the transition starts to the recognition sequence, and it comes through a narrowing down of those who might be inclined to pity, since pity is all too clearly what Orestes has been showing (1197–1202).

The altar which received Clytemnestra's futile offerings earlier in the play, during the dialogue that featured in the Second Workshop, has a significant role in the recording of this scene (**Recording 8**). There is only one, indicative chorus member, but the actor playing Electra has a great deal of space in which to work her version of the central monologue and the exchanges with Orestes that frame it. You will see that she also uses moments of physical contact at different points in the scene, conjures up the figure of their mother in the scene building behind the performers, and casts herself to the floor in a contrasting stillness. Orestes and Pylades are able to act together explicitly at a number of points in the scene, and to maintain a necessary sense of their own, overall purpose.

Feedback and rounding off

Work on this scene concludes the Fourth Workshop, and with it the series of Workshops, and it demands great skills from the performer: to realize grief in the terms that the script etches for us, to moderate the flux of power in the performance, to interact with other performers, and to give life to a property that supposedly carries the dead, but which proves to be an empty vessel. Rather like the opening of *Antigone*, it is a scene that people can rush to do, because it looks as if it is painted in primary colours. However, the primary colours can prove to be the hardest to handle.

I hope that what has emerged in this Workshop is that it is not the authenticity of the property—its visual resemblance to an object that may be pictured in some kind of illustration, painted or carved, from ancient Greece—that is important but the value that is placed on it. We are certainly dealing with material objects, even if we do not know whether they were found or made, or of what they were made. But they are all dramatic objects, which bear a limited relation to those in the world outside the theatre, and they are inscribed with precisely what is required dramatically. We have to accept that this as true of the children as of the inanimate properties. We do not know anything about Medea's children, or about Astyanax, whether they were bad-tempered when they were hungry, or even if they were fond of their father. All we know about Astyanax is what other people see in him or expect of him, and the same is more or less true of Medea's children. It is their futures in which trading takes place, so to speak, and in both cases it is to their loss.

If establishing and maintaining the autonomy of the property should be the major focus for feedback, and insistence on it relentless throughout the Workshop, then we should not ignore the other vital aspect of these scenes, which is the work with and for others. It is perfectly possible to watch an actor working solo up to fever pitch with an old plastic pot, and to wonder just how awkward it can be to have two other actors and representatives of a chorus standing around, detached from that action and so from each other. The property is the focus of the scene, or part of that focus, and how other performers respond to it and to the emphasis on it is part of the scene. This, indeed, is an aspect of the autonomy of the property. In theatrical terms, it does not belong to the performer who is closest to it, but it does help to define the performer in that scene. Think of Orestes as a playmaker in the scene from Sophocles' *Electra*—he gives the property to Electra, and makes her perform the part of mourning. Then he takes it away. If, as the actor playing Electra, you think the chorus is not looking and involved in your work with your urn, then you are going to be surprised by their prompt reaction at the end of your riff. If you are not, as an actor, to some degree playing to these people, who are your partners in this scene, then you are not playing the scene. You are in your living room, pretending to be a tragic actor performing the part of Electra.

If those seem like harsh words, then they are not meant to be. It is simply, at the end of the process, a last warning against what we roughly call ego, which is never so dangerous as when it can plead that it has art on its side. If you want to look at this particular danger of too much absorption in a role, then I might recommend a scene from Euripides' tragedy *Orestes*, which might profitably be added to those in this workshop. The dramatic moment is a short while after the murder of Clytemnestra, and Orestes is sleeping off his latest bout of insanity, while Electra keeps watch and cares for him. The action is outside the palace. The chorus, as it arrives, is told by Electra to be quiet; but Orestes awakes, and rises quickly into madness, attempting to shoot the invisible Furies with the bow Apollo gave him. His sister is distraught, while the chorus looks on fearfully, and at the edge of being in danger itself.

The actor must work frantically with the bow, and the beguiling invitation is to play madness extravagantly. But the scene also demands close interaction with the other performers. The script of the scene finally offers Orestes the opportunity to register pity for his sister, who has to bear the weight of all his troubles, and is sitting with her head covered. While the madness of Orestes is in one respect a temporary lack of awareness of the existence of others around him, when sane he is highly sensitive to their presence and support. So the scene can offer, if you like, a kind of metaphorical moral to us all.

In addition to the criterion the measure of autonomy created for the property, the second topic for feedback should be the degree of interaction between the performers, and the third topic should be the use of space, notably how actors use the object to activate the space. Actors should also be clear how the property prompts and plays its part in transactions, and the extent to which properties successfully evoke characters or figures not present at the time. It is as well to remember that the introductions to the presentations—which summarize the situation at the start of the play, the tipping point or change to circumstances, and the action up to the moment that the chosen scene begins—remain just as crucial to the process in the Fourth as in the First Workshop. Performers themselves should always be aware of how their scene changes or directs the course of the play, although this should not form part of the introductions to their presentations.

LAST THOUGHTS

Looking Back, and Forwards

Any form of theatre practice that finds itself expressed in words is going to suffer limitations and quite probably distortions. Yet in the modern world, most forms of practice are expressed in words, and we accept that because we are in favour of their distribution. People want to know, and to have access to different kinds of training and knowledge. Perhaps the simplest example here comes from the popularity of leading books on the creative use and training of the voice, written by those who have extensive experience. Nothing could be more physical and less typographical than the voice, and yet we are willing to embrace print to 'get at' exercises and the accompanying insight that we can then deploy ourselves live and in space.

It is even the case that theatre forms that we tend to associate above all with in-body training have written accompaniments that were meant to be treated with almost scriptural reverence. I am thinking here of Japanese noh and ancient Sanskrit theatre. Zeami Motokiyo, who established the pre-eminence of noh through a broad range of developed skills including dramaturgy, voice and singing, and movement and dance, wrote a series of treatises and observations on those arts as he saw them and wanted them, almost certainly, to remain. Although compiled in a very different way, and much earlier in human history, the *Natyasastra* is a compendium of the means of producing a codified and rigorous system of danced and vocalized mythology. In these two cases the written code, so to speak, had the role of insisting on what we might loosely call standards, and inscribing the upkeep of those—through strict and demanding discipline— respectively under a mystical and spiritual (Japan) or sacred (India) value-system and purpose.

With those august precedents we need hardly fear that a little bit of writing will destroy our ability to realize a modern art of performing Greek tragedy through the trusted resources of the body and intuition. In fact, it may well be the case that that the body and intuition will not lead us very far without some kind of guidance, since there is no continuity at all from antiquity in this artform. What has been offered in these four Workshops is not an attempt at the rediscovery of the lost art of ancient acting, but a modern approach to understanding the implications of the scripts predominantly through the study of transactions. The idea is that if we get a sense of how transactions are working in the play and within scenes and sequences, we shall not be looking to unlock the secrets of a style, but aiming to render the emotional sense of thought, word and action with some confidence firstly to each other and subsequently to an audience.

I should like to emphasize that dual value, and the attention to confidence. All the understanding in the world will be of no use to an actor without confidence, and confidence without understanding is what I have had to watch rather too often, and in considerable pain. That is why the approach given here is set out in Workshops, which are in principle for performers only. The creation of understanding and confidence both take large amounts of time, and in my view they should ideally be separate from the preparation for a specific production. There really should be no kidding yourself. What is the point? You need to work hard, consistently, thoughtfully and reflectively, critically, and to ask more of yourself almost constantly. You may then have something. That something may then serve the purpose of a specific production, and the demands of an audience.

What you should aim to have is an approach which you understand, and which you can apply. The test of that may be to take other passages from Greek tragedy and see if you can discuss them successfully in terms of transactions, and work through a rendering of the script that modulates in the right way, bringing across the particular qualities of that piece in relation to the action of the play as a whole. That may seem rather a mundane and prosaic description, but that is what acquiring an approach should mean. It should be a transferable skill, a way of working, rather than a formula stuck to learned and supported pieces of work. The supported pieces are where you acquire the approach, combining your work on a number of them to create the confidence that will be based in a disciplined adjustment and development of your skills. Material from another culture, or even another era of one's own culture, can never be handled successfully with only an intuitive response, which it will elude and exceed without the slightest difficulty, and to your intense frustration.

It should, I hope, be evident that an approach is not a method. For those who are unsure, the difference I would propose is that an approach allows you to unlock the distinctive qualities of a scene, revealing a form of action in that scene that may actually be unparalleled in the rest of the artform. The point here is that plays are original conceptions. They are not merely repeating modes of thought and action that are found elsewhere just because (from our perspective) they 'belong' to an era or a convention of theatre or drama. We should not assume that we know what a scene contains until we have spread it out, and seen what it is, and how it works. That constitutes an approach, in my terms, in the simplest outline.

By contrast, a method will give you more or less the same results each time, coaxing or coercing the material through vocal and physical preconceptions into the same style of performance. 'This is how you do it' presupposes that 'it' remains conveniently and submissively constant, that tragic emotion takes certain fixed forms, that Medea's grief is the same as Electra's grief. The intended effect is that an audience will deduce that this is Greek drama from seeing the striking externals of performance, and will with luck gradually pick up some of the specifics of this play and these scenes.

Yet the danger with a method is that instead of allowing access to what is happening, those in the audience are given not much more than an experience with a strong flavour, which makes them nervous of believing that they might actually understand what is going on. Obviously, some actors like that kind of theatre and relationship with the audience, and so they will look elsewhere for their induction, which will probably concentrate largely on externals, such as symbolic gesture and the vocal expression of emotion. The problem there is that, without understanding and a sensitive approach, it will never be very clear what precisely a gesture is symbolizing, or what specific emotion is being expressed. There are no short cuts in performance, or none that are not short-lived.

It is fair to say that one will never know what a director, a producer, a company, an ensemble of lively actors may want to do with a Greek play in a public production. They may be puzzled, intrigued, excited or even mildly bored, and they will all come with their own 'handles' on remote and rather awe-inspiring material. One can usually expect quite a lot about the gods and fate, both of which are used to explain actions by human characters that we don't readily understand, or wish to recognize. Some may be interested by the idea of transactions if that is explained to them, but it is unlikely that it will be seen as a 'way into' production or even rehearsal by someone to whom it is new. So what is the value of acquiring an approach if it will be ignored by others with whom we will be working?

The answer to that is that it is a form of preparation which you can adopt no matter in what direction the production is heading. I would always advise that in any case: that an actor should have ways of preparing work on existing scripts that do not prejudice the tone of the production, but do not leave her totally dependent on what is given her (and, in many cases, not given her) in the process. I have no doubt that many performers would not rely exclusively on the physical training or exercises provided in the rehearsal process, and would have their own warm-up at least, and possibly a course of vocal and physical activity running parallel to professional involvement. So there is absolutely no reason why a similar attitude to skills or readiness should not be adopted in relation to scripts, even if it may take time and some luck to introduce performers to a reasonable range of suitable approaches.

In that respect, it seems obvious to me that at some stage an actor should spend time on the rhythms and breathing of blank verse and their relation to sense in Shakespearean drama. This is the kind of work that I still admire in John Barton's *Playing Shakespeare*, which in an odd way has been an influence on me, which I am happy to acknowledge. What Barton was saying was that speaking Shakespearean verse was dependent on an understanding or appreciation of emotional as well as semantic sense. It should not rely on a ranting style of force and cadence that could be applied with equal effect to any passage unfortunate enough to be exposed to it by virtue of being composed in blank verse. There was, in other words, not a method of speaking Shakespeare's scripts which somehow indicated your professional competence and status, but an informed and sensitive approach to playing them. I suppose an alternative title for Barton's work might have been 'speaking sense', which would be a good watchword for any material that attracts too much reverence and not enough respect.

I should return here to my emphasis on limitations and distortions, and make some observations about the recordings attached to this book at www.actinggreektragedy.com and about the chorus. Firstly, most of you will be familiar with at least some of the basic arguments about the inadequacy of the recording of live performance as a reproduction of it. The camera is not a pair of human eyes, it directs vision often from a fixed spot, and this limitation is only complicated by the addition of more cameras, which is more satisfying to us but no more like live reception. The recordings we made were with one raised and fixed general view, and one camera on a stand with an operator, 'takes' which have been mixed. This was the bare minimum, and one might call it clinical. The performances were undertaken by the actors after a course in the approach more or less as detailed in the four Workshops here, but were prepared separately, and recorded without the presence of a group. The choice was to record them end-on, and so to present the scenes in a way that could be recorded from that perspective.

While the decisions made by the actors under my guidance are closely related to the analysis and considerations advanced for that scene in the book, they are only one version, and they are not authoritative. I regard them as indicative, and that is their function, the reason for their inclusion. Some indication is bound to be helpful, and the absence of any would be frustrating, and a shortcoming of a written version. But we should be explicit about the limitations and the distortions.

For a start, I would rarely expect a scene to be played end-on in a workshop. End-on to whom? As a reader of the book, you are entitled to be a viewer of the recorded performance that acts as a kind of embodied illustration of what you are reading. So there is a case for the end-on performance of the recordings that have been made for you. But as a member of a workshop, there is no reason why you should be in any particular or fixed relationship in space to the presentation by your fellow participants.

Possibly the worst assumption that anyone can have is that it is the purpose of the workshop to reproduce in a studio some kind of imitation of the shape of a Greek theatre, and that will somehow release the essence of the scenes. It will not. Realizing that the Greek theatre was an open space, outdoor not indoor, without a proscenium arch or a boxed set, with one main door into a dramatically defined building and two side approaches into the space from 'elsewhere' is undoubtedly important. Realizing that most characters of a Greek tragedy are in public all the time, in the open, and that speech is correspondingly expressed 'outward' in the broadest sense is also important, perhaps essential at least after the First Workshop. But trying to become a puppet in a scale model of an ancient theatre will not help you to communicate, to take the plainest term of those available to describe what we are doing. It is rather like the sofa or the chair on stage, and what used to be the cigarette on which the actor relied when he had not the slightest idea how to play the scene: it is, in crude terms, the kiss of death.

So, above all, make an allowance for the end-on character

of the recordings, and take a vow not to repeat it in your own work. That will immediately release you from any temptation to reproduce what you see, to imitate the rendition that should only be an illustration. Instead, think of your audience as those who are learning with you, of whom you do not need to be apprehensive, but whom you can deploy as you see fit. Here I can offer at least a couple of dispositions that are radically different from the end-on.

Many scenes will work very well with an audience roughly in the round, for the simple reason that you can remain performing outwards wherever you are, and those you are performing with will also be subject to that same effect. It is very simple, but in many cases as good a default disposition as you might find. In fact, the final recording in the sequence (**Recording 9**), which I have included although there is no discussion of the scene in this book, is of a version that was originally conceived for performance in the round, and which has been turned end-on for the recording.

One clear alternative to working in the round is to dispose the workshop members, individually or in small groups, through the space so that you can walk amongst them. This is particularly effective with a monologue, where individuals can be addressed by the performer as and when she chooses: remember, an individual can be as much an audience as the group. I can assure you that a performer's back can be quite disturbing, if that performer may on an impulse turn on you and shove some of her script in your face.

Do think about what tragedy is meant to do. Is it meant to make people reverent with its solemn dignity? Or scare the life out of them when they may not be expecting it? Reverence and solemnity, or apprehension and terrifying vitality? All that matters in the Workshops is for participants to support the performers in developing the skills of expressing tragic scripts fluently and in an emotionally articulate way. The performers need to make use of the space, possibly to identify the location of the scene-building within it, but above all to use the other workshop participants to achieve the coherence of the scene, and its impact on those in the space who are not characters. You will find your own ways of doing this; you may need a focus, you may to define specific spaces, but you should always seek for maximum involvement and engagement. Forget about the passive audience, and do so by *not* forgetting about anyone in the room: there should be no escape from tragic characters and their actions, just as there is so often no escape for them.

One thing leads to another, and the major limitation of what can be effectively reproduced in a book or in these recordings is the relative absence of the collective character played by the chorus. I have indicated at times in the discussions how the chorus is involved in the scene, and I have pointed out how it is almost part of the physics of Greek tragic performance that characters express themselves to the chorus, about their feelings or about another character, or *through* the chorus to another character. This is a public form, not just in terms of a watching public, but for the characters, as we have so often said. The fact that individual characters are outside is one with the fact that they are expressing themselves in the hearing and view of a collective character played by the chorus, and individual Greek tragic characters expect to be doing just that. We have noted a few times and occasions when this may be less true than normal, but the exception does prove the rule.

Some of the workshop participants should form a chorus, since the acting needs to feed through their presence, in one form or another. Indeed, the truth is that our whole emphasis on tackling the problems of acting is setting Greek tragedy on its head, because the primary element in Greek tragedy is its chorus. This is a matter of history and original form, but it also continues with the primacy of the chorus in the *Oresteia* of Aeschylus, and the way in which the chorus can be seen to demand action from characters even in plays composed much later, those by Sophocles and Euripides. But despite how much the chorus serves to impress the sense of the public on Sophoclean and Euripidean characters, these workshops set out to establish an approach to the portrayal and realization of individual characters, and the scenes that take place with them and between them. So this approach cannot apply directly to the full tragic role of the chorus, which poses very different problems of interpretation for the modern theatre.

So to use the chorus just to enhance and make sense of realizations of the script for actors is a major distortion, but one that is necessary. Any modern approach to the totality of the chorus would have to be established through a totally different process to that required by individual actors, and it depends on decisions made for each and any production. What we are doing here is highly selective and strictly functional, granting priority to the characters and subordinating the chorus to a presence that serves that end.

In the recordings there is at times a notional presence of one performer, indicative of the chorus at the margins of perception, and in many cases there is none at all. This is by no means ideal, and is certainly not meant as a model. In the Workshops, it would almost always be best to designate a group as a chorus, provide them with an adequate sense of role and definition, and play them into the scene. What matters is that those in the chorus are engaged, which they should be in any case as participants, and above all that they are responsive to the characters, not solely when they are directly addressed. These are the functions that they should have, and there should be no attempt to create choreography for the workshops, since this is fundamentally meaningless without attention to their own, elaborate script in the songs and dances of the tragedy.

Yet a chorus may well be physically involved in the action, in response to a character's movement or needs, and accordingly differentiated from the role and engagement of other workshop participants. It will probably be a mistake in these Workshops if a chorus becomes seen rather than perceived, the object of attention as well as or instead of characters. But it will be a contrasting mistake if they are not perceived, and cannot contribute to the creation of meaning and apprehension in the scene. The productive use of the chorus is in itself a discipline, like everything in these Workshops, something that can be done slackly or brilliantly well, facilitating attention and concentration, or detracting from it.

As with everything else, it all depends on what you want, and how much you are prepared to put in. There are no easy answers, or quick fix. I would think that exposure to the Olympics has taken most of us beyond the naïve belief that some people are naturally good at running, and don't need to practise that much. Yet some people still believe that they can immerse themselves in a particular form of actor-training, and then be pretty much equipped to handle anything from that base of skills—or be shown relatively quickly what the additional or variant skills are. I doubt the validity or the value of that assumption.

Acting Greek tragedy is a specialist area, and I would say that there is no end to working on the set of skills suggested in this book, in understanding and practice. When I have worked with actors who have no investment in complacency, then I have found the results remarkable. Some of those performers are in the recordings that accompany the book, and they will inevitably progress well beyond what they have offered you here as an illustration. I am immensely grateful to them, and for the time spent with them.

I hope you gain as an actor from the support given by this book. Thank you for reading it, and good luck.

Thanks

Thanks to Peter Hulton and Chris Mearing for setting up and operating the two cameras for the recordings, and to Chris Mearing for painstaking cross-editing to create the version that you can see on the dedicated website at www.actinggreektragedy.com. Thanks also to Jon Primrose for setting up that site. The scenes were recorded in studios at the Drama Department at the University of Exeter during 2012 and 2013. The actors in the scenes gave their time and care to the project, and I am very grateful to them; you will see their names attached to the individual recordings. These students, along with others, had studied on the course I ran with the same title as this book over a number of years in the Department. So they were only lightly directed by me, with much of the realization coming from their own work.

As I stated in the Introduction, the translations from Aeschylus and Sophocles are taken, with permission granted by Orion Books, from Michael Ewans (ed. and trans.), *Aeschylus: The Oresteia* (London: Dent, 1995) for passages from *Agamemnon*; from Michael Ewans (ed.), *Sophocles: Four Dramas of Maturity* (London: Dent, 1999) for passages from *Ajax* and *Antigone* (trans. by Michael Ewans), *Young Women of Trachis* (trans. by Graham Ley), and *Oedipus the King* (trans. by Gregory McCart); and from Michael Ewans (ed.), *Sophocles: Three Dramas of Old Age* (London: Dent, 2000) for passages from *Electra* (trans. by Michael Ewans).

Finally, my thanks must go to Simon Baker at University of Exeter Press and to my colleague Michael Ewans, for their constant support for this and other projects.

ACTING GREEK TRAGEDY

Recordings
www.actinggreektragedy.com

The recordings are illustrations for nine of the scenes discussed in the course of the Four Workshops, and can be found at the above web address.

They were recorded with two cameras, one static and elevated, and the other tripod-based and manually operated on the ground. The camera operator was Peter Hulton, and the recordings were edited by Chris Mearing. The recordings were made in studios in the Drama Department at the University of Exeter in 2012 and 2013. With one exception, the performers studied in the Department on the course taught there, but the recordings were made after the course had concluded.

The scenes are recorded end-on, all in approximately the same manner, so they do not reproduce the effect of a live presentation as it would be experienced in the Workshops. But they are instead illustrative of a number of aspects of the discussion of the scripts made in the book. At times, the recordings include a chorus member as a functional reference point for the actors in the scene. But there is no audience and no attempt to involve members of a chorus fully, as there would be in the Workshops.

The full list of actors, in order of their appearance in the recordings is Richard Brindley, David Johnson, Dan Smith, Olivia Bussey, Lizzie Southall, Kate Rayner, Beth Kennedy, Joe McDonnell, Penny Simons, Jess Philips, Martin Harvey. I am very grateful to them for their time, commitment, and skill. Martin Harvey is a director, and a member of the Drama Department staff who has contributed to the course.

The full list of recordings is:

First Workshop—monologue

Recording 1 – Herald, from Aeschylus' *Agamemnon* – Richard Brindley

Recording 2 – Hippolytus (with Nurse), from Euripides' *Hippolytus* – in two versions, by David Johnson and then Dan Smith (with Lizzie Southall as the Nurse)

Second Workshop

Recording 3 – Clytemnestra and Electra, from Sophocles' *Electra* – Olivia Bussey and Lizzie Southall

Recording 4 – Hermione and Andromache, from Euripides' *Andromache* – Kate Rayner and Beth Kennedy

Third Workshop

Recording 5 – Deianira, Lichas, Old Man, from Sophocles' *Young Women of Trachis* – Jess Philips, Joe McDonnell, Martin Harvey. The actor playing Iole is masked.

Fourth Workshop

Recording 6 – Medea, from Euripides' *Medea* – Kate Rayner

Recording 7 – Hecuba, from Euripides' *Trojan Women* – Jess Philips

Recording 8 – Orestes and Electra (with Pylades), from Sophocles' *Electra* – Richard Brindley and Kate Rayner (with Joe McDonnell as Pylades)

Additional scene—dialogue

Recording 9 – Oedipus and Jocasta, from Sophocles' *Oedipus the King* – Joe McDonnell and Penny Simons. This scene does not form part of the discussions in the book.

The chorus role is taken in some of the scenes by actors from this list.

The mask of Iole in the scene from *Young Women of Trachis* was made by Teresa Rodrigues.

Index of Greek names and characters

General index

Words such as tragedy and transactions, space and playing-space, chorus and character, are not listed since they recur constantly throughout this book.

241

122–23, 127,132, 135, 137,
140–42, 144–45, 148–52,
157–58, 171, 176, 184–87,
189, 191, 196, 198, 206,
212, 216

iambic trimeter 12
impiety 74, 88, 152
inheritance 10, 33, 43, 46, 96,
    196–97, 199, 202–3, 205
injustice 77, 99, 170
interaction 64, 73, 123
invocation 40–41, 57, 80, 86, 89,
    130, 133, 174
irony 22, 40, 47, 66, 73, 89,
    105–6, 122, 133, 145, 159,
    161

justice 21, 24, 51, 82–83, 87–88,
    94, 99, 106, 127

lament 26, 44, 48, 69, 90, 94,
    132, 198–99, 203, 217
law 20, 25, 44, 47, 69, 84
letter 168–83
loyalty 5, 7, 9–11, 44–45, 54, 61,
    64, 88, 93, 107, 132, 210,
    213

madness 116, 181, 219
magic 40, 123, 136
marriage 4, 31, 36–38, 43, 62,
    77, 80, 84, 92, 96, 99–100,
    102–3, 107, 123, 125,
    129–30, 133, 153, 175, 184,
    186–87, 191, 196, 202
masks 14, 52, 112, 124, 132, 163,
    234–35

monologue 11, 14, First
    Workshop 17–51, 54–55, 58,
    65, 67, 72, 75, 90, 95, 97,
    103, 112, 123, 144, 146–47,
    157–58, 163, 189, 190,
    193–94, 197, 205, 215–17,
    227, 234
mourning 86, 194, 198, 200,
    205–7, 215–16, 219
movement vii, 14, 25, 55, 67, 112,
    131, 157, 159, 164, 214, 221,
    229
murder 24, 38, 40, 42, 44–45,
    48, 57, 61–63, 66–68, 89,
    93–94, 97, 115, 124–25, 133,
    177, 185, 188, 194, 199, 206,
    210, 216, 219
myth 1, 22, 33, 50, 56, 106, 120,
    195, 201, 222

Natyasastra 222
noh theatre of Japan 221–22

oaths 3, 32–33, 57, 138, 143,
    170–73, 192
objects 166–67, 173, 175, 181,
    183, 190, 194, 204, 212–13,
    218
offering(s) 8, 9, 23, 28, 38, 41,
    44, 48, 64, 80, 85–89, 94,
    106, 108, 117, 122, 124,
    133, 140, 166, 172, 184–85,
    188–89, 206–7, 212, 217
opening situation 56–57
orchestra 13
oracle 56–57, 133, 142, 159

pace and timing 164